RELIGIOUS LIFE: A PROPHETIC VISION

Diarmuid O'Murchu, M.S.C.

RELIGIOUS LIFE: A PROPHETIC VISION

Hope and Promise for Tomorrow

AVE MARIA PRESS   Notre Dame, Indiana 46556

International Standard Book Number: 0-87793-463-0

Library of Congress Catalog Card Number: 91-72116

Cover and text design by Elizabeth J. French

Printed and bound in the United States of America.

Acknowledgments

I am deeply indebted to my provincial, Fr. Tim Gleeson, MSC, who made available to me the time and resources to write this book. Much of the research took place at the Multi-Faith Center, Birmingham, England, under the guidance of Dr. Mary Hall, director of the center. I owe a debt of gratitude to Mary for her advice and encouragement; I also thank her secretary, Yvonne Swain, whose practical help and personal support was much appreciated.

Through the Multi-Faith Center, I drew on the wisdom and resources of many people, particularly the following: Dr. Anthony Fernando, Dr. Harish Trevedi, Dr. Khalid Alavi, Bishop Patrick Kalilombe, Eleanor Nesbitt, and Bahadar Singh Anjaan; to each I am immensely grateful for stimulating conversations, knowledge generously shared, important reference materials, and, not least, their keen interest and support for my research and exploration.

Fr. Stephen Gowers, OCSO, of Mount St. Bernard Abbey, Leicestershire, England, shared generously of his experience with Zen Buddhists in Japan. He also made available to me a number of monastic journals from the monastery library. I also deeply appreciate the many Cistercians who have inspired and encouraged me over the past twenty years.

My correspondence with Edith Turner proved to be a source of great affirmation. I am grateful to her for assuring me that I accurately reflected the profound insights of her late husband, Victor. I am also indebted to Karma Lekshe Tsomo for sharing information from her research on female forms of religious life in the great Eastern religions.

I wish to acknowledge the following permissions to reproduce copyrighted material: Veritas, Dublin, for material taken from my earlier book, *The Seed Must Die*, and *Lumen Vitae*, Brussels, for permission to reproduce an article originally published in *Lumen Vitae*, vol. 37 (1982), pp. 95–103.

While writing this book I was the beneficiary of home and hospitality from the Sisters of St. Paul at Selly Park,

Birmingham; their kindness and care I deeply appreciate. Sr. Teresa Burke excelled in a thorough and meticulous proof-reading of the typed text, and for that kind turn I record my deep appreciation. Finally, I thank my religious confreres and friends, both within and outside my own congregation, without whose love and support I could not continue to grapple with the profound questions that confront men and women religious today. Whether in the daily experience of religious life or in the more formal setting of chapters and renewal programs, I have shared much of the joy and pain that characterize the vowed life today. In love and gratitude I dedicate this book to all those who share in this exciting and challenging pilgrim journey, from the depth of our historical past to the breadth of our evolutionary future.

Contents

Introduction

The dawn of the third millennium lights up the horizon, illuminating our world with expectancy and anticipation, but with no small measure of anguish and apprehension.

The very mention of a new millennium generates a feeling of hope and vitality. But can we honestly hope, in these final hours before the sunrise of the new millenium, to rectify the wrongs, to reconcile the differences that fragment and desecrate our world? No doubt we will try, because if we don't there may be, in fact, no planet worth saving.

Why do I begin a book on religious life with these complex global issues? Because I believe this is what religious and monastic life is (ought to be) about today. In fact, I believe that this is what religious life always has been about: the transformation of life (human and earthly) into what Jesus called the kingdom of God.

The kingdom agenda continues to be the blueprint, posing for religious today a profound pastoral and theological challenge. We are emerging from a protracted era of cultural and spiritual suffocation that has all but smothered the prophetic and global ambience of the vowed life, not merely in Christianity but in the other religions as well. Let me attempt to explain the transition with diagrams.

The Old Model

To illustrate the transition, I use the Catholic model of the religious/monastic life, simply because it is the one I know best. Diagram A (p. 10) depicts the old model that dominated Catholicism up to the Second Vatican Council. In this illustration, the church (3) stood between this world (4) and the world hereafter (1), and religious life (2) was perceived to be an integral dimension of this exclusively institutional model of church.

This world (which usually meant planet earth as there was little sense of the cosmos in the church prior to the 1960s) was considered to be materialistic and transitory; it was passing away tinged with sin and decay. Thus, "this

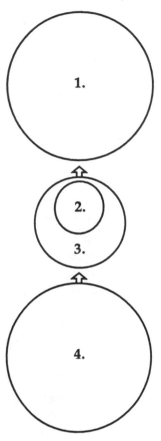

world" was not to be taken seriously. By contrast, the afterlife (1) was considered to be eternal, not subject to death or decay, the only abode of bliss and happiness (hence, all the arrows point toward the next life). The church stood between the two worlds as a permanent reminder to this world that its ultimate and only worthwhile destiny was the world hereafter.

Note that all three circles are closed; the three major realities (1, 3, and 4) are perceived to be self-contained and independent. It is a rigidly mechanistic model, which emulated perfectly the cultural reality around it. Unknowingly, and paradoxically, religious life (and the church) of this model was absorbed by the world. Many religious alive today were formed and molded in this model, a fact that has profound ramifications for living the vowed life in our time.

The New Paradigm

The new image — which throughout this book I argue to be the authentic image of religious life not only in Christianity but in all faiths and cultures — is significantly different. Since the Second Vatican Council we have been rediscovering the theology of the kingdom of God: the new reign of godliness, inaugurated in our world by Jesus, with a lifestyle marked by right relationships, justice, love, and peace. This new reign is in the world, but not confined to it; experienced in time but not time-conditioned; profoundly human yet cosmic; concerned with physical reality yet essentially spiritual. In diagram B, kingdom (1) and world (3) intersect; the church (2) coexists within both, and religious life (4) exists at the points of intersection between kingdom and world. Note that all the circles are open; it is precisely in this openness

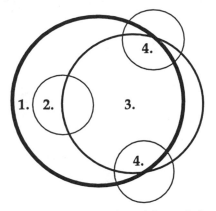

that they mutually enrich one another.

This diagram illustrates a new model of religious life which speaks to present needs. I believe we are moving into a new world in which old models will be of little use. Increasingly, religious themselves acknowledge that the old models are dying from encumbrances and irrelevancy. This book is an attempt to explain that death experience and more importantly to discern the process of resurrection of new life and fresh hope for the future of religious.

Religious are intended to be kingdom-spotters; their vocation is to be kingdom people. They belong to both church and world, to the here and hereafter; and yet, they are invited to transcend all these categories and respond to the supreme prophetic task of *advaita*: the re-creation of life in the depth and unity of the One who holds all things in being.

Part
ONE

The Global Context
of Religious Life

1
A Panoramic Overview

Of all the ages of religious life, perhaps this is the one in which the sharing of stories is most important.
— Evelyn Woodward

When I began the study of the history of religious life in the early 1970s my mentors informed me that I was dealing with a uniquely Christian phenomenon. I was advised to waste neither time nor energy studying the monastic systems of the Far East; these other developments had nothing to offer Christianity. The advice I was given sounded so derisory. One might wonder if the Eastern monastic systems had anything to offer even to their own religious traditions.

The tendency to study Christianity in exclusive context is the fruit of a restrictive consciousness. It has dominated reflection for much of the post-Reformation era. It began to disintegrate in the 1960s, when an ecumenical consciousness encouraged us to transcend traditional denominational boundaries. Meanwhile, with expanding travel and telecommunications, the East-West encounter opened up new vistas and we began to realize how constricted our Western vision had been.

The interfaith exchange is still in its infancy. It is not surprising, therefore, that most books on religious life ignore the non-Christian aspects, but it is a gap that is no longer justified. With the parallels in all the major world religions, it is culturally and spiritually stultifying to ignore or dismiss kindred spirits. We are dealing with a global reservoir of vision, wisdom, and inspiration.

In scanning this horizon, our initial task is to clarify terminology. As a descriptive phrase, religious life has a distinctive Christian meaning referring to sisters (nuns), brothers, and priests who live the vowed life, usually in community, and serve humanity in a pastoral capacity. Some

14

opt for a more secluded and prayerful lifestyle which we call the monastic life. (Throughout this book, I use the terms "religious" and "monastic" interchangeably.)

Christian writers often differentiate between the religious and monastic life. For the first 800 years of its existence (400 –1200), Christian religious life was almost exclusively monastic. With the emergence of the Mendicant Orders — the Franciscans, Dominicans, and Carmelites in the thirteenth century — religious became predominantly apostolic and have remained so ever since. The terms "apostolic" and "monastic" are best understood as complementary aspects of one reality.

In Hinduism and Buddhism, reference is made to the monastic life (but not to religious life). As we shall see, the vowed life in the East closely resembles that of the West but because the apostolic aspect is underplayed, the term "religious life" is best avoided. In Islam and Sikhism, we speak neither of monastic nor religious life, but if we refer to religious orders both Muslims and Sikhs will know what we mean. Both religions have groupings known as "orders," which, however, signifies something quite different from the Western connotation. Finally, Judaism does not accommodate a monastic system but readily acknowledges its existence elsewhere.

Where the different systems converge and differ becomes clear when we examine each tradition. Before doing so, it is necessary to state that our research is not confined to the major religions of humanity. Along with the institutional forms of the religious/monastic life, we have what I wish to call "religious-life values." At no stage in history have these been confined exclusively to official orders and congregations. In today's world there exists within (or on the margins of) all the religious traditions a vast array of self-constituted groups, cults, or sects whose adherents profess a radical and simple lifestyle. By any set of standards, their way of life must be considered evangelical.

Our ambience stretches even further afield. Before formal religions ever came to be (about 2,500 B.C.), there existed in prehistoric societies sages and holy people who played an important part in the spiritual life. Among these was the shaman, a saintly figure whose lifestyle and value system has a remarkable affinity to the vowed life in all the religious traditions.

The Hindu Sannyasi

Hinduism is the oldest world religion, dating from about 2,500 B.C., and today claims some 600 million followers. It is the seedbed of formal religious life. For the first fifteen hundred years there are no records of organized orders, but from the beginning there did exist a strong monastic orientation reflected in the four stages of human development: (a) *Brahmachari*: a celibate student, one studying under a spiritual master; (b) *Griastha*: a householder, one embracing marriage, home, and family; (c) *Vanaprastha*: one who is retired (husband or wife) who retreats to a quiet, remote place (a forest dwelling) and prepares for eternal happiness; (d) *Sannyasi*: the monk living alone, in a community (ashram), or monastery (matha). Female ascetics are known as *sannayasini*. Only the last stage belongs properly to the vowed life.

Today, there is an estimated one million monastics in India alone. It is believed that the number of monks living communally (in either ashrams or mathas) slightly outnumbers those who live alone. Since there is a great deal of fluidity and mobility, the situation can vary greatly from one year to the next. Since the Indian ashram is much more flexible and open-ended than the Christian monastery or community, there tends to be a continual flow of spiritual seekers, single and married, some of whom may stay only a few days but many of whom remain for six or twelve months.

From earliest times, the monastic life in India transcended all the social and cultural divisions of the caste system. For this reason, the sannyasi has always been cherished by the marginalized and less well off, especially the untouchables of the Shudra caste. It is an interesting paradox that the monks and nuns have been allowed to disregard one of the most sacrosanct of Indian customs, the allegiance to caste. The gradual erosion of caste, since independence in 1949, seems to have contributed to the diminished cultural impact of the sannyasi and sannyasini in contemporary India.

Flight from the world is an important aspect of Hindu monastic teaching. Rarely has the theory been matched by practice. Like the early Christian ascetics in the desert, Hindu devotees often attracted several hundred seekers until the places of quiet refuge became cities. There is also a trend for Hindu monastics to be involved in education, hospitalization, and care for refugees, but how extensive these practices are (or have been) is very difficult to establish.

In terms of apostolic service, "The only service that every ascetic is expected to perform for patrons or clients is the giving of personal advice on many matters, including religion, philosophy, private donations, management of money, choice of career or marital life."[1] There is a tradition of Hindu monks contributing to agriculture (since many monasteries have their own farms), education, health care (quite a few monasteries operate dispensaries), and the provision of shelter and refuge in monastery guest houses.

In India today, the monastic life is taken for granted and the four stages outlined above are not closely followed. These stages, however, are of immense historical and cultural interest, indicating that the monastic life exerted an undefinable but powerful influence on Indian life. From earliest times it was assumed that the vast majority of those in the Brahmachari stage would marry and take up a secular task in the world. Nonetheless, the schooling of a celibate student under a spiritual master was considered to be important in the young person's growth and maturity. Deprived of this opportunity, the youth was considered immature and unsuitable for the responsibilities of adult life. There are some intriguing parallels here with the monastic schools of the West and the tradition of Christian education, long associated with religious life.

The third stage of the Vanaprastha is profoundly meaningful. The departure from the "world" can be understood as similar to the Christian tendency to escape from the evil and sin to prepare to meet God and attain the eternal happiness of the "next world." But that would be a misunderstanding of the Hindu intent. In Hinduism there is no "afterlife." There is an ultimate stage of bliss called Nirvana. It is believed that this final state can only be achieved after many cycles of reincarnation (samsara). But the cycle can be broken

much sooner if one has prepared more assiduously for it
during one's earthly life.

The Vanaprastha stage, therefore, is an option for a life
of prayer, solitude, and penance in the pursuit of ultimate
liberation. The sannyasi undertakes a similar program of
austerity (tapas) but in a more institutionalized and clearly
defined context. At the third stage, the man may take his
wife with him; as a sannyasi, he must become a full-fledged
celibate. The monks and nuns take three vows: poverty,
chastity, and reverence for elders (very similar to the West).
They are accountable to a spiritual master (guru) until such
time as they may choose to go it alone and live an eremitical
life of prayer and simplicity.

The Hindu monastic person strives to attain liberation by
the practice of the "three jewels": right vision, right knowledge, and right conduct. Four great virtues enhance this
spiritual development: universal friendship, seeing the good
side of others and rejoicing in it, universal compassion, and
tolerance of evil-doers (nonviolence). It is within this broad,
universal set of aspirations that acts of renunciation are
practiced.

A notable absence in Hindu spirituality is that of the
desert. In the Indian tradition, especially in Buddhism,
monks withdraw to the forest. This is a dimension of the
Eastern monastic tradition that has a profound spiritual
meaning which often escapes the Western observer. The forest can be any place of solitude and quiet, not necessarily the
woodland. However, the connotation is one of encountering God in the unperturbed and uncontaminated solitude of
nature, not in the "desert" of demonic conflict and sensory
deprivation advocated in Western monasticism.

Hindu monks and nuns, who live on their own, beg for
their food on a daily basis. Buddhist ascetics have a similar custom, and there are traces of it in the Islamic orders.
People give generously on the understanding that their gen-
erosity earns them "merit" to facilitate their achievement of
moksha (salvation). This idea is quite close to the Christian
concept of indulgences.

Indians treat their monks with a mixture of bewilderment and admiration. Even today the monastic presence is

cherished by most Indians, although few can say why. The marriage of Christian and Hindu monastic forms, as in the Christian Ashrams, of which there are about one hundred in India, has great promise for the revitalization of Hindu monastic life.[2] It has helped to tone down the mysterious, individualistic orientation of the ascetic sannyasis and opened up the monastic experience to a greater range of people. It also highlights the potential for social as well as spiritual enrichment. In this way, an earlier tradition of monastic spirituality, which focused on the liberation of people into the fullness of their God-given humanity (cf., Griffiths, 1979), has once again emerged.

As a religious system, Hinduism is unique for its freedom and flexibility. Its monastic system too, has been, and continues to be, marked by great variety of lifestyles and spiritualities. While one cannot easily delineate its unique features and apostolic impact, one can be in no doubt that it exerts, even to this day, a significant spiritual and cultural impact on Indian life and culture.

The Buddhist Sangha

In 563 B.C., Gautama the Buddha was born (some traditions date his birth to 623 B.C.) in Northern India and founded what is, today, one of the most widespread religious systems in Southern and Eastern Asia. Buddhism has many branches, arising from its two main strands of historical development: the Theravada and Mahayana. The latter, known as the great vehicle, could be described as liberal Buddhism which interpreted Buddhist teaching and sought its application in relation to a variety of different social and religious contexts. The Theravada, on the other hand, was noted for its strict adherence to the letter of the tradition, which was guarded with utmost devotion.

Buddhism originated as a monastic religion. The Buddha himself was a monk and passed on to his followers a well developed monastic system which took its main ideas from the Hindu sannyasi. But from the beginning, it set out to reform what it perceived to be a chaotic and disorganized system. The main goal of Buddhism has been the elimination of suffering (dukka) by the cessation of desire. Consequently, ascetical practices of self-denial and prolonged disciplined meditation became the main features of a monk's life. To this day, this individualistic pursuit of perfection (so reminiscent of traditional Christian asceticism) dominates religious life in the Theravada Buddhist tradition.

From the beginning, however, there was an enforced form of community life (subsequently known as the *Sangha*). The place where monks or nuns live is called the *Vihara*. Because from June to September the monsoon rains made it impossible for the monks to travel, they settled as groups and cultivated a communal lifestyle. In its origins, therefore, Buddhist religious life, like that of Christianity, had a variety of communal and individual forms. To this day both categories flourish, with life in the monastery perceived as a preparation for the more authentic, solitary existence of the hermit.

The Buddha left his monks a precise body of teaching. Three outstanding virtues were to govern their lives: nonviolence, chastity, and poverty. These virtues worked in opposition to the capital sins of passion, hatred, self-deception:

> This, O monks, is the noble truth of the way: it is the way that leads to the cessation of sorrow, the holy way with eight branches; rightness of opinion (attitude), rightness of intention (thought), rightness of word, rightness of bodily activity, rightness of the means of existence, rightness of effort, rightness of attention, rightness of mental concentration . . . .

And elsewhere in the rules for monks (*Vinaya Pitaka*) we read:

> To abstain from killing any living thing and from taking what is not given, to resist every temptation against chastity, to keep from lying, from fermented drink, from eating after midday, from dancing, singing, playing music or attending worldly festivals, from carrying garlands and from the use of perfumes and cosmetics, from using large or raised beds, from accepting money.[3]

There are obvious parallels with the Christian vows. To this day individual monks and nuns live frugally, a witness sometimes contradicted (as in the West) by elaborate buildings, highly ornate temples, and wastage of food and clothing. Since Buddhism has no priesthood, the monk has become a ritual functionary, which militates seriously against the witness to simplicity and communal sharing. (Hinduism has always differentiated between the priest and the monk.)

Most Buddhist monks were celibate until the late nineteenth century, when under the Western influence adopted by the Meiji reform, monks in Japan began to abandon celibacy. Today, nearly all Japanese Zen monks marry, but spend most of the time at the monastery or temple away from their wives and families. Schloegl claims that the monks lost a great deal of respect and influence with the abandonment of celibacy.[4]

Eastern forms of religious life have no real equivalent to the vow of obedience, as popularly understood in the West. In Hindu ashrams the key person is the spiritual guru, whose role is almost identical to that of the spiritual father in the Christian tradition.[5] His authority is not organizational or administrative and, even in a community, the context of his service is to each individual within the group rather than to the group as a whole.

In the Buddhist tradition, there also tends to be a superior, whose role is primarily administrative. This office was, and still is, imposed by government requirements of "law and order." By the same token, the monks often wield powerful social and political influence both for themselves and for the people who live near their monasteries. Politics and religion are not mutually exclusive as in the West.

There is a great deal of variation in the pastoral involvement of the monks among the people. In all parts of the Buddhist world, participation in temple worship brings monks and people together. Monasteries also serve as places for quiet and retreat, although there is no obvious tradition of the monks passing on their wisdom and skills of meditation to the people.

In much of South East Asia, the monks are involved in social and political issues and are looked up to for their wisdom and inspiration.[6] Ironically, this pastoral consciousness is accompanied by a tendency for married men to abandon wives, families, and homes, and opt for the monastic life to better ensure their individual salvation.[7]

In Buddhism, there is a long tradition of begging monks. Each morning the monks leave the monastery and go in search of food. Usually, they acquire more than they can ever hope to consume because people consider their contributions to be a very effective means of acquiring merit for afterlife:

> The one essential point in acquiring merit is this: it is not the giving of money or food or other things that produces merit, but it is the fact that the gift is accepted. Hence, the very great importance . . . of the monks. The monks are the ones who accept the gifts to make it possible for the laity to acquire merit.[8]

In this custom, we glimpse something of the rapport that exists between monks and people. It defies description and analysis. Over the centuries, abuses have crept in; for example, since the monk cannot redistribute the food, there tends to be scandalous waste. But there is within the Buddhist tradition an interdependence between monk and people which can enrich religious life.

Although Buddhism has always had both male and female forms of the monastic life, male religious life has always overshadowed the female forms. Historical records of the unique and longstanding contributions of female religious are virtually nonexistent. However, sisters of the great Eastern traditions (like their Western counterparts) are assuming ownership of their rich and diversified heritage and demanding recognition of the contributions of women religious.[9]

Buddhist monks do not recruit; the people try to ensure that there is a constant supply of candidates. It is common, therefore, to hand over one or more members of the family to the monastery, usually at the tender age of nine or ten. Older people enter voluntarily but these are a minority. Because of the young age at which people enter, huge numbers leave in their twenties or thirties — an average of one hundred each year in Sri Lanka alone. Overall, numbers do not dwindle, however, because of fresh intake in large numbers of young children.

In the Buddhist tradition, commitment is theoretically for life, although one can disrobe and leave at any time.

We have no precise record of how many monks there are. There is an estimated one million in Thailand alone, many of whom are very young and some of whom live married, family life. One is on much safer ground in counting the number of monasteries (which is what textbooks tend to do). They run into thousands except for China, where apparently, the monastic life is not very extensive. Numbers in any one monastery can range from fifty to five hundred.

As a cultural, spiritual movement, Buddhist religious life has a widespread and inspiring influence. There are remarkable similarities with Christianity, and a Buddhist-Christian dialogue could fruitfully commence in an exchange between monks and religious on both sides. In fact, that dialogue began in the great monastic conferences of Bangkok (1968), at which Thomas Merton died, Bangalore (1973), and Sri Lanka (1980). Unfortunately, there has been no similar concrete follow-up with the Christian-Hindu ashrams of India.

The Muslim Tariqahs

After Christianity, Islam is the largest world religion with an estimated 900 million followers. It is particularly strong in North Africa, Central Asia, Turkey, Arabia, and India, with a growing presence in many Western nations. From its origin, propagation of the Islamic race and the development of the Islamic Empire were fundamental moral and personal duties. Consequently, a monastic system embracing celibacy and ascetical withdrawal from the world have not been amenable to Muslim thought.

Shortly after its recognition as a formal religion, early in the seventh century, there emerged the Sufi mystical tradition. It has always been closely associated with Islam although scholars differ greatly about its origins. Some claim it sprang from within Islam; others suggest that it predated it. Within Islam, the Sufis emerged in the eighth century acting in a countercultural way. According to Muslim scholars, they adopted the following orientations: a) withdrawal from the politically turbulent Islamic Empire in favor of a life of prayer and contemplation; b) free and creative thinking to obviate the dry orthodoxy of the major legal schools of Islam; c) efforts to address an intellectual barrenness in Islamic theological thought; d) protest of the moral laxity brought about by prosperity; and e) Christian monasticism as a working ideal for life.[10]

The Sufis tried to live out their mystical vision while remaining fully pledged to orthodox Islam. They generated both fear and admiration and occasionally disdain, especially when some opted for celibacy. From the eleventh century on, the Sufis organized fraternities, today called orders (tariqahs). Many of these orders survive to the present time despite a serious decline in the nineteenth century. They have had a profound impact not merely on Islamic life but on world culture as a whole.

The tariqahs (tariqah means "road" or "path," hence, followers of the way) are not religious orders in the strict sense. There are some obvious parallels, and there seems no doubt that they are intended to serve as a monastic model within the Muslim faith. They have a strong reputation for holiness and learning on par with many of the great orders of Christianity. Although not ascetical, Sufis have tended toward a simple and frugal lifestyle. In the tradition of orthodox Islam most have married; however, a significant number have remained celibate. Because the great Sufi masters frequently refer to the burden of being married and the spiritual distraction it causes, I would suggest that the celibate archetype is as strong in Islam as in any other religious system. It simply has never been granted the approval which it merits.

An interesting feature of the tariqahs and the Sufi movement in general is its apparent success in communicating mysticism to the total culture. While disapproving of materialism and worldliness, the religious are cherished among the Muslim people for their involvement and social concern as well as their spiritual devotion.

> Their role is manifold: they add an emotional and spiritual dimension to religious devotion; they contribute to the ultimacy of social life; they are associated with trade and craft guilds; they have provided staging posts and hospices for travellers and merchants; and they have served as credit and finance institutions .... Their functions then range from leading souls to the highest

levels of spirituality to providing guidance and support in the requirements of everyday social, political and economic life.[11]

Most interesting to the Western reader, perhaps, are the authority structures. Each Muslim order has a superior general with a hierarchial structure governing subsequent groupings down to each local community. At the local level the leader demands and receives absolute obedience since he is presumed to communicate God's will for the members. The novice to the order must submit to the leader as if he were a corpse (this image is frequently used in Sufi texts). According to Lawrence, this form of blind obedience is alien to the theology of early Islam.[12] The close resemblance to trends in the Catholic tradition of the recent past is obvious.

There has always been an uneasy relationship between the Sufis and mainstream Islam. Nonetheless, the Sufis, and particularly the orders, are still admired and appreciated for keeping this tradition alive. Even political figureheads consult the spiritual masters. And yet, many textbooks, only briefly, if at all, refer to this movement.

Today, there are over two hundred orders in Islam. Half of them were originally founded in the heyday of the twelfth and thirteenth centuries. This, too, was one of Sufism's illustrious epochs, especially under the influential and inspiring Al Ghazali (1058–1111), considered by many to be the next greatest prophet after Muhammad himself.

In the first half of the twentieth century, the orders dwindled considerably in influence and importance. This was the result of the political opposition and possibly of a serious internal malaise of the orders themselves.[13] The orders had become powerful and wealthy but also spiritually introverted. They failed to activate the social and spiritual revitalization which characterized their golden age (1200–1500). Since 1950, a revival seems to have been underway, but precise information is difficult to obtain. A. H. Jones, in his contribution to the 1987 edition of *The Encyclopedia of Religion*, claims that the history of the tariqahs in the twentieth century has not been written and is in danger of being lost to posterity.

Other Traditions

Though Hinduism, Buddhism, and Islam have all contributed dramatically to the monastic/religious life of the
Asian continent, there are a variety of smaller but significant traditions that merit attention. Jainism (numbering some
three million followers) is believed to have arisen in northern
India in the sixth century B.C. as a Hindu reform movement.
It had (and still has) a strong monastic presence in accordance with its very strict philosophy of nonviolence.

Sikhism (now numbering fifteen million followers)
evolved in the early sixteenth century in protest to the deca-
dence, intolerance, and persecution caused by Muslim raids
in north India. It attempts to transcend the Hindu/Muslim
division by incorporating important aspects of both faiths
and by emphasizing the unity of all people under one God.
From its Muslim source it inherited a strong sense of propagation of the species and, consequently, rejects celibacy and
strict asceticism. Nonetheless, in its short history of 450 years
it has developed a mystical and broad monastic system in
India and even in parts of the Western world.

Because of Buddhist influence, we would expect other
Eastern religions — such as Shintoism, Confucianism, and
Taoism — to have monastic systems. But information on this
is not available because, apparently, a lack of research.

The Bahai faith came into being in the middle of the
nineteenth century. It claims to be a global religion and has
some four million followers. It transcends many of the sec-
tarian elements of other creeds, and largely rejects the reli-
gious/monastic life, in agreement with Islam.

Judaism

Judaism has twelve million followers in today's world.
In pre-Christian times, we know of two monastic movements, the Therapeutae and the Essenes. Both groups were
celibate and lived a communal and austere life. It is suggested that the Rechabites, referred to in Jeremiah 35, also
deserve to be considered as monastic, although they were
not celibate. A Jewish rabbi, G. Bernheim, addressing a
symposium held in Paris (March, 1987), suggested that

the three vows of the Nazir (cf. Numbers 6) were to abstain from drinking wine, cutting hair, or touching a dead person for thirty days. There is a parallel here for monasticism. Neither of these Old Testament examples seems entirely convincing, but they may serve as yet another example of archetypal values seeking a context in a religion that has no formal system to explore and articulate these values.

Judaism, like Islam, considers the propagation of the species to be a divine imperative for every Jew. Family life is of paramount importance and both Jewish ritual and morality are very much family centered. For these reasons, the vowed life is alien to the Jewish value system. But as in other religions, the monastic archetype tends to break through, usually in marginalized or mystical contexts. Examples in contemporary Judaism are those of the theosophical movement known as the Kabbalah (which originated in medieval times and contributed greatly to the spread of Judaism). There is also the disciplined, intellectual pursuit in Talmudic studies known as the Yeshiva, which has schools worldwide. Finally, there is the well-known Kibbutzim. Over 300 flourish in Israel today with an estimated 95,000 participants.

Religious Life And The "New Religions"

A contemporary assessment of religious life outside traditional Christianity would be incomplete without reviewing a controversial phenomenon of our times, namely the upsurge of several sects, cults, and "new religions" exhibiting features we traditionally associate with the vowed life. Movements of this nature always have existed and, no doubt, always will, but their proliferation in the recent past and the lifestyle they tend to adopt pose questions. I contend that these questions can only be addressed appropriately in a religious life context.

For a start, we note that this trend is not peculiar to Christianity. Wallis, while not referring explicitly to religious, offers an insightful analysis of the new groups that explicates some significant archetypal values. Among the groups he notes three dominant attitudes to the world: a) those

who reject the world, such as ISKON (Krishna consciousness), the Unification Church or Moonies, Love Israel, the
Manson Family; b) those who affirm the world, such as Sci-
entology, the T.M. Movement, Nichiren Shoshu of Japan, the
Human Potential Movement; and c) those who accommodate the world, such as many of the pentecostal/charismatic
groups in the United States, Pak Subuh (a Muslim mystic
movement), the Aetherius Society.[14]

All these groups are united in a common aspiration,
namely the transformation of the world. Devotees often
admit that they perceive this to be the task of the church.
But it fails to a lesser or greater degree; hence, the shift to an
alternative movement which is presumed to succeed where
the church has failed. This is the same myth which gave
birth to Christian monasticism and has fueled the prophetic
vitality of religious life through the centuries.

Many of these groups assume a monastic/religious-life
orientation. Some adopt temporary or long-term celibacy.
They tend to share wealth and resources (a fact often shad-
owed by the publicity accorded to a wealthy "guru"). Most
groups pray, reflect, and discern together, and very few are
without a leadership structure. They all focus on community.

This reawakened community consciousness became the
compelling myth of the new groups throughout the 1960s
and 1970s.[15] No longer does this issue make the headlines,
but the myth continues to flourish, broadening from local
attempts at communion to more global efforts at unity and
partnership. The myth is most creatively grounded in what
we call basic Christian communities, local ecclesial groups of
Latin America (an estimated 160,000 religious are involved)
which are inspiring many similar experiments across the
Christian world.[16]

The fact that the new groups adopted the communal
myth as their basis is historically, culturally, and spiritually
significant. In Catholicism, at least, we are emerging from
a long phase (the whole post-Reformation era) of legalistic,
individualistic, and institutionally-dominated parochialism. Clark suggests that the entire Christian church suffered
from this petrified orthodoxy.[17] The swing to "community,"
therefore, was, and continues to be both a reaction to an

oppressive leadership and a rediscovery and a restatement of a fundamental dimension of the Christian faith. (We will examine the whole phenomenon in greater detail in subsequent chapters.)

What I have attempted in this section is to outline the scope, diversity, and variety of movements which embody religious-life values. They exist in all the major religious systems, but because Christianity is more amenable to the community archetype, their impact on Christian life is greater.

The African Continent

Christian religious life owes much to the African continent. Egypt is the birthplace of many eremitical and communal movements which inspired the monastic ideal in the West. Over the centuries, Egypt has maintained this tradition with a number of revival movements emerging in recent times.[18] There is no evidence to suggest that monks travelled from Egypt to other parts of Africa, possibly because much of the continent was unexplored. Apart from the original upsurge in Egypt, we look to Europe for subsequent developments in Africa.

According to Beaver, male and female monastic communities were widespread in North Africa during the fourth and fifth centuries.[19] Much of the original inspiration seems to have come from St. Augustine. Subsequently, the Canons Regular and the Mendicant Orders established foundations. The main growth came in the nineteenth century when several missionary congregations established small communities throughout the continent.

Along with Christian communities, many of the Islamic orders flourish, especially in North Africa. Unfortunately, we know nothing about forms of religious life articulated and expressed in the native tribal religions. This is a rich reservoir of archetypal, primordial values that many in the West dismiss as being archaic and cannibalistic. The limited evidence suggests quite the opposite. Many contemporary anthropologists marvel at the delicacy, balance, and deep spirituality of prehistoric peoples in general.

Religious of the Christian tradition continue to struggle with the African reality. The early Christian missionaries were often ruthless in their imposition of Christian values. Today, there is a growing respect for native ideologies, along with an enabling of the African people to live in the modern world. How to be prophetic and genuinely ecumenical in such a culturally diverse situation is a challenge continually facing religious in Africa today.

The Female Contribution

If historians of religious life are culpable of any sin, it surely must be their deplorable neglect of the female contribution. Most historical records are compiled by men and focus largely or exclusively on the male aspect. Yet in the Catholic church today, women outnumber men by three to one, while in Hinduism and Buddhism female ascetics and communities have existed from earliest times.

In the Muslim tradition, the picture is a good deal more complex. To the best of my knowledge there are no female orders, although at least in the past " . . . there were Convents reserved for women. Female Sufiyya either belonged to one of the existing (male) Orders or led a religious life on their own. When associated with men, as pupils or teachers of mysticism, they generally sit segregated from them and separated by veils or curtains."[20] Since the only option, in most cases, is to join a male group, most female religious opt instead to be individual ascetics.

In Buddhism there seems to be a huge number of female religious, conservatively estimated at 150,000, with 20,000 in Thailand alone. Apparently the Buddha in his lifetime instituted a female form of the monastic life in conjunction with the male one, but due to political unrest and religious persecution, the female form became extinct. Since the line initiated by the Buddha was broken, any revival was considered unorthodox, a rigidly legalistic attitude that prevails to the present day.

Things are changing, however. At an international conference of 150 Buddhist nuns held in India in 1987, a vociferous and enlightened group of women displayed a fierce determination to uplift their religious status. In many ways this gathering is reminiscent of the courageous and visionary stance adopted by sisters of the Christian tradition — especially in the U.S.A. — in recent times.

Toward Convergence

In this chapter, we have scanned a vast territory, and a diverse range of monastic/religious-life experience. There are many points of convergence, as will become clear in exploring religious life in the Christian tradition in subsequent chapters. It is not my purpose to establish that religious life in the different traditions is essentially the same. There are common elements but there are also distinctive differences which must exist if we are to respect the cultural and spiritual uniqueness of each ethnic group. I am not trying to create a monastic/religious syncretism.

My objective is of a much more fundamental nature. Behind the diverse expressions of the vowed life, there seems to be a basic set of aspirations shared by all humans in every age and in all cultures. Consequently, we see the monastic/religious life arising quite independently at various times and in different cultures.

Our task, therefore, is to identify the shared cultural values that generate the diverse expressions of the monastic/religious lifestyle. In this way, we connect with archetypal, primordial values that unite us as a human species. What binds religious together, therefore, is not so much the fact that we belong to a movement that exists with remarkable similarities in diverse religious and cultural systems, but that we share a common vision and a potentially unifying set of archetypal aspirations.

Ever since the Second Vatican Council, religious in the Catholic tradition have been standing on the hill of Calvary, confronted with death and decline (dwindling numbers, diminished apostolic impact, questions of irrelevancy, etc.). The fact that we belong to such a potent and pervasive global movement is in itself a poignant reminder that it is inappropriate to remain at Calvary. At the present time, I suggest that religious move to the first Easter morning and stand at the mouth of the open tomb, striving to enter into the bewilderment, wonder, and hope of those who met the Risen Lord, only to be told that "...he has risen, he is not here .... He is going ahead of you to Galilee; that is where you will see him, just as he told you" (Mk 16:6–7).

Our task for the remainder of this book is to tread the pathway of resurrection: to remember (rather than record) our sacred story of divine liberation, a story that is deeply rooted in our prehistoric ancestry. In the light and inspiration of our sacred past, we are called to project a vision for the future, a dream of hope and promise as we stand at the threshold of the twenty-first century.

Tomorrow is another country. We do things differently there. If we really want to live, we had better start at once to try; If we don't it does not matter. We shall start at once to die (W.H. Auden).

2
Liminal Identity

With the development of modernity, the whole map of liminality and protest has developed in new directions which are connected both with the growing social differentiation. . . as well as with far-reaching transformations in the symbolic field.

— S.N. Eisentadl

Religious life has existed in every major culture of humanity. It is a universal reality. Throughout its long history, it has adopted a variety of norms and customs while maintaining a remarkably similar value-system across ethnic and religious boundaries. In all known situations, it tends to be a lifestyle of simplicity and austerity, of prayer and devotion, and frequently an apostolic commitment to poor and marginalized people.

We don't know when religious life began. We know of its existence in early Hinduism around 2,500 B.C. with a style and structure very similar to early Christian forms. Hinduism is the oldest of the major world religions, which may lead one to assume that religious life could not have existed prior to the emergence of the Hindu faith. This, in fact, is not the case. There are known individual prototypes of the religious life predating Hinduism, and chief among these is an intriguing character called the shaman.

Shamanism

The renowned anthropologist Mircea Eliade wrote an entire work on Shamanism[1] in which he describes the shaman as the numinous religious personality among tribal peoples, a person who by contacting the sacred absorbs and communicates a special mode of sustaining and healing power.

Sr. Donald Corcoran[2] outlines five stages of the shamanistic spiritual journey: (a) The devotee renounced the world and entered into the solitude of nature (the desert); (b) there followed a long period of spiritual discipline, including fasting, heroic deeds, and celibacy; (c) there are various accounts of symbolic encounters with evil forces;[3] (d) gradually, a deepening experience of personal wholeness and integration takes place; and (e) finally, the devotee is deemed a full-fledged shaman and is reintegrated into the societal context as healer[4] and mediator. According to Eliade, this latter role is not to be identified with the priestly task of offering sacrifice.[5]

Parallels with ancient Christian ascetics (for example, St. Anthony) are easily identified. It has been suggested that the shaman is a prototype of the prophetic figures of the Old Testament times, who in turn are considered to be prefigurations of the Christian religious life, a link we will explore in chapter four.

Shamanism is known to have existed as early as 10,000 B.C. The literature focuses largely on the male model; females (shamanesses) also existed but little seems to be known of their role and function. Shamanism still prevails in contemporary tribal groups, notably in Central and Northeast Asia, North and South America, Malaysia, Indonesia, Australia, and in parts of Africa. The shaman is not a priestly figure with a specific cultic role. His mediating task is effected more through trance and sacred dance (acted-out petitionary prayer?) than through sacrificial rites which tend to be reserved for the cultic priesthood. Consequently, the shaman, in his functional role, is perceived more as a healer than as a priest.

For prehistoric peoples, however, it was the symbolic and spiritual significance of the shaman, rather than any functional role, that held prominence. He was a person marked out and set apart, spiritual enough to mediate divine benevolence for the people, yet human enough to share their hopes and fears, their needs and aspirations. There was something ambiguous about the shaman: feared and yet admired, felt to be close to the people yet kept at a safe distance. These contradictions were held together in Eliade's cryptic description of the shamanic role as, "the defence of the psychic integrity of the community."[6]

Quite extensive literature exists on Shamanism, much of which focuses on the esoteric and, at times, bizarre behavior associated with shamanic trance and ecstasy. One is reminded of the parallel tendency in many lives of the saints to focus attention on outstanding ascetical achievements. This focus of hagiography runs a great risk of missing the essential message embodied in these special personages.

The literature refers only to individual shamans (as far as I can discover). There are no records of communities or groups of shamans, although Eliade does refer to a shamanic fraternity[7] and to an auxiliary group called "sons of the Shaman."[8] But there is a very definite communitarian ambience: recognition as a shaman is bestowed only by the whole community,[9] and many aspiring shamans renounce the profession if the clan does not grant unanimous approval.

Eliade suggests that shamanism is better understood in a mystical rather than a religious context.[10] He notes the comparison with monks of the Christian tradition but chooses not to develop this seminal observation. He describes shamans as "the elect" whose ecstatic experience gives them access to the sacred on behalf of the wider community; parallels with the Old Testament prophetic tradition are readily recognizable.

The decision to become a shaman is described as a vocation. Hereditary transmission seems to be the primary means of conferring the vocation, but what Eliade calls a "spontaneous vocation"[11] also seems to be quite common. There is an initiatory period of solitude and austerity culminating in the first consecration, a process described by Eliade as a "death and resurrection."[12] The consecrating ceremony is celebrated by the community to which the shaman will minister.

In line with traditional religious life, the shaman was set apart from the people, even to the extent of being donned with a special costume[13] (the prototype of the Religious habit?). His life was one of prayer, simplicity, and communication with the divine. There is nothing in the popular literature to suggest that he was celibate (in the modern sense of the term), but there is much to indicate a desire for celibacy as we find in contemporary religious life traditions

of Zen Buddhism and Islam.[14] Eliade makes several references to intimacy, intercourse, and marriage with angelic
figures, reminiscent of the mystical marriage which features
strongly in early Christian literature and hagiography.

Although "set apart," there is no sense in which the
shaman is either cloistered or set in opposition to his people.
Indeed, there is little in the entire cultural history of the
religious and monastic life to mark the quality of integration
between the people and this sacred personage. Something
of this unique spiritual interdependent relationship can be
gleaned from this description of the shamanistic spiritual
journey:

> ...these contemplative experiences are equivalent;
> everywhere we find the will to transcend the profane,
> individual condition and to attain a transpersonal per-
> spective. Whether there is a reimmersion in primordial
> life in order to obtain a spiritual renewal of the entire
> being, or...a deliverance from the illusions of the flesh,
> the result is the same — a certain recovery of the very
> source of spiritual existence, which is at once "truth"
> and "life."[15]

The Concept of Liminality

Much of our information on Shamanism focuses on the
function, behavior, and lifestyle of the individual shaman.
Little has been written on the cultural context of Shamanism
itself. Is this phenomenon marginal and abnormal, or is it
somehow central and important for mainstream society?

To address this question we employ an anthropological
concept, much in vogue at the present time, namely, liminality. In 1908, the anthropologist Arnold Van Gennep coined
the term "liminality" to denote the periodic separation of
a person from her family (as in Rites of Passage). In recent
times the term has been adopted by Victor and Edith Turner
and given a whole new meaning to explain features of small
groups and communities in their relationship to, and interaction with, mainstream society.

Liminality may be described as "an ambiguous, sacred,
social state in which a person or group of persons is separated for a time from the normal structures of society...."

Every society has a structure, and a liminal community both clarifies the structure of society and can be instrumental in changing it."[16] In a sense, therefore, every society creates its own liminal groups — unconsciously for the greater part. There seems to prevail in human culture a tendency to embody in a radical and profound way the values we cherish most deeply. Unconsciously rather than consciously, society sets aside certain individuals and groups and endows them with intensive value systems. It projects on to these liminal groups its deepest hopes, dreams, and aspirations, and requests the liminal person or group to embody and articulate for society at large the deepest values the society holds sacred.

Put more simply, we seem to need models that will embody for us the ideals we deeply believe in. Yet, society can be very ambivalent about such persons or groups; sometimes it dismisses them as totally irrelevant, often persecuting (even executing) them, while at the same time admiring them, however begrudgingly. We use these liminal groups to articulate our archetypal values. Society has always done this and there is good reason to believe that it always will.

Endress suggests that liminality serves two main functions.[17] First, it provides a mirror-type image in which society at large can perceive and understand more clearly the values best suited to its own evolution; thus the liminal group provides a social and cultural critique, usually expressed in negative fashion. Second, " . . . by throwing the structure of society into sharp relief and illustrating its deficiencies and stress points, the liminal group is often instrumental in bringing about a dissatisfaction with the status quo."[18] Activating change, especially at a structural level, is a primary liminal task.

It is often in hindsight that a specific person, group, or movement is deemed to be liminal. Liminality is not something one sets out to create. Rather, it is the product of the creative imagination, seeking to respond to the pressing needs of the contemporary world, fueled by a new vision of the future. The initial inspiration tends to be embodied in one person (for example, founders or foundresses of religious orders) but rarely comes to fruition without a group which that person gathers around himself or herself.

According to Turner, liminality strains toward universalism and openness.[19] It may, therefore be expressed transculturally as in the anti-colonial movement of the 1950s and 1960s, the student protests of the 1960s and early 1970s, or the alternative health movement of the 1980s. Turner suggests that sports, games, pastimes, and artistic endeavors can also serve a liminal purpose by lifting us out of our daily preoccupation with structure, organization, roles, and functions.[20] This he names the liminoid. For the greater part, however, liminal groups tend to be more specific; some outstanding examples of the present time would include the missionary movement of Mother Teresa of Calcutta, Taize, the basic Christian communities of Latin America, the Sojourners Community in Washington D.C., the Findhorn Foundation in Scotland, and many of the small cooperatives which articulate alternative values in terms of the work ethic, industrial relations, inventive skills, and holistic vision.

Liminality and Religious Life

I suggest that religious life in its varied expressions across the different religions and cultures is one of the most pervasive forms of liminality. Indeed, it may well be the primary and most authentic expression of this reality. Consequently, we can assume that religious-life values are inherent to human civilization and will tend to seek expression in a liminal framework. In other words, human civilization needs the values of the vowed life, but in a manner that challenges and inspires in the context of each new age. When religious fail to produce the appropriate counterculture, liminality doesn't die. It simply shifts its focus elsewhere. For Turner, there is a transcultural dimension to that shift which has led him and his wife to explore pilgrimages as another dominant medium for the articulation of liminal values:

> Of course as the history of monasticism has shown, the orders become decreasingly liminal as they enter into manifold relations with the environing economic and political milieu . . . But the religious, though relatively numerous in the heyday of the historical religions, were

easily outnumbered by the ordinary worshippers, the
peasants and the citizens. Where was the liminality? Or
was there, indeed, any liminality for them at all?...For
the majority, pilgrimage was the great liminal experience of the religious life.[21]

There is no age or culture without an accompanying
liminality that may be individual, communitarian, or both.
In prehistoric times, the focus seems to have been on individuals, the shaman or the person undergoing Rites of
Passage. In early Christian monasticism, and extensively in
the monastic systems of the Far East, individual holiness
(eremiticism) seems to enjoy priority over the communal
context. However, even in the most individualistic cases,
there tends to be somewhere in the background a group
or communitarian expression. Many of the early Christian
"hermits" belonged to a *lavra*, an organization consisting of
"...a row or cluster of solitary cells round a common center
including a church and bakehouse."[22] An identical institution called the *Avasa* prevailed in early Buddhism. I suggest, therefore, that liminality uses the group or communal
medium as its primary mode of expression and articulation
— hence the interchangeable use of "communitas" and "liminality" in all Turner's works. Moreover, individual people,
serving in a liminal capacity, tend to veer toward a "community" to check out and authenticate their liminal aspirations.

As already stated, we do not set out to invent or create
liminality. It seems to arise from what Carl Jung called the
"collective unconscious," that repository of psychic and spiritual energy which pervades our universe and channels our
collective hopes and aspirations into broad cultural channels. The liminal, therefore, complements the institutional.
Human beings need both; society needs both. The liminal
without the institutional destroys itself in a perpetual fascination with novelty, experimentation, and dreamlike vision.
The institutional without the liminal grows "fuzzy and like
the ancient dinosaurs, dooms itself to extinction by its inflex-
ibility in the face of needed changes:"[23]

> Indeed, if structure is maximized to full rigidity, it
> invites the nemesis of either violent revolution or un-
> creative apathy, while if communitas is maximized, it

becomes in a short while its own dark shadow, totali-
tarianism, from the need to suppress and repress in its
members all tendencies to develop structural indepen-
dences and interdependences.[24]

The Shifting Liminal Focus

Today, we seem to be experiencing a shift in liminal
possibilities.[25] No longer do religious orders serve a liminal purpose since many (most?) are closely identified with
the institutional church and, in some cases, with secular organizations. The liminal function of religious life has been
subverted and is now reappearing in strange and unexpected
places. A vast array of grassroots movements have surfaced
all over the world. The range includes basic Christian communities, new age movements, industrial and agricultural
cooperatives, spiritual regeneration movements, cults, sects,
Green politics, feminism, ecology groups, and a host of others. I do not wish to suggest that these groupings are authentic and orthodox in every respect. They merit attention
since they are clearly the exponents of the contemporary
counterculture and consequently the main focus of liminality
for our time.

Where does this leave religious life? In something of a
dilemma, I suggest. The dominant image in both East and
West has lost its liminal appeal and cultural relevance. In
the West, it has become excessively institutionalized and too
closely identified with both church and state; in the East, especially in Buddhism and Hinduism, it has veered so much
to the margin and sought to sever itself from the mainstream
to such a degree that it has turned the liminal space into yet
another institutional format. Consequently, ordinary Hindus respect the monk for what he does but sees little affinity
between the monastery and the world.

Reclaiming liminal identity is not an issue for direct address. It's not the liminal space that needs our attention, but
rather the cultural and spiritual stance we adopt toward the
modern world. What are religious saying to the world of today? Do they understand this world with "its expectations,
its longings, and its often dramatic characteristics"?[26] Only
when religious address the world, sensitive to its needs and

evolution, with a view to responding in a manner eminently appropriate to the present, can they hope to become liminal once more. The agenda for this conversion — it does involve drastic and profound change — is what we explore throughout this book.

We conclude our reflections stating again the broad cultural framework within which religious life values originally emerged and within which they continue to unfold; namely, the liminal context. Liminality is that indefinable, ambiguous space thrust upon a person or a group. Simultaneously, it is a position of privilege and of pain; it is inviting and frightening. It may be described negatively as marginalized, alienated, and alone, set over against the mainstream of society. It may be perceived positively as a countercultural movement on the frontier, opening up new horizons, dreaming new possibilities. It exists not for its own sake, but for society at large to articulate the deepest hopes and aspirations of people; that is, their archetypal values. What these perceived values are is the subject of our next chapter.

3
Archetypal Values

The encounter with the archetypal world is no small venture.

— Myriam Dardenne

Reference has already been made to the value system of religious life that enables it to serve humanity in a liminal capacity. Once again we recall that it is the function of the liminal group to mirror for the wider culture the deepest hopes, dreams, and aspirations of the people. Sometimes, the people will find this "mirroring" highly attractive; at other times, challenging and inspiring. Frequently it will be found demanding and frightening; occasionally, the truth becomes too bitter and people either ignore or seek to destroy the liminal person or group.

What Are Archetypal Values?

The value system which we attribute to the authentic liminal group we describe as archetypal values. "Archetype" is a difficult concept to grasp. It originates from two Greek words: *arche*, meaning first or original, and *tupos*, meaning type or form. Far from being a modern term, it was already in use in late antiquity; it is found in Cicero's letters to Atticus in the first century B.C. and was adopted by writers of Greek, Judaic, and Christian backgrounds. In its early usage it depicted a cosmogonic principle, namely that the evolution of the universe exists as a primordial image in the mind of God under whose creative plan the world began to unfold. Conceptually, it is quite close to the Platonic notion of the "idea" which precedes the "appearance."

During the twentieth century the term has been rehabilitated by religious historian Mircea Eliade and psychologist Carl G. Jung. For Eliade, archetypes have a supernatural or transcendental origin.[1] They are divine endowments of the human psyche which evoke a spiritual response, conscious or unconscious. For Eliade, therefore, humans are innately spiritual and they seek to articulate their spiritual thirst in mythical stories and ritualistic behavior.

Formal religion is intended to be the primary medium of this articulation but often fails to mediate the appropriate feelings and aspirations. In its absence, humans (consciously or unconsciously) invent spiritual outlets such as excessive devotion to money, power, or pleasure, or escapist, ritualized behavior centered around recreation, pastimes, and entertainment. The result is, in Eliade's own words, "a regression into chaos."

For Jung, the term archetypes denotes a set of values, hopes, dreams, and aspirations which all humans are assumed to possess because we all share in that universal consciousness which Jung called the collective unconscious.[2] According to Jungian theory the collective unconscious is mediated to us through archetypes, predominant ways of thinking and feeling which all humans share, leading to universally shared forms of behavior and ritual. "I have often been asked where the archetypes or primordial images come from. It seems to me," writes Jung, "that their origin can only be explained by assuming them to be deposits of the constantly repeated experiences of humanity." Elsewhere, Jung writes: "The archetype . . . as well as being an image in its own right is at the same time a dynamism which makes itself felt in the numinosity and fascinating power of the archetypal image."[3]

There is also a biological aspect to archetypes which Jung calls instinct for which he also uses the analogous term "pattern of behavior." But of greater significance is the "authentic element of spirit" which archetypes embody and represent. Formal religion exists to express and mediate archetypal, spiritual aspirations. Consequently, one finds in most religious systems similar symbols (for example, bread, water, wine, candles, incense, statues, etc.) and concepts (such as light, darkness, wisdom, power, glory).

Hart makes the following list of prominent archetypal themes:

... wresting power from the Gods — fate and freedom, questions of danger, vengeance, retribution; of change, rebirth, old age, death; the passage of time, the revolutions of the seasons; origin and continuity — of man and the earth; food supply and the earth's fertility; the context of the sexes and its derivatives — masculine concept and feminine intuition; good and evil, innocence, justice; the relations of family and the struggle between generations; ordeal and trial, the test by outrageous onslaught. What we have in such lists are timeless questions and timeless answers. It belongs to the archetype to run in this direction.[4]

Archetypal Values and Religious Life

That way of life called the religious or monastic life is intended to be the primary embodiment of archetypal behavior. Religious life is intended to be a tangible realization of some of the deepest cultural values of humanity. This, I believe, is the main reason why religious life exists in every human culture with very similar characteristics in virtually all religious systems.

I deliberately use the phrase "intended to be" because religious life, also an institutional reality, can become detached from its life-giving myth and thus incapable of serving the archetypal values it is intended to articulate. When this happens — and I believe it is happening today — the collective unconscious throws up new archetypal models, new embodiments for the articulation of mythic (meaning-bearing) values. Jung informs us that when cultural canons become exhausted and when symbols decline, the collective unconscious becomes volcanic and erupts with new archetypes.

Religious life in both East and West has lost a great deal of its vitality and appeal. It has become excessively institutionalized, choked and stifled amid a plethora of archaic legalism, insipid spiritualism, and, especially in the West, excessive activism. Many religious-life values are now more clearly expressed and more creatively embodied in "new age" movements, communal experiments, some cults, and in other liminal groups.

What are the main archetypal values which monks and religious are intended to embody on behalf of humanity?

First, the relationship of religious with the sacred is fundamental to their well-being, human and cultural. Women and men whose lives are "set aside for God" are reminders of that fact.

Second, religious mediate for people their ideal relationship with the cosmos. They need to distance themselves from created reality to be able to wonder and admire its sacredness and not be absorbed by its transitoriness and superficialities; hence, the hermit experience and the need for solitude. It is in togetherness that religious relate most coherently with God, life, and each other. As humans, relatedness (relationships) is a basic element of life and destiny; hence, the communal experience.

In the Christian tradition, spiritual writers tend to oppose the eremitical and communal lifestyles, and consider the former to be the more perfect. Historically, I suggest that the latter is more basic and more important. The two should be understood as complementary rather than in dualistic opposition.

Third, the relationship of religious with the earth is basic to their existence, although it is rarely articulated with clarity and conviction. The vow of poverty is not so much about sacrificing or depriving oneself of wealth and property, but about the archetypal, primordial focus of caring and responsible stewardship of the earth and the goods of creation. The contemporary ecological consciousness is a great deal more than a reaction to the nuclear threat or to the denuding of the tropical rain forests (issues which, in themselves, merit serious concern). It expresses something very deep in the human search for meaning.

Fourth, religious note their relationship with all human beings. Several archetypal values operate at this level but two merit special mention:

Emotional and affective intercourse — the deep, interpersonal interaction in which we humans mediate our need for warmth, intimacy, affection, affirmation, and love. Our sexuality is central to this experience whether we are married, single, or celibate. The vow of celibacy articulates something of this depth and richness, reminding us that our affectivity (our need to give and receive love) is deeper and more

all-embracing than our need for genital relationships, suggesting, therefore, that even in the married state there is a
deeper union of love and self-giving than that expressed in
the intimate bond of marriage. In a society avid for gratification and sexual fulfillment, a celibate lifestyle is considered
to be freakish and even bizarre. Consequently, its deeper
meaning is largely unappreciated. It is important to realize that it is the "collective consciousness" of society that
has created this archetype. We will return to this topic in
chapter nine.

Cooperative interaction.   Here we touch on issues relating to authority and leadership, what the traditional vow
of obedience seeks to express. There is a popular perception
— false and naive — that obedience is about the subjuga-
tion of some people to the commands and dictates of others.
Archetypally, the fundamental meaning is inherent in the
word itself: *obaudiere*, which means to listen attentively; that
is, listen to one's inner voice, to God, to others, to life's circumstances, to nature; and, in response, to act in a manner
that enhances growth and progress.

The acting is primarily communal and cooperative, that
of equals in partnership, not competitive and hierarchical,
that of bosses and servants. The ideal which the archetype
seeks to express is one of mutual participation in which every member feels cherished and wanted, and all have a voice
and feel part of a common enterprise. This may seem quite
alien to contemporary practice — in the family, social systems, state agencies, and church and state leaderships. What
has happened is that structures alienate people from the
archetype because the myth (the ideal) has become encrusted
in norms which have outlived their time.

Thus far, I have outlined five major archetypal values
which have dominated human life and culture in the sense
that they continue to find expression in liminal groups, predominantly those we label "religious orders." I refer to them
as dominant relationships with (a) the sacred — "God" (or
by whatever name one uses); (b) the cosmos — solitude and
community; (c) the earth — the vow of poverty; (d) other
human beings in terms of affective sexuality — the vow of

celibacy; (e) other human beings in terms of partnership and cooperation — the vow of obedience.

These are some of the chief archetypes that impinge on our existence, although many people may not readily acknowledge it or agree that they are universal to humanity. Historically and culturally, religious orders seem to be the chief embodiments of these values. However, one notes a similar orientation in many African tribal groups (particularly in rituals pertaining to Rites of Passage), in basic Christian communities of Latin America, and even in some of the cults and sects which feature strongly in contemporary society. Even such controversial groups as the Moonies and the followers of Bhagwan Shree Rajneesh espouse an archetypal value system (or at least aspire toward such values). Their attempts to articulate and live out such values may be misguided, but the underlying aspiration is more genuine than is generally recognized.

Archetypes and Individuation

Jung's interest in archetypes arose from his work as a practicing psychiatrist, initially with people experiencing emotional trauma, but later with many of those same people who continued therapy long after their recovery from illness. This led Jung to postulate the concept of "individuation," the unfolding, over time, of that growth and integration which enables a person to experience life in its fullness.

Here we are dealing with a frequently misunderstood notion of Jungian psychology. Individuation is, first and foremost, a primordial (archetypal) concept, an ideal all humans strive to attain, but one never fully realized in this life. It is not something an isolated individual sets out to attain. Its realization (rather than achievement) is dependent on the ability to integrate and hold together the diversity of human experiences, positive and negative, not only at an individual personal level, but also in a social, global, and universal sense.

> Individuation is a conscious attempt to bring the universal program of human existence to its fullest possible expression in the life of the individual.[5]

Individuation may be described as the ultimate (fundamental) archetype. I suggest that it provides a contemporary
exposition of the ancient pursuit of perfection for which the
monastic/religious life was perceived to be the primary
means. As the goal of perfection has often been miscon-
strued in a narrow, individualistic sense, we need to found
our consideration of archetypal values in the broad global
and holistic ambience to which it belongs.

Vows and Archetypes

Archetypal values are clearly related to the traditional
vows of celibacy, poverty, and obedience. However, they
recast the vows in a radically new context with broad cultural applications. As archetypal values, the vows are not
just for religious; indeed, they speak to all human beings.
The vowed life is not just for the holiness and perfection of
those in religious orders and congregations; it is a movement
of challenge and inspiration (at least, it is intended to be) for
all humanity. Far from being a set of legal requirements with
strong institutional connotations, the vowed life is, first and
foremost, a sign or sacrament, a focal point for articulating
and celebrating those values which concern people at the
deepest levels of their hopes and aspirations.

When we consider the vows in this context, we are left
with a dilemma. We readily identify with the idealism of this
renewed vision because archetypal aspirations are engraved
deeply in our hearts. But we also confront the daunting and
discouraging accumulation of legal and devotional trimmings which have so institutionalized the vowed life that
it is no longer capable of being an effective witness for the
surrounding culture. We are faced with a massive salvage
operation; we'll review its implications in part two.

Karl Marx said that context governs consciousness. If our
frame of reference for the vowed life is institutional ambience, then we run the real and grave risk of being squeezed
to death by our narrowness of vision. The vowed life is a
creation of the collective unconscious; it is a dimension of
the liminal space that human beings have invented and continue to create in order to express and articulate their deepest aspirations.

When we broaden the context — which is not a deviation but a return to the source where water is purest — a different consciousness begins to prevail. A sense of unity and common pursuit arises; old dichotomies (for example, secular v. sacred) break down completely. At the archetypal level, life is one; opposites are seen as complementary. The vowed life, far from being the exclusive domain for those seeking perfection, becomes the focal point for encounter, for community, for dialogue, for incarnation. The monastery is, and I believe always was intended to be, the apex of the *sequela Christi* where the Christ (of all religions) becomes radically incarnate and visible as a sign of hope and vitality for God's people on their pilgrim journey.

At the present time — for a variety of historical and cultural reasons — religious life is in a state of limbo. This book is intended to offer some guidelines for hope and revitalization. In this chapter, we have attempted to connect archetypal, primordial roots with that fundamental value system that seeks re-expression and fresh articulation in each new era. Next we return to the fundamental value system and explore its articulation in the ministry and service of God's people.

4
Prophetic Possibilities

True prophecy is a dynamic movement which combines
criticism of the oppressive present, graced remembrance
of the past, and the liberating exhibition of alternative
futures to convert potentially destructive energies into
the saving waters of life.

— Thomas E. Clarke

In Jungian terms, the collective unconscious (with its accompanying archetypes) is primarily positive, benign, and
life-giving. People familiar with Jungian thought, however,
are also aware of the shadow — the negative, dark side
which can also influence, mislead, and misguide.[1]

When we refer to archetypal values (as a basis for the
vowed life) we need to keep in mind the negative dimensions, whether we trace their source to the shadow or to
original sin. There have been some very saintly people who
were grossly misguided in their perceptions and in their
pursuit of holiness. There have also been appropriate and
inappropriate embodiments of archetypal values. What
I now wish to explore is one possible context that helps
to authenticate these values, and that I call the prophetic
dimension.

In prehistoric times and in many of the great world religions, the role or ministry of prophecy belonged to the
individual. We identify prophecy primarily with the greatest prophets of the Old Testament: Samuel, Isaiah, Jeremiah,
Amos, etc. It is worth noting that these outstanding individuals have much in common with the shaman of prehistoric
times. When we come to New Testament times we encounter
quite a different model. There is no outstanding prophetic
movement, as in the Old Testament, apart from the ministry
of Jesus himself. Christian scholars explain this by claiming
that the prophetic movement finds its ultimate expression

and fulfillment in the life and ministry of Jesus, and consequently needs no further elucidation.

A few scholars, notably John Davies, opt for a different interpretation: with the coming of Christ and the birth of Christianity, the prophetic focus shifts from the individual to the community.[2] Consequently, in the New Testament prophetic vision and values are found not in individual people (perhaps, not even in Jesus himself) but in communities. We suggest that Jesus is truly prophetic not so much in his individual identity but rather in his trinitarian identity. Immediately we can glean something of the mysterious and complex nature of the kingdom which Jesus sought to establish — it is marked by right and just relationships.

Prophetic Characteristics

The prophetic tradition, both personal and communal, channels archetypal values into apostolic options. How this is achieved is lucidly outlined by Walter Brueggemann,[3] whose synthesis is eminently suitable to the religious-life context and has been adopted by a number of contemporary writers.[4] According to Brueggemann the following are the chief characteristics of prophetic witness:

— The task of the prophet is to criticize while, at the same time, not de-energize people. Reading the signs of the times is a supreme prophetic challenge. This implies a critical evaluation of what is oppressive, manipulative, consumerist, and unjust. But it means also that the prophet must enable, empower, and energize people to rise above their human and spiritual plight.

— The prophet is called to articulate alternative futures to the "royal consciousness." In the Old Testament, the king is the guardian of the status quo, upholding the existing power structure. The task of the prophet is to continually question the underlying assumptions, the strategic values of the status quo, and propose (dream) better ways of serving people. The status quo may be the way of church or state, of sacred or secular institutions. In the ecclesial context, what is being suggested is not the creation of an alternative church but, rather, exploring alternative ways of being church in the context of today's world.

— The prophetic outreach is one of sensitivity and imagination. It connects readily with pain, hardship, suffering, and injustice. It is the task of the prophet to help people confront the numbness of death. It seeks to alert the oppressor to the plight of the oppressed. It draws attention to those systemic tendencies which blind or inoculate us against our own pain (for example, drugs and alcohol) and that of our neighbor, home or abroad.

— The prophet empowers people to engage in history. Prophecy is not merely a here-and-now movement, so immersed in present reality as to be absorbed by it. Because it dreams and imagines, remembers and re-enacts, it seeks to draw on the wisdom of the past and on the collective wisdom of humanity.

— Prophets seek to promote justice and compassion, without which love cannot become the binding and healing force of our world. It is in this context that many religious orders today deliberate on how best they can make a preferential option for the poor and oppressed.

— Because the prophetic vision arises from imagination rather than from rational, linear thought, the creation of new symbols and education in symbolism is a prophetic task. Without appropriate symbolism, humans can neither dream nor imagine at a depth that celebrates appropriately the ambiguities and challenges of life.

— The prophet is called to foster hope. Precisely because the prophetic person or movement engages with the pain and contradictions of life and refuses to be overcome by evil, the prophet seeks ways to negotiate growth and encourages perseverance.

Prophecy, as outlined above, denotes the complementary side (in terms of yin and yang) of the organizational, institutional, hierarchical, and human urge to structure and control. By fostering imagination, creativity, spontaneity, freedom, and challenge to grow, the prophet seeks to create a mature and holistic balance.

Every healthy organization needs a prophetic dimension. Yet, organizations by their nature tend to subvert and even suppress the prophetic. Many of our churches feel uncomfortable with or threatened by the suggestion that an important dimension of the Christian mission belongs to the extra-institutional sphere. This fear and suspicion rests with the church's slowness to explore the meaning of prophecy in the contemporary world and the consequent ignorance and mistrust that accompanies most attempts to dialogue about this phenomenon.

Prophetic movements are not intended to be, nor do they set out to be, alternatives to the main institutions. In fact many of the people who create the liminal groups and aspire to become liminal persons are deeply committed to the renewal of the institutional church. We need liminal groups to mirror to the institutions their limitations and possibilities. Liminal groups are intended to be the purifying agents for our institutions.

We need both institutions and frontier groups, or in Victor Turner's terms, we need structure and anti-structure. Being predominantly rational creatures, especially in the Western world, we give emphasis to structures, often subverting anything that poses the slightest threat to our institutions. So doing, we ensure the premature death of many institutions by attempting, with mistaken and shortsighted perceptions, to safeguard the integrity of that which we deem to be permanent and absolute.

Brueggemann's characteristics of prophetic ministry serve as criteria for liminal witness and the articulation of archetypal values. I do not wish to suggest that the ensuing discernment is easy or automatic. In fact, it may be a long and tedious process, as it has been for many women and men religious in recent times. Uncooperative attitudes of church officialdom can further exacerbate frustration, but such opposition, which can be necessary and fruitful, should not discourage discerning and seeking a new vision. History affirms the determination and perseverance of visionaries.

Such discernment seems to demand a group context for full fruition. Mutual support, encouragement, and affirmation are all important if a new vision is to be given birth that can address the needs of the contemporary world and creatively respond to the religious congregation's own charism. It is a fortunate group that can welcome prophetic vision (whether articulated inside or outside one's congregation),

accommodate it in appropriate structures, and allow it to call
forth its members, often along pathways we would rather
not go.

Religious Life As Prophetic Ministry

The emerging theology of religious life is primarily that
of people and communities called to prophetic ministry.
We're not suggesting that orders and congregations can
claim to have a monopoly on prophecy. All people are called
to a mutual enrichment and a ministry to one another that
is essentially prophetic. It is out of the depth of that call,
shared in the universal search for meaning, that the collective unconscious generates liminal groups and articulates
archetypal values in a prophetic manner. Historically and
culturally, religious, whether active or contemplative, are
intended to be the primary bearers of this vocation.

Religious life, therefore, contrary to popular perception
and traditional teaching, exists for people and for the world.
Consecrated life segregated from humanity in its pursuit of
individual perfection is a deviation from the tradition of religious life as a universal, prophetic movement. There is no
domain of human life that religious can consider to be beyond or outside their focus of attention. Religious are called
to be a "shock therapy"[5] for political structures, economic
systems, ecological concerns, enterprises pertaining to health
and education, scientific pursuits, and ecclesiastical institutions. Any project that touches human reality and the well-
being of our planet (dare we say the entire cosmos) must
resonate in women and men religious and in the communities to which they belong.

A perennial challenge facing religious life throughout
the world is the need to explore an alternative context for
its life and mission. Religious, in many cases, are far too
closely aligned to ecclesiastical structures to be able to serve
humanity in a liminal, prophetic capacity. Primordially,
historically, and culturally, religious life is not intended to
be an ecclesiastical structure. It is neither a secular nor sacred
reality; it transcends both. It is distinctly spiritual insofar as
its primary focus is the universal search for meaning, but it
is also explicitly human, earthly, and worldly in its mission

to serve people in a liminal, archetypal, and prophetic way. It is inappropriate for religious to be overidentified with any one realm of human and earthly reality. This leads to categorizing, which impedes the universal, global nature of the religious-life vocation.

Religious life should not be elevated to a superior, exclusive stance. As humans, we all need structures and institutions. But today we live in a world of interconnections and interdependence. Old categories, divisions, and dualisms are proving to be fragmentary rather than unifying. Our world is essentially an interconnected web of relationships.[6] The old mechanistic paradigm, the birthchild of Newtonian science and Cartesian philosophy, is in decline,[7] while a new holistic vision of one people, on one earth, in one world is a growing aspiration of our time. We are encountering a new awareness calling for new liminal spaces and new prophetic options. Religious are called to be at the cutting edge, the front line as trailblazers for this new dream; their vocation is to be in the "vanguard of mission."[8] If religious fail to respond, others will fill the void. The collective unconscious will generate its own protagonists, those who respond when the Spirit calls. They become the "new religious."

Religious life will always exist because it is an integral part of human culture. It flourishes or declines according to its ability to address the crucial issues of meaning within changing cultural patterns. It is oversimplistic to suggest that religious seek to inculcate permanent values in an ever-changing world. It is the task of religious to empower and enable people to grow, to change, to adopt, to find meaning amid both the permanence and fallibility of earthly life. Religious are essentially change agents and social catalysts, people whose task and privilege it is to loosen up congealing systems so that those systems can energize rather than hinder people in their growth and development.

Accordingly, religious should feel very much at home in an atmosphere of change. In the Christian context, at least, this view is substantiated by the creative and dynamic response of religious in some of the great epochs of European history. Recall the impact of the early Benedictines in Europe of the sixth and seventh centuries: the monks pioneered important developments in agriculture, commerce, education, and political life. The Mendicants of the thirteenth century became a powerful humanizing influence, while the emergence of the apostolic religious groups in the sixteenth century laid the foundations of contemporary health care and education.

In all these examples, orders and congregations grew and flourished despite adverse political and economic conditions. There is also an abundance of historical evidence (which we will explore in chapter five) to indicate that orders and congregations decline and die when they become overconcerned with their own growth, identity, and survival; that is, when they become overinstitutionalized. Frequently, this means overspiritualized, so (en)closed and anti-worldly that they begin to ignore and dismiss the world they are called to address in a liminal and prophetic way.

The call to be prophetic demands a constant listening and attentiveness to what the creative Spirit of God is doing in the heart of the world. Where are the vibrations of new life? What are the new aspirations of our age? What are the emerging paradigms of our time, and what is their cultural and spiritual significance? What is God saying to us in the cry of the poor and oppressed? These are the perennial questions for prophetic discernment, questions that cannot be fobbed off with yesterday's solutions, questions which in today's rapidly changing world demand novel and flexible responses.

On the Margins or at the Frontiers

What we call the prophetic movement and the liminal space is not an enterprise out on a wing, although the popular culture will tend to perceive it as such. It is much more akin to a frontier movement throwing out "feelers," animating new ideas and fresh possibilities, exploring alternative ways for the pursuit of growth and meaning, proffering hope. It is not a deliberate choice to be unorthodox, but it becomes very difficult for a group to be liminal or prophetic if members are forever looking over their shoulders to check their orthodoxy with the bishop or some guardian of the faith. Prophecy flounders in this environment; in its efforts to be "respectful," it is likely to become cynical and embit-tered. For the prophetic to survive and exert its influence in a life-giving way, there needs to exist a climate of mutual trust with open and frequent communication.

Because we live at a time of extensive and rapid change affecting the quality of global life to a degree not previously recorded, we can expect to encounter a good deal of prophetic contestation. It will take a variety of forms, ranging from the traditional contemplative monastery (reminding people of the primacy of the spiritual) to the local cooperative (challenging traditional industrial institutions) to the basic Christian communities of Latin America (offering an alternative way of being church) to the Philipino peace and justice group (that leads a protest march on behalf of marginalized fishermen). In all cases, new frontiers are opening up for a better world and a more meaningful human existence. "False prophets," a label frequently and prematurely attributed to any movement that challenges or opposes the status quo, may exist, but they rarely survive for long. They tend to capitulate to their own narcissism.

Finally, a note of caution! Prophecy has nothing to do with the popular idea of foretelling the future. There is a quality of prognostication, sometimes accompanied by warning and even doom, which can arise from prophetic discernment. For the greater part, however, the future orientation tends to be one of expectancy and hope; the negative dimension tends to focus on what has to be done or undone to make possible a better future. This redemptive element seems to be an important criterion of genuine prophecy.

Throughout this book, we accept and assume the prophetic ambience to be the primary and the most appropriate context for living and understanding religious life. I realize I am projecting a vision that has few concrete expressions in contemporary orders or congregations. However, the concrete expressions do exist, most often outside the formal context of religious life and occasionally outside the churches.

It is not my intention to create confusion or to add to the apathy and disillusionment which already prevail in religious life. Many orders and congregations are in decline; some are dying. I, too, share the anguish and ambivalence

of that painful situation, but I do not believe in a meaningless death. As a Christian, I believe resurrection is always a
possibility — in fact, the supreme possibility! What I have
attempted to do in these opening chapters is to plant the
seeds of resurrection, to reconnect with life-giving roots, to
rediscover the source where water is purest. This will not
guarantee survival, but it is a crucially important element in
the process of revitalization, a subject I'll explore in detail in
part two.

Conclusion to Part One

Reflecting on the experience of the Second Vatican Council in 1978, the late B.C. Butler, bishop and abbot, wrote:

> "But few of us seemed to have very clear or distinct ideas about the theology of religious life; or if we did they proved singularly out of harmony with the general theological renewal that was taking shape within the Council itself. In default of a good and dynamic theology our temptation seemed to be to take refuge behind the bastions of Canon Law."

The main document on religious life to emerge from the Council, *Perfectae Caritatis*, although hailed at the time as a significant breakthrough, is essentially a revamp of the theology of the vowed life outlined by St. Thomas Aquinas in the thirteenth century. It retained an image of religious life as unique and exclusive to Christianity and continued to interpret the vows in a predominantly ascetical way. A new and significant contribution was its orientation for renewal, marked by a return to the scriptures and to the spirit of the founder or foundress. While this directive engendered some hope and promise, it failed to connect religious with the deeper and wider ambience of their vocation. But it has opened up hearts and minds and enabled us to redress the theological imbalances noted by B.C. Butler.

In today's world, we theologize not on the basis of theory but of experience. For religious, therefore, their experience is their primary theological data. The resources for that reflection are primarily our globalization and our history. No longer can Christian theologians dismiss or ignore the universal nature of the vowed life — that dimension of the giftedness (the charism) which religious life is to the world. It is of relative importance whether Christian religious life is influenced by Buddhism, or whether Muslim forms are related to those of Christianity. And it is intellectually and spiritually naive to suggest that the respective forms of Hinduism, Christianity, Islam, etc. are of a totally independent origin. Both arguments misconstrue the essential nature of religious life, which transcends all formal religions and is

more appropriately understood as a dimension of culture
and spirituality.

It is beyond the scope of this book to explore the historical impact of religious life in its various cultural settings. In
fact such a study has not been done in any of the major religions (to the best of my knowledge) apart from Christianity
(see chapter five). How the historical consciousness and experience can be integrated into our theological reflection is a
subject I treat throughout subsequent chapters.

Both the global and historical aspects are inherent to the
considerations of the present section. Those experiences we
name liminal, those values described as archetypal, and that
apostolic orientation we call the prophetic create the context
in which we can examine, explore, and discover anew the
deeper and richer meaning of the vowed life. Instead of an
institution, buttressed and often stifled by the "bastions of
Canon Law," we encounter a global movement spearheading
a unique human and spiritual enterprise. We are only beginning to tell the real story of religious life which enables us
to break out of the imprisonment of exclusiveness into an
arena of hope and freedom wherein we can celebrate anew
the giftedness (the variety of charisms) with which God has
endowed the world.

Part
TWO

The Christian Context:
Rise and Decline

5
The Historical Paradigm

No reality is more essential to our self-awareness than history.

— Karl Jaspers

It is extremely difficult to date or document the origins of religious life in Christianity. Most historians opt for the second half of the third century (250–300 A.D.) and trace the origins mainly to Northern Egypt. But a number of eminent monastic historians express reservations about the primacy of the Egyptian model, opting instead for Syria as the probable birthplace of the monastic/religious life (more on this in chapter six). Moreover, if the prophetic tradition of the Old Testament becomes predominantly a communitarian movement in New Testament times (cf. pp. 50–51 above), is it not possible that the early Christian communities referred to in Acts 2:44ff. and 4:32ff. are, in fact, the first "monks"? St. Pachomius took the model of Acts as the prototype on which he modelled his first monastic communities.

There is yet another possible biblical prototype, that of the beloved disciple and his followers in John's gospel. It is the view propounded by Oscar Cullmann and Raymond Brown[1]: that is, the gospel of St. John presupposes a Johannine community, a closely-knit group represented by the beloved disciple (Jn 13:23–25; 18:15; 19:26ff.; 20:2–8; 21:20), to whom Jesus addressed a much more personal, distinctively spiritual message, exemplified in John 14–17. According to this theory, Jesus would have had two groups of followers: one arising mainly from official Judaism in Judea and Galilee, the apostles represented by Peter, and concerned with apostolic activity; the other arising from a less orthodox form of Judaism in Jerusalem, namely the Johannine circle,

represented by the beloved disciple, and concerned mainly
with the deepening of faith in Christ himself.

According to John's gospel, there may have existed a
non-institutional, charismatic lay group, which stood in creative confrontation with, or in a complementary relationship
to, the institutional clerical element of the early church. Furthermore, movements of the first Christian centuries, such as
Gnosticism and Encratism, both of which claimed to be authentically Christian in the light of the Johannine New Testament writings, elucidate a form of spiritual life and practice
with a distinct monastic flavor.

These questions may seem academic, but they merit
consideration because they reveal a tendency toward liminal
and prophetic witness in Christianity from the beginning.
What eventually came to be accepted as the monastic life
in Egypt and Syria is probably the final development of an
important undercurrent prevailing from the time of Christ
himself.

By the beginning of the fourth century, religious life
was well launched. Monks, most of whom were hermits,
and many of whom were female (living in their own homes
rather than in hermitages), began to flourish in the Middle East, especially in Northern Egypt. Gradually, the new
movement spread westward, especially under the pioneering work of John Cassian (360–435) and the inspirational life
of St. Anthony compiled by St. Athanasius. Not until the
time of St. Benedict (480–540), however, did the Christian
monastic movement leave a marked imprint on mainland
Europe.

The Evolving Pattern

I do not wish to record the various developments which
enabled the vowed life to spread throughout the Christian
world; that type of information is readily available in other
sources.[2] Instead, I wish to examine the evolving patterns
that mark the different epochs of religious-life development,
recorded by various historians. In this way, I hope to capture
the underlying dynamism that makes religious life a unique
feature of culture and religious belief in every epoch of human history.

The analysis that follows is an attempt to decipher a series of cyclic developments covering Christian religious life from its suggested origins in the third century to the present time. The theoretical framework was initially outlined by the French Jesuit, Raymond Hostie.[3] His theory makes many generalizations, is based on a number of unproven assumptions, and is modeled exclusively on male orders and congregations. Nonetheless, it carries a ring of truth and makes sense of historical developments that otherwise remain disconcerting and baffling.

The subsequent research of the Marianist Brother Cada and associates[4] endorsed Hostie's historical findings with sociological evidence (which I will examine in chapters seven and eight) and further enhances Hostie's theoretical framework.

The kernel of Hostie's theory is summarized in these words:

> Religious institutes have a hardy life. They need a period of gestation from ten to twenty years. To consolidate, they need almost double that time. Their full development, if not postponed by a period of incubation, takes almost one hundred years. They remain stabilized during an almost equal period of time. Then suddenly they begin a downward curve, which in its turn can last from fifty to one hundred years, after which, according to circumstances, extinction is duly registered. . . . The complete life-cycle of groupings of religious life stretches out over a period varying between 250 and 300 years.[5]

Within each life cycle we identify five consecutive phases:

(a) *The foundation phase*:   This period consists of some twenty to thirty years, a time of grace and charism with a strong sense of integration and cohesion centered on the founding person.

(b) *The expansion phase*:   This comprises a minimum of fifty years during which the original charism or inspiration is institutionalized. This process can involve certain organizational crises; for example, the initial efforts to establish the Cistercian lifestyle, solved by the introduction of the general chapter. The early Franciscan debate on poverty is another good example.

(c) *The stabilization phase*:   This may last for a century or more. A feeling of success pervades the group, and the group's cultural and spiritual influence has a wholesome, redeeming effect both on its members and on those to whom they minister. However, this success is a breeding ground for stagnation: activism begins to dominate, work satisfaction displaces the centrality of Christ, and members tend to be carried along by the sheer inertia of the community's activities rather than by deep personal commitment. A feeling of overall well-being rules out the necessity for change, and a hidden type of rigidity begins to set in. This is the phase in which wealth begins to accumulate, poverty becomes problematic, and prayer life recedes into the background.

(d) *The breakdown phase*:   This period of disruption and disillusionment may take place quite rapidly or in a matter of a few decades. This phase begins with a minority's dissatisfaction with the internal life of a group or the relevance of its external commitments. Institutional structures and belief systems give way to widespread doubt and stress. Going back to the time when things were going well is an illusive dream. The sense of crisis grows, membership decreases, and internal abuses increase. The breakdown may be so severe as to force a group to withdraw from many of its long-established apostolates.

(e) *The transition phase*:   Any one of three outcomes is possible:

1)   Total extinction: This has happened to 76 percent of all groups of male religious founded before 1500, and to 64 percent of those founded before 1800. Historically, this would seem to imply that most groups of religious in the church today will eventually become extinct.

2)   Low level of minimal survival: A low profile can last for several centuries. Of all male groups, only five percent of those founded before 1800 have a current membership larger than two thousand.

3)   Those who survive and enter a period of revitalization: Three characteristics tend to accompany this revival: a transforming response to the signs of the times; a reappropriation of the founding charism; and a profound renewal of the life of prayer, faith, and centeredness in Christ. This

upsurge of new life demands deep, personal transformation, coupled with insight and vision. A new theory emerges which will guide the community in its search for new modes of living and working.

The Major Historical Cycles

When this model is applied to the history of religious life within Christianity, we can establish the following historical cycles:

First Cycle: c.200–500; the original foundations of Syria and Egypt, the bedrock tradition of Christian religious life.

Second Cycle: c.500–900; the first Benedictine era, marking the upsurge of religious life in the West.

Third Cycle: 900–1200; the second Benedictine era, consisting mainly of the Cluny reform and the rise of the Cistercians.

Fourth Cycle: 1200–1500; the Mendicant era, during which the friars came to prominence.

Fifth Cycle: 1500–1800; the era of the Apostolic Congregations, with an orientation toward popular missions, education, and care of the poor and sick. This era saw the emergence of such groups as the Jesuits, Vincentians, teaching brothers, and nursing sisters.

Sixth Cycle: 1800 to the present day; the Missionary era, consisting of many new groups of priests, brothers, and sisters with distinctive missionary apostolates.

Unprecedented upsurges can and do take place within different cycles; for example, the rise of the Cistercians in the third cycle: this group emerged when the basic model of the second Benedictine era was already declining. It succeeded in halting the rapid decline which followed the Cluny reform, but only for a period of about fifty years, after which time the Cistercians themselves, immersed in secular affairs, lost much of their spiritual and cultural vitality. Another unprecedented upsurge is that of the canonical congregations (a form of religious life for secular clergy) which has occurred at various times between the fourth and nineteenth centuries. However, the thesis is valid insofar as it claims that religious life in each cycle hinges on one basic image — the mendicant, the apostolic, the missionary, etc. — and within that perspective religious groups enjoy a renewed spiritual growth and cultural impact. It must also be noted that many congregations initially founded for a specific purpose — the Jesuits in the apostolic era, or the many French congregations of the nineteenth century — readily identify with the wider apostolate peculiar to that cycle.

Each cycle is unique, yet all are remarkably similar in their pattern of growth and expansion. We will now examine in further detail the unique features of each cycle, a process which, hopefully, will clarify considerably the historical forces at work in religious life today.

First Cycle: The Original Foundations of Syria and Egypt

This cycle is unique not merely because it contains the bedrock tradition, the roots, of religious life in Christianity (explored in greater detail in chapter six), but because it retained for over two hundred years the vitality, spontaneity, and freshness of the foundation phase, which lasts for little more than thirty to fifty years in the other cycles. Cada claims that the foundation phase is marked by a transforming experience in which

> ...a new appreciation of the message of Jesus leads to innovative insight on how the condition of the church or society could be dramatically improved or how a totally new kind of future could be launched. A new impetus to live the religious life in all the totality of its demands is felt, and a new theory emerges that is at once a critique of the present, an appropriation of the past, a compelling image of the future and a basis for novel strategies.[6]

The depth of human concern, described by Cada, coupled with an equally deep and vital spirituality existed in a unique way among the early Syrian groups and in the monasteries of St. Basil, as we shall see in a later chapter.

Despite the spiritual and cultural impact of these early groups, their downfall came about quite rapidly. In 451, the Council of Chalcedon drew up a code of legislation for the founding and governing of monasteries, an act that seems to have initiated the first phase of decline in the history of religious life. The decline happened rather slowly with the

Basilian monasteries, but in Egypt the decline was much
more rapid. Accumulation of wealth,[7] bitter strife caused
by the intrigues of ecclesiastical politics,[8] and an introverted
withdrawal from society by the monks (even to the extent of
prohibiting priests from visiting the monasteries) accompanied the decline. By 500 little had remained of the Egyptian
model except what had been transferred to the West by John
Cassian.

Second Cycle: The First Benedictine Era
   St. Benedict wrote his Rule about 540, some 100 years
after John Cassian had implanted the Egyptian model of religious life in Europe. Benedict, like all the great founders,
was a man of simplicity and personal sanctity, and was
endowed with a deep love for humanity. Contemporary
writers[9] are much attracted to Benedict's Rule and the lifestyle which it engendered. As happened in the first cycle,
this original vitality seems to have lasted well into the second century of the Benedictine era.
   Benedictinism became a powerful cultural, educational,
and social influence during its expansion phase, winning
wide approval among church and state authorities around
600–700. This public image brought about the inevitable
corruption, which took place during the latter half of the
stabilization phase, commencing about 750. The downfall
was first detected by political leaders — for example, Charle-
magne — who initiated a monastic reform program at the
beginning of the ninth century. With great enthusiasm Benedict of Aniane set about implementing the reforms, effecting
a new cohesion and a stronger unity in all the monasteries
of Europe. His effort came too late. In fact, it now seems that
the breakdown phase of this cycle had already commenced
when Benedict started his reforms in 817. The ensuing corruption and strife has been well documented.

> Take for instance this picture from the celebrated mon-
> astery of Farfa. In 936 two of the monks murdered the
> abbot and seized the abbey. For years they ruled as
> joint heads, carrying on a perpetual struggle with each
> other, squandering the convent's [i.e. the monastery's]
> estates on their followers and soldiers. One of them was
> the father of seven daughters and three sons, whom he

> ostentatiously brought up in princely luxury. . . . Each
> had a mistress with whom he lived openly. That these
> might not be without finery, the consecrated vestments
> were turned into dresses, the altar dressings melted
> down into earrings and brooches. In spite of all at-
> tempts at reform by the brothers of Cluny, this state
> of affairs went on for fifty years.[10]

Fortunately, Church history does not record many episodes of this nature, yet similar events have occurred many
times in the history of religious life. They well depict the social and spiritual chaos of the breakdown phase, paving the
way for the inevitable dissolution at the end of each cycle.
Somehow, revitalization always takes place and religious life
enters a new cycle of growth and expansion.

Third Cycle: The Second Benedictine Era

As a reform movement Cluny remains one of the most
outstanding in the history of the church. However, its short-
comings lay in its methodology: it sought reform within the
system which had caused so much decay and destruction.
It worked within a feudalistic structure which it had converted to its own needs, but in time the needs of the system
dominated, the eagerness for reform faded, and apathy and
disillusionment set in once more.

Nevertheless, it produced one of the few successful efforts at revitalizing a former model of the religious state.
The Cistercians, in their effort to recapture the purity and
originality of Benedict's rule, temporarily revived the cal-
iber of religious life. However, their withdrawal from the
thoroughfare of life was an inadequate — indeed, irrelevant — response to the new materialistic and intellectual
mentality of contemporary Europe. The Benedictine ideal
continued to decline. Political, social, and spiritual life lost its
vitality.

In the third cycle the freshness of the first thirty to fifty
years was followed by a long expansion phase. The rise of
the Cistercians in 1098 marks the final stage of the stabilization phase and the onset of the breakdown phase. The breakdown phase in this cycle is quite intriguing; the Cistercians
were prepared to learn from the mistakes of history. To shun
the inevitable accumulation of wealth (with its consequent

downfall), they asked for marshy land away from the thoroughfare of public life. To devote themselves more fully to
prayer and contemplation they formed a new group, the
lay brothers (*conversi*), to work the land and administer the
needs of their monasteries. However, the lay brothers converted the marshes into huge agricultural terrains and by the
end of the twelfth century the Cistercians found themselves
back in the business world. Although the Cistercians themselves continued to flourish, their spiritual impact dwindled
considerably. A new spiritual thirst arose in Europe; it met
with a poor response from the monks. The time was ripe
for a new image; a fresh cycle in religious life was about to
commence. Europe needed a new charismatic vision: Francis
emerged to fulfill that need.

Fourth Cycle: The Mendicant Era
     With the founding of the Franciscans in 1209, religious
had taken their first major step away from the monastic
world which had dominated the Western scene since the
time of Benedict. The Franciscans, the Dominicans, and, to
a lesser extent, the Carmelites and Servites showed that the
church was not to be identified merely with monasteries or
institutions. Christ could also be encountered in the marketplace and in the classroom.
     Inner strife and friction, which by now had become a
familiar to religious life, left its mark on the mendicants,
too. Plague-stricken Europe reduced the manpower of these
groups. Also the abuses of church life generally crept into religious orders, and with the dawn of the Renaissance (1450–
1500) the mendicant charism dwindled considerably.
     This cycle is particularly interesting for the unique na-
ture of its foundation period. "Nowhere else in the history
of religious life," writes Veilleux, "can we discover such a
combination of poetry, charm, and mysticism as we do in
the origins of the Friars Minor."[11] Francis and Dominic were
innovators and offered models of religious life which were
strange, yet highly relevant for the needs of the time. They
faced adverse circumstances, as church life generally was in
a state of disarray, and in 1215 the Fourth Lateran Council
ruled:

> Lest the extreme diversity of Religious Orders lead
> to confusion in the Church of God, we firstly prohibit
> anyone else to found a Religious Order. But whoever
> wishes to enter the Religious Life, let him join an Order
> already established. Similarly with anyone wanting to
> set up a new Religious house, let him choose a rule
> and form of life from among the approved Religious
> Orders.

Dominic acknowledged this directive and adopted the
Rule of St. Augustine, giving it an orientation that made the
Dominican rule practically a new one. Francis continued to
insist that the only rule he wished to adopt was the gospel
message of Jesus himself, but a group of Friars prevailed
upon him to compile a new rule, which despite the canonical
prohibition of 1215, was approved by Pope Honorius III in
1223 and came to be known as the *Regula Bullata*.

The courageous and daring initiative of Francis, Dominic,
and the entire mendicant movement in its foundation phase
has important implications for crisis periods in religious
life (the present one included): no matter how entrenched
religious life becomes in any one historical, cultural, or spiritual mold, the Spirit will call forth prophetic leadership to
pioneer new possibilities in response to new needs. Unfortunately, the old, well-established groups rarely seem to be
prepared for the moment, and fade into oblivion. Yet, religious life continues to flourish.

The rapid growth of the mendicant model is of particular historical interest. Already in 1220 Francis had attracted
some three thousand followers, most of whom were laymen.
This, in fact, was the last major lay development in the history of religious life; henceforth the clerical image prevails.
Francis died in 1226 leaving his followers with many unresolved problems, poverty being the most acute. For the
following three hundred years poverty was to remain divisive among the Franciscans, leading to the emergence of
many splinter groups, including the Spirituals, the Laxists,
the Moderates, and the Capuchins.

Despite this internal crisis, which existed almost from the
very beginning, the Franciscans enjoyed an expansion phase
of spiritual vitality, cultural impact, and numerical strength,

accommodating 35,000 members at the eve of the Black
Death in 1347. This observation seems to suggest that no crisis, whatever its intensity, can offset the upward growth and
expansion which the Spirit generates in the opening decades
of each cycle.

At this juncture the historian is forced to ask: Are we
dealing with a form of historical inevitability — an inevitable
growth rate in the first half of a cycle, and a predetermined
decline in the latter half? One suspects that a solution to
this dilemma does not rest in a philosophical interpretation of history but rather in a humble recognition that the
Holy Spirit promotes the growth and decline of religious
life within the mysterious plan of the divine economy. The
history of religious life seems to be food for prayer and contemplation rather than for intellectual evaluation.

Fifth Cycle: The Era of the Apostolic Congregations
The mendicants had opened up new avenues for the
witness of religious life. Starting with the Jesuits, a number
of new groups, both male and female, gave religious witness
a more distinctively secular flavor. This cycle is marked by
a great variety of apostolates and a close liaison between the
hierarchical church and groups of religious, the latter largely
manipulated and controlled by the former.

This era was dominated by an expansion phase of some
150 years when men and women religious pioneered many
new initiatives in education, hospitalization, and popular
missions. It also marks the beginning of emancipation for
women religious. Prior to 1500, practically all nuns were contemplative and cloistered. Various attempts were made to
break out of this mold, only to be frustrated by the decrees
of the Council of Trent, which imposed cloister on all nuns
and punished violations of cloister with excommunication.

But the inventive Spirit of God was not to be thwarted.
Visionary people like St. Vincent de Paul and Angela Merici
of the Ursulines found ways of circumventing repressive
legislation. Loosely-knit groups of women, without formal
rule, habit, or cloister, usually living in their own homes,
united around special apostolic projects on behalf of the
poor, the sick, and the marginalized. They gave birth to

female apostolic religious life, one of the most powerful and creative resources the church has ever known. Of the early Daughters of Charity, St. Vincent de Paul wrote:

> They are to have no monastery but the houses of the sick, who have for cells only a lodging or the poorest room, whose chapel is the parish church, who have the streets for cloisters. They are enclosed only by obedience; they make the fear of God their "grille," and they have no veil but their own modesty.

The female contribution added variety, depth, and humanity to the apostolic image of religious life while also contributing uniquely to the growth in valor and holiness within the church at large. In 1750 there were few public indications of impending decay, yet by 1800 the apostolic model was falling to pieces under the expulsions of both church and state. What brought about this unexpected and unprecedented downfall?

This breakdown phase merits special attention. It is a stark reminder of the provisional and fragile nature of institutions of religious. Two factors in particular seem to point the way to impending disruption.

One was an introverted spirituality. A strict, individualistic spirituality prevailed, heavily tinged with the Lutheran emphasis on man's total sinfulness and alienation from God. Hence, religious, despite their admirable apostolic endeavors, tended to turn within themselves and away from the world of sinful humanity to seek salvation within the spiritual security of their communities. A second factor was excessive church control. It was during this era that religious life was first subjected to a canonical form of papal and episcopal control (hence the distinction between orders and congregations), thus generating a new identity for religious life as an institution within the church. "Religious are an elite of dedicated and militant servants of the church with a high level of individual holiness, and a readiness to defend the church on any front. . . ."[12]

An introverted spirituality is a continual threat to a religious group, particularly where cultural, historical, and theological insights are considered to be irrelevant or even dangerous. The original inspiration for religious life arose from a charismatic lay group working in close liaison with the ordinary members of the local church, bearing witness to evangelical values which were and continue to be essential to the growth and progress of humanity. Religious are in the world, for the world. Flight from the world, as understood in the Egypt of Cassian's time, is a culturally determined concept with a strong apocalyptic or end-time overtone (see chapter thirteen). Humanitarian witness and concern — especially for the poor, the outcast, the rejected — lies at the heart of the most authentic forms of religious witness. This was the kernel of Basilian monasticism, with its strong incarnational flavor. Perhaps it was from this background that religious life came to be known as "the following of Christ" (Sequela Christi). How appropriate this ancient description could be in a renewed theology of the religious state.

Efforts by church authorities to structure and control religious life have not been very successful. The Syrian groups had no "superior" other than the head of the local church, the bishop. This early liaison between religious and the hierarchical church seems to have been positive, creative, and immensely beneficial to the church.[13] Even in Basil's time the same healthy relationship persisted. In more recent times the relationship between these two groups has been somewhat strained and uncertain because of a variety of historical and cultural circumstances.

The first break with the official church seems to have occurred in Egypt, where the hermits tended to opt for a solitary life in protest against the increasing institutionalization of the church.[14] Some of the early fathers took this belief to an extreme in encouraging the monks to shun ordination to the priesthood. Had they known the more authentic Syrian tradition (outlined in chapter six), such an approach would not only have been unnecessary, but would have been seen as meaningless.

From quite an early date, bishops in the West sought to establish monastic conditions for their clergy, in the hope of fostering better quality in the secular priesthood. Orders of Canons Regular continued this tradition up to the sixteenth century. The eventual institutionalization of clerical celibacy is just one outcome of this move.

Throughout the sixteenth century, several congregations originated with the aim of improving the quality of priesthood and priestly formation within the church. Among these groups were the Theatines (1524), the Barnabites (1530), the Somachi (1532), and, perhaps best known of all, the Oratorians (1564). An unfortunate repercussion of this otherwise timely movement was a tendency to "clericalize" religious life, a tendency which became even more pronounced within the Counter Reformation. Religious priests were perceived to be more valuable (and more useful) as priests rather than as religious; in time, even sisters were forced to assume an institutional role which identified them with the clergy and undermined the lay aspect of their liminal and prophetic vocation.

The picture becomes much more complex when we examine the historical evolution of religious exemption. The anomalies of this practice are neatly summarized by Rees:[15]

> Prior to the Council of Trent the history of exemption fell into two periods. Until the twelfth century, exemption was a general condition for the establishment and development of monasteries. From the twelfth century until Trent it was a source of widespread contention because the privileges granted to monks were so extensive that they seriously curtailed the authority of local bishops. To alleviate this tension the Council of Trent inaugurated a reform which, while not reducing the privileges of the regulars concerning the inner lives of their communities, nevertheless restored the authority of the bishops in matters of pastoral ministry and public ecclesiastical order.

From these observations it becomes clear that the relationship between religious and the official church has rarely risen above a functional level. This seems to be particulary true of post-Reformation times when the church sought to exert strict control over all movements within its ranks. When this was coupled with the narrow, individualistic spirituality of the seventeenth and eighteenth centuries a progressive state of spiritual stalemate seems to have set in, leading to the rapid decline and virtual extinction of the apostolic model (the fifth cycle) toward the end of the eighteenth century.

Sixth Cycle: The Missionary Era

Prior to the expulsion of the Jesuits at the end of the eighteenth century there were an estimated 300,000 male religious in the Catholic church. It is estimated that there were little more than 40,000 when the Jesuits were officially restored to friendship with the church in 1814. Bearing in mind that the latter number includes a handful of new foundations, one can safely estimate that the apostolic model had lost almost 90 percent of its manpower in less than forty years. Such is the harsh reality of the breakdown phase leading to virtual extinction in the history of religious life.

Apart from the Jesuits, very few of the older groups were restored to their original numerical strength. The onus of growth in the nineteenth century rests with several new congregations of sisters, brothers, and priests (many of which were founded in France) who became the backbone of the Catholic missionary movement. To our day, this movement absorbs large numbers of men and women religious.

The missionary era enjoyed the original vitality and progressive expansion of all former cycles, reaching approximately 80,000 members by 1850 and growing to a massive 1,330,000 (one million females and 330,000 males) members in 1960. The sixth cycle seems to have reached its zenith point in the early 1960s. Numbers have been declining since then, reaching an estimated 940,000 in 1990, registering a 35 percent decline in the thirty years since 1960. On this reckoning, the missionary cycle will have run its course sometime between 2050 and 2080, thus verifying once again the classical cycle of 250–300 years.

However, outright extinction is never registered. A small percentage will succeed in the revitalization process, but far more important is the reassurance of history that the Holy Spirit will activate new initiatives, a renewed model, and with it the dawn of a new cycle. Indeed, the first indications of new life, seeds of resurrection sprouting forth, may be discernible in movements of the twentieth century, such as Taize, the brothers and sisters of Charles de Foucauld, the sisters and brothers of Mother Teresa of Calcutta, the basic Christian communities of Latin America, and the vast array of Christian communities that continue to spring up across the world.

The turning point in the sixth cycle (the early 1960s) indicates that the missionary model was already declining prior to the Second Vatican Council. The proposed reforms of the council may have highlighted or even intensified the declining process, but it is historically inaccurate to suggest (as some writers have done) that the Council caused the present crisis. There is a historical timeliness (appropriateness?) about the diminishing impact of religious life today. Why the decline is taking place and what to do about it are considerations of subsequent chapters. We record and acknowledge the historical facts, not for the purpose of plunging us into despair and despondency, but to alert us to the possibilities for the future.

The Impact of History

Whatever its limitations, the cyclic model is useful and enlightening to the extent that it delineates factors which identify both decline and decay and possibilities of revitalization. I suggest that the historical model traces the symptoms of decay and the process of breakdown much more clearly than the process of revitalization. The sociological analysis of chapters seven and eight offers more on how revitalization can be activated and enhanced.

Another issue worthy of comment is the distinction which today must be made between religious life in the church of the first world (Europe, the U.S.A., and Australia) and the church of the third world. In the third world generally, religious life is more vibrant and prophetic. Vocations tend to be more abundant and religious life seems to have a brighter (albeit, a struggling and often painful) future. While religious life in the Western world seems to be well on track in terms of Hostie's paradigm, this is clearly not the case in third world developments. Are we dealing with two different models? Or does the upsurge in the third-world church mark the beginnings of a new cycle? I would opt for the latter interpretation with its inherent invitation to explore ways and means of opening our hearts and minds to what God's Spirit is doing in the young churches. I am not advocating a transfer of a Latin American or Asian model to European soil, but I do believe that the vitality and new vision of the south can activate and animate new possibilities elsewhere in the Christian church. While respecting cultural differences, I don't believe we can separate these two realities.

We are arriving at a complex ecclesiological question. On the one hand, we accept the unity of the church and, consequently, we strive to keep open the possibility of one part, sector, or experience of the church being revitalized by the other. On the other hand, we cannot ignore the stark reminder of Mark 2:22 that new wine must not be poured into old wineskins. Is it possible, therefore, that the old models of church and of religious life still prevailing in much of the northern hemisphere must actually die before the new creative models of the south can take root? Why it should happen that way is baffling and mysterious, but not for those among us who can accept Hostie's historical analysis. It has happened many times. And the reality that died has quickly been supplanted each time by a vibrant new vision.

How does the historical evidence help us address the current decline in religious life? I attempt a response to that question in chapters seven and eight when I align the historical insights with sociological considerations. Meanwhile, I return to the origins of religious life in the Christian context, outlining what scholars of recent times have been discovering. Our roots are very sacred and contain some vital clues for our ongoing growth and development. The bedrock tradition of religious life in the West is quite a fascinating story. We take it up in the next chapter.

6

A New Look at the Origins of Religious Life

We have to rediscover the past, but discover it in its ambiguity, so that it can give us courage in a present, moving into the future. This is the difference between dynamic Christian hope and static religiosity.
— Thomas F. O'Meara

The historical renewal of religious life always seems to originate within the decline of a former model. Thus, the Mendicant movement arose as Benedictinism faded into the background. The Apostolic image emerged as the Mendicant movement lost its original vitality. The Missionary movement came into prominence with the expulsions at the end of the Apostolic era. Every new impetus seems to have a number of common factors — the original grace, charism, spirituality, vitality — dominating the first twenty to fifty years, which then, after the death of the founding person, gradually fades into the background and frequently disappears.

One historical cycle seems to have retained its original vitality for the greater part of its life span and, therefore, merits special consideration. Contrary to popular opinion, its story is not a tale of outstanding ascetical prowess, but an unfolding exploration of how the Spirit of God calls forth and invigorates a great diversity of gifts and charisms.

The Egyptian Model

Religious life is said to have originated in Egypt in the third and fourth centuries of the Christian era. St. Paul of Thebes (whose life was written by St. Jerome) retired to the desert about the year 250 and thus seems to have been

79

the first Christian hermit. Much better known, however,
are the exploits of St. Anthony (251–356), who attracted
a large number of disciples to serve God in mortification,
prayer, and seclusion. Our main source of information on
St. Anthony is his biography compiled by St. Athanasius.

Anthony's reputation is largely associated with eremitical
asceticism, that lifestyle whereby the monk withdraws to the
desert, entrusts himself to a spiritual master, and lives a life
of intense prayer and mortification. Dissatisfied with certain
aspects of this lifestyle, Pachomius (286–346) developed
a communal system to which Western monasticism owes
its origins. John Cassian (360–435) is mainly (though not
exclusively) responsible for transferring this model to the
West.

Both the eremitical and communal lifestyles were transferred to the East, to Palestine and Syria by St. Hilarion and
Palladius, to Judea by St. Euthymius, and to Mesopotamia
by one called Mar Awgin (Eugenius). A simultaneous upsurge of ascetical devotion in Asia Minor is presumed to
have arisen from Egyptian influence, an opinion which is
no longer widely held.

By 500, the ascetical movement (which in the twentieth
century we call the "religious life," incorporating a variety of
forms, contemplative, mendicant, apostolic, etc.) had spread
throughout the entire Roman Empire, attracting large numbers of disciples and establishing numerous hermitages and
monasteries.

The original impulse to enter religious life centered
largely on the desire to withdraw from the world to lead a
life of prayer and austerity thus ensuring the salvation of
one's soul. A number of factors motivated this withdrawal.
One was a yearning for a simple lifestyle in an age of political and cultural upheaval; the Roman Empire was beginning
to disintegrate. Another factor was a sense of disillusionment
with a church which, in its efforts to establish itself, had accommodated secular models and standards: "Monasticism
then in one of its aspects was a protest against the growing
secularization of the church which had ceased to be a community of saints and was now a school of righteousness with
many reluctant pupils."[1]

The Edict of Milan (313) procured peace and granted recognition to the church, thus bringing to an end a long phase of persecution in which the martyr was the hero of the church. This factor motivated ascetics to emulate the heroism and sanctity of the martyrs (they came to be known as "white martyrs").[2] A fourth factor was a renewed acceptance that the end of the world was at hand. It was therefore considered futile to promote secular growth, or even address the welfare of the human species itself. One's main duty was to prepare for God's judgment. This conviction, held by many contemporary heretical groups, was particularly strong among the Montanists and Messalians.

In its origins then, Christian religious life (at least the Egyptian model) was a rather strange phenomenon. It consisted almost entirely of lay people. Indeed, its members seemed to have a dislike for clergy and church officials and adopted a nonconformist attitude to both church and state. It was held suspect by the church, although subsequently many of its strongest advocates were themselves church leaders (for example, Basil, Jerome, Augustine). Over the centuries the church has accepted this rather ambiguous model and has frequently encouraged religious to draw strength and inspiration from it.

The renewal advocated by the Second Vatican Council initiated a new search for roots and for the bedrock tradition of religious life. Many scholars considered the Egyptian model to be inadequate and based on sources which were not above reproach.[3] Religious have not felt obliged to live religious life exactly as was done in Egypt of the fourth century. But many argue that certain aspects of Egyptian spirituality — for example, the division of active and contemplative life, the state of *apatheia*, the charity of the passionless man, the stripping of the mind in prayer, and withdrawal from the world — have dominated religious life and may be a contributing factor to the contemporary crisis.

The Covenanters in Syria

Questioning of this nature (largely confined, unfortunately, to monastic scholars) has led to new discoveries,

which, in time, may exert a profound influence on the
renewal of religious life. The general tendency has been not
to abandon the Egyptian model, but isolate its positive com-
ponents and further explore their origins. This exploration
has led scholars away from Egypt to an earlier strand of asceticism prevalent in Syria.

Arthur Voobus[4] is the pioneer in this field, and much of
his research is based on the works of Aphrahat (Aphraates),
Ephraim, and Theodore of Cyr. Although his critics note that
these sources have not been exhaustively studied, further
research of the past twenty years has augmented rather than
disproved Voobus' convictions.[5]

According to Voobus, an ascetical movement of a communal nature existed in Syria, possibly as early as the second
century, a movement which predates Egyptian eremiticism
and is considerably different in both spirit and content. This
movement is best exemplified in the groups known as the
Benyai Qeiama and the *Benat Qeiama* — the Sons and Daughters of the Covenant (hence, Covenanters).

Initially this group consisted of baptized members of the
Christian church at a time when, apparently, baptism involved commitment to an ascetical life, including celibacy
and probably a form of communal living.[6] With the expansion of Christianity, however, baptism became synonymous
with membership in the Christian church; those formerly
committed to a special lifestyle now became a group apart.
In this new capacity their commitment came to be known
as the second baptism, a term frequently used in Christian
literature to describe religious profession.

The following are some of the outstanding features of the
Covenanters:

1)   They did not leave their towns or cities and search
for seclusion.[7] Veilleux and Gribomont are of the opinion
that anchorites and hermits were unknown at this early
stage.[8] The available evidence seems to suggest that the communal ascetical movement predates the eremitical one, one
of the outstanding differences from the traditional Egyptian
model.

2)   Celibacy and singleness of heart are the unique features of these groups. Although commitment to the *Qeiama*

was considered to be lifelong, vows were apparently unknown at this early stage.

   3)   It was a lay organization and seems to have been
well integrated with each local church, existing side by side
with ordinary Christians, and like them subject to the bishop.
Superiors and internal governmental structures do not seem
to have existed among the Covenanters.[9] There is some evidence to suggest that a leading charismatic figure, known
as the "spiritual father" held certain status within the group;
his role, however, was one of spiritual rather than functional
leadership. There are no indications of the male dominance
that prevails in later religious life; women and men seem to
have enjoyed equal status in the Syrian groups.

   4)   In terms of service to the local church, the Covenanters seemed to function mainly in the preparation of liturgical celebrations and the service and care of the sick and
needy. Burkitt describes them as the backbone of the Syrian
church,[10] which tells us little about their functional role, but
indicates the high respect in which they were held among
the people.

   5)   In contrast to Egyptian groups, excessive mortification, long fasting, and social isolation seem largely unknown
among the Covenanters. "The Rule of life which he (Aphrahat) sketches out is quite dignified and temperate, with no
special features of observance of asceticism."[11]

   6)   Celibacy is regarded as superior to marriage. But, un-
like in Egyptian monasticism, marriage is not considered as
essentially evil, belonging to a sinful, material, and passing
world. The Syrian attitude to celibacy (virginity) is beautifully portrayed by Aphrahat:

> For those who obtain this portion there awaits a great
> reward, because it is in our freedom that we bring it to
> fulfillment and not in slavery or under the compulsion
> of any commandment; for we are not forced thereto
> under law. Its model and type we find in scripture.
> And we see in the triumphant the likeness of angels; on
> earth it is acquired as a gift. This is a possession, which
> if lost cannot be recovered, nor can one obtain it for
> money. The one who has it loses it and does not find it
> again; the one who does not have it can never race to

pick it. Love, my beloved, this charism (machabta: gift)
which is unique in the whole world.[12]

Standard textbooks on church history attribute little importance to early Syrian asceticism and its unique form of
monasticism. What is even more misleading is the brief reference frequently made to bizarre and extravagant feats accomplished by mystics of the Syrian church, such as Simon
the Stylite who is reported to have spent thirty years on top
of a pillar. Such claims are not entirely false and are more
easily understood in their historical context.

The Covenant groups seem to have flourished during the
third century. Then at the beginning of the fourth century
began a long phase of persecution under three successive
emperors, Shaphur II (309–379), Vahram IV (388–399), and
Jazgard I (399–421). Because of their benevolent attitude to
slaves and other oppressed groups, the Covenanters were
often the victims of attack. Many of their monasteries were
destroyed, their lifestyle was disrupted, and many fled to
the mountains for shelter and safety. Thus began a new
strand of Syrian asceticism which in due course seems to
have accommodated Egyptian influence; it became much
more individualistic and quite severe in terms of its demands. (There is evidence to suggest that recluses did exist
in Syria from an early date, but it was only after the perse-
cutions that they gained prominence and outnumbered the
Covenanters.)

Fortunately this was not the end of the Covenanters.
What was salvaged for posterity has come down to us
through one regarded unfavorably by the Christian church,
Eusthatius of Sebaste. Eusthatius, described as a "zealous
propagator of monasticism in Asia Minor,"[13] seems to have
been the crucial link in transferring the *Qeiama* model from
its Syrian homestead to its more structured format in Basilian monasticism.

The Basilian Model

Scholars have noted the unique features in the tone, style,
and structure of the monasticism propagated by St. Basil.
Few have attempted an explanation of the differences, but
accepting the Egyptian model as original and authentic they

tended to dismiss the Basilian model as a fringe group of monasticism. On close examination one detects all the main features of the Covenanters in Basil's monasteries: brotherly love, simplicity, moderation, and compassionate care for the sick and underprivileged.[14]

Commentators on the Rule of St. Benedict are quick to point out that the rule espouses elements of Basilian monasticism. If such elements do exist they are largely undetectable under the more obvious influence of John Cassian and the then prevalent rule of the master. What is much more important is the spirit as distinct from the letter of Benedict's rule,[15] fostering a lifestyle which seems to have contained a remarkable degree of originality, flexibility, and moderation.

Although Basil had no direct influence on the West, the spirit of Basilian monasticism has been frequently detected, particularly in the opening decades of each new era of growth, expansion, and decline of religious. Why do these qualities of the bedrock tradition resurface at regular periods throughout history? Is the Holy Spirit striving to lead us back to some original vitality and simplicity? Is the Spirit striving to establish the basic qualities of the bedrock tradition as the permanent values of religious life?

Before concluding, we must return briefly to the Egyptian model. When Cassian came to Europe, he confronted a monastic endeavor consisting largely of wandering monks for whom he set out to create a uniform and universal structure. He modeled that structure on the Christian church in Egypt, especially in Alexandria, not on the Pachomian communities as is often presumed. In fact, Cassian never seems to have visited the Pachomian monasteries. Having devised a structure, he sought to spiritually enliven it with the principles and lifestyle of Egyptian eremiticism.

As a monastic organizer, Cassian cannot be faulted. However, few scholars today would accept his writings as authentic accounts of Egyptian monasticism, particularly Pachomian monasticism.[16] It is now widely accepted that Pachomian monasteries were, in many ways, similar to Basilian monasteries in both spirit and lifestyle, and the traditional progression from eremiticism to cenobitism in Egypt is no longer tenable. Rather, it is postulated that a variety of forms existed from an early date (c. 200), possibly arising initially from groups considered at one time to be orthodox but later deemed to be heretical (for example, Encratism).[17]

Conclusions

In its origins, Christian religious life seems to have arisen in a variety of forms across a wide geographical area. A simple, prayerful lifestyle, including celibacy and a form of community life — even the cells of Egypt consisted of at least three people — seem to be the main ingredients. A close liaison with the hierarchical church certainly existed in Syria, possibly in Egypt too. In all the areas we have considered, the monastic movement consisted almost exclusively of lay people.

What is most striking to the modern reader is the originality, simplicity, flexibility, and moderation found in early asceticism. The members do not seem unduly concerned about structures, works, rules, and regulations, which we associate with religious life today. The early ascetics seem to have been very much in the world, close to people in their struggles and aspirations. Yet clearly they do not belong to the world. Are we dealing with an "original purity" which subsequent generations will forever strive to reinstate but are never likely to succeed in doing?

But subsequent generations have not entirely failed. As indicated above, Benedict recaptured this original vitality; so did the Cluny reformers, Francis, and Dominic in the thirteenth century, St. Vincent de Paul in the seventeenth century, and, in our own day, pioneer religious such as Roger Schutz of Taize, Mother Teresa of Calcutta, and Chiara Lubich of the Focolari movement.

It is my conviction that the Holy Spirit seeks to establish in the church permanent witness to the qualities of the bedrock tradition, and that the challenge of history confronts each religious person and every religious group in the renewal of their religious lives. Moreover, there does not seem to be any blueprint for either individual or group to confront this task except history itself. It records the triumphs and the failures, the abiding truths and the passing realities, the factors which precipitate decay and those which lead to revitalization. History is a source of enlightenment and hope; it is a beacon of light which none of us can afford to ignore.

7
The Vitality Curve:
Growth and Decline

The important thing for this age to remember is that
there is nothing wrong with death with dignity, provided
that it is ringed with resignation, rather than with de-
nial. In fact, this acknowledgment of services ended may
be the last great gift these groups can give.

— Joan Chittister

In 1979, Brother Lawrence Cada and some colleagues wrote
an important book, *Reshaping the Coming Age of Religious Life,*
in which the authors supplemented Hostie's historical analysis with contemporary sociological insights on the rise and
fall of institutions. They rooted the historical paradigm in the
lived experience of women and men religious and were able
to name different dimensions and experiences of religious
life in its unfolding complexity. Of particular significance is
their use of the vitality curve and its application to the evolution of the religious state.

The ability to model and name a social phenomenon
is immensely helpful in comprehending its opus operandi
and predict its likely evolution. When applied to groups
and organizations, the vitality curve describes with clarity
and imagination the various stages of group evolution, the
patterns of human behavior that are likely to predominate at
various stages, and the strategies likely to augment life and
vitality.

The model is applicable to secular and ecclesial groups
alike, and it may be used to assess an international movement such as a religious congregation, a national enterprise
such as a state organization, or a local grouping such as an
industrial plant. My intention is to use the model in its application to the life span of a religious congregation; it may

also be applied to the life cycle of a province or even a sub-section of a province.

THE VITALITY CURVE

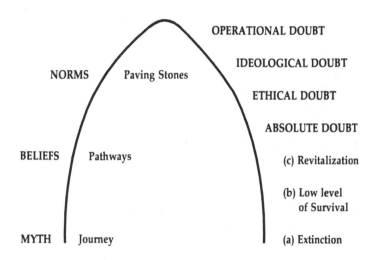

The nature of the various phases of each cycle of the rise and fall of religious life becomes clearer as we treat the different stages of the vitality curve. Practically every religious congregation in the Western world is experiencing something of a decline; consequently, understanding the downward curve merits primary consideration. However, the possibility of revitalization challenges us all, and I believe that it is God's will that we all should become renewed and revitalized. The fact that this rarely happens is attributable, I suggest, to the unwillingness to die, to let go of old models.

We cannot treat revitalization without a thorough understanding of the upward curve because the renewal process is essentially one of rebirth and refounding. Therefore, I treat initially the upward slant with its respective stages of myth, belief, and norms.

A Story That Invigorates

The mythic stage is that of laying foundations. There does not exist a well thought-out plan, but there is a

powerful vision that unites the founding group and ener-
gizes it for action. It is as if the group is carried along by
some, perhaps unnamable, supernatural force. In the case of
a province, the (re)founding members may bring a very specific image of religious life (from another province or from
the founder/foundress) but their desire and effort to enculturate it in the new area is what gives drive and dynamism
to the enterprise. It becomes their story and in some deep
and mysterious sense a story, too, for the recipients of the
new vision.

The story arising from this type of experience we call
myth; it is not a legendary, fanciful tale with no foundation
in reality, but a story loaded with emotion and meaning
which grasps those who tell the story, projects them on a
new course of action usually based on an understanding of
reality radically different from the existing order.

Myth has its own inner driving force, transcending that
of individual vision and even binding together those who
may differ on details. That is not to say that cohesion will always emerge. Frequently a movement never moves beyond
the mythic stage, petering out from an unfocused enthusiasm
which, in time, drains energy and dissipates vitality. This
may not be the fault of the myth-makers; the collapse may
be brought about by the threatened protectors of the status
quo rather than the euphoria of the innovators.

There is a good deal of historical evidence to suggest that
the (re)founding members of a congregation or province succeed, to the degree that they respond to the contemporary
needs of those they serve. Where there is an attempt to impose a message from outside, with little recognition of local
needs and culture, then the effort is likely to fail.

The authentic myth for a religious group seems to demand two preconditions: 1) A profound awareness of the
contemporary world and the wisdom to respond appropriately and creatively to the "signs of the times," and 2) a
founding or refounding group, which I believe will tend to
be a small group rather than an individual.

Historically, we attribute the launching of a new order
or congregation to a founder or foundress, a person fired
and imbued with a new, creative vision. What is frequently

underestimated, and sometimes ignored or forgotten, is the group (two, three, or maybe ten people) who accompany the founding person and play a crucial role in grounding the vision. I feel we have underestimated the group nature of new foundations. Without the accompanying group, the original founding vision may never have become a shared story and, consequently, may never have become the myth that energized a new movement.

We may compare the mythic stage to a journey in which group members travel together, perhaps unclear about their destiny but convinced that it is a journey worth pursuing and one that can be undertaken if they travel together. Here we have a liminal group in its most profound sense, absorbed in new vision and carried along by a psychic energy. It is highly appropriate that the founding charism "explodes"; it is of equal importance that it becomes streamlined into the next stage of belief, which we will now explore.

Beliefs and Convictions

In due course, the story produces a set of beliefs and convictions which give the group a clearer identity and indicate preferential options for lifestyle and apostolic action. The vibrancy and enthusiasm of the myth is still very much alive, but now it is channeled along more specific lines. Instead of a superiorless community, the group chooses to explore alternative forms (one or many) of leadership and authority.

At this juncture, the group must create some appropriate structures to facilitate more effective dialogue, discernment, and decision making. This may cause a temporary crisis in the life of the (re)founding group; parting with the fluidity and flexibility of the myth and opting for a more structured approach may take some time and effort to negotiate.

At this point, also, the group will tend to review its terms of entry and commitment. At the mythic stage, practically anybody who shares the enthusiasm can "jump on the bandwagon." Only the more committed will persevere, and these will tend to become more selective in admitting others to their ranks.

The theological and theoretical underpinnings of the new experiment become important. It is imperative for the group to build on solid foundations; the prophetic members of the group will come to this realization. Thus, the new vision is enunciated and clarified so that it can be shared by all who participate in the experiment.

The second stage, therefore, involves the translation of the dream, the story, the myth, into a set of statements that articulate what the group wishes to achieve. Metaphorically, we may say that the journey is being channeled into pathways. This progression is as necessary for the group's growth and development as it is for its exchange and dialogue with the wider world. Without this step, the myth dissipates, the innovators lose heart, and the dream fizzles out.

It is at this stage in which myth and belief are held in contemporary tension that the group can be a powerful catalyst for change. It is acknowledged and respected by mainstream institutions, but has not been accommodated by them; it is greeted with both fear and respect, and sometimes, paradoxically, with scorn.

To maintain this position for any length of time is difficult; nor indeed would it be to the benefit of the group itself or to society at large. Once the group has raised the level of consciousness, it must engage in formulating policies and strategies and articulating this new awareness through appropriate structures and services.

Rules and Regulations

The normative stage is that of laws, rules, and regulations. At this juncture in the history of orders and congregations, constitutions become important. There is a historical misconception that a family of religious only comes into existence when a new constitution has been approved by the Holy See. This is not always the case, and even when it is, as with the early Franciscans and Dominicans, the constitutions play a very minor role in the group's evolution for at least the first fifty years of its existence.

It is inappropriate for a (re)founding group to outline laws and regulations before embarking on a new enterprise.

This will not guarantee success or make the initial experiment more orderly or fruitful. Most likely, it will have an adverse effect.

At the normative stage, the group or movement may seek to establish itself in the mainstream of society. Because this process is largely unconscious (as are the processes for the former stages) there is a distinctive risk of the new movement being absorbed by the major institutions of the dominant culture. (This, in large measure, is what has happened to the religious orders in the Catholic church of our time).

It is essential for the group's growth and survival to clarify for itself its own commitment and lifestyle and articulate the parameters for its liaison with other movements and organizations in society. The supreme challenge — the pivot on which so many movements succeed or perish — is to retain the myth as the basic source of inspiration and animation. In biblical terms the dilemma is one of holding together the law and the spirit (of the law).

How the group at this stage handles issues such as power, control, and influence is all important. The danger is to emulate what already exists in dominant institutions. This is a sure sign that the group has largely lost or abandoned its myth, and leads to self-destruction. Structures and procedures must be animated by the original dream and inspiration. The group must find the time and space to continue dreaming, imagining, projecting, and praying, even though the supreme temptation is to devote all its time and energy to the task and to rules and regulations that will guarantee the survival of the project.

Formalizing beliefs into a set of rules and regulations provides a sense of identity and security, guaranteeing not merely survival but the opportunity to reform the value system of the surrounding culture. It also provides the opportunity to move into the mainstream society, which is not the same as being absorbed by the dominant institutions of that society. If the group fails to move to this stage, it cannot leave a long-term imprint on the surrounding culture. But it is also the stage of many pitfalls, which may be unavoidable without the wisdom and insight of the enlightened few.

Updating the Constitutions

Ever since the Second Vatican Council, religious have been trying (unconsciously for the greater part) to apply remedial action at the norms stage. The name of the process has been "rewriting" or "updating constitutions." Whether such action could enliven a group remains obscure. Indeed, quite a number of religious would concur with the verdict of O'Meara: "The outcome is always dubious when Christians start renewing their institutions by rewriting laws and creeds. . . . Meeting with the purpose of solving problems entirely through legislation and administration can only fail."[1]

Updating and rewriting constitutions has been an enriching experience for many religious, deflated somewhat by the reaction of the Holy See requiring tedious modification of words and phrases. One wonders, however, if the new constitutions have been or can be a life line for new vitality.

In terms of the vitality curve one questions the wisdom of rewriting constitutions. The implication seems to be that revitalization can be fostered by recreating the normative process, thus bypassing the stages of a new myth and a new belief system. I don't believe that is possible. Nor can I accept the suggestion that a comprehensive overhaul at the normative stage will automatically reawaken the values of the mythic and belief stages. This view is based on an erroneous perception that the myth (and its accompanying beliefs) remains unchanged over time and that the constitution, which embodies the myth, is a central part of the congregation's sacred story. The perception alleges that the founding charism always remains the same, and that all we need to change is the institutional framework which embodies the vision. Thus we set about revising norms (expressed in constitutions and statutes) and explore ways of internalizing the new norms.

Intervention at the normative stage is not entirely new. There are many historical examples, within both sacred and secular institutions. Consistently, the result is similar. Reform is superficial and shortlived. The group doesn't reconnect with its life-giving myth; at best, it deals with a myth that has outlived its time and usefulness. Giving it a new normative context will make it look more attractive and, perhaps, more meaningful, but it will fail to generate the (re)founding vigor and enthusiasm and set the group on a new vitality curve. Only a new myth can do that.

There have been some notable attempts at a new story (myth) in renewal programs of recent years. These are often encapsulated in renewal documents, future statements, and vision statements. Religious often ask what weight these statements have and how they relate to constitutions. Insofar as these statements may be articulating a new myth, they are significantly more important than constitutions. They may not have canonical approval, but they articulate the (re)founding dream and story. Many of these statements are sacred stories, with primal and primordial underpinnings, which are a great deal more profound than rules and regulations.

The Utopian Flaw

To an outsider this stage is easily recognizable. Whereas at the norm stage, group members may claim, "We do things this way," in this stage, they are saying (unconsciously, and, sometimes, consciously), "And our way is the best, perhaps, the only valid way to do things." Power and arrogance have taken over, to a degree that becomes self-destructive; the myth has become a blind conviction, an ideology. How the policies and strategies may serve the common good is no longer an urgent question. The survival of the group itself has become its primary agenda. This begins the downward slide to ruination, a process that is practically impossible to reverse.

The group has lost touch with the myth. The life force that energized the enterprise is abandoned (not consciously or deliberately) for a compromise with the accompanying cultural forces (secular and ecclesiastical). It seems to be difficult to recognize the shift from the life-giving, upward curve to the declining process within the stabilization phase of the vitality curve. Some scholars claim that it is the inevitable destiny of all groups and that it just cannot be averted. Perhaps, at some higher stage in our evolution, we may attain the wisdom to retain the creative myth in a more enduring way. For the moment, we are aware of our sinful condition which condemns every good intention to a limited destiny.

The Downward Curve

The stages of the downward movement of the vitality curve are easily identified, and the process clarifies a great deal of what is happening in orders and congregations today, especially in the Western world. Doubting and questioning characterize all four stages. It is not the doubts, however, that cause the problem; they result from the problem, a process of decline and decay that seems well nigh impossible to reverse.

Operational Doubt. In this stage, people become uncomfortable and uneasy with the way the system is working. The doubt tends to be free-floating and not aimed at any specific apostolate or aspect of lifestyle. People feel that something is going wrong but they don't know what it is; consequently, they are unable to address the problem. To relieve anxiety, people change or modify externals, as illustrated by the attempts in the 1960s to make religious houses more homely and comfortable and the modifications of religious habit. These gestures were necessary and had merit, but they failed to address the real problem.

At the level of a province or local community, this stage is marked by a feeling that things are not going right. Leadership is perceived to be inept; work continues as normal, or may even increase in quantity (as a compensation). Doubts about the effectiveness of the operation are frequently expressed, but nobody seems to have either the energy or good will to address the doubts. Often the doubts are dismissed as being superficial and not to be taken seriously, or a rationalization, which, in fact, accentuates the problem.

Not all members of a congregation will share this anxiety. Initial concern about the effectiveness of ministry or the relevance of lifestyle results in a twofold response. For some members, the questioning and unrest becomes more pronounced. For the majority, defense mechanisms come into play. The problem is denied and the doubters blamed, and the unease is attributed to lack of personal faith or to secularizing influences. A rift emerges between the "radicals" and "conservatives."

Ideological Doubt. It usually takes a number of years to identify those areas where the breakdown is manifesting itself. Initially, the areas tend to emerge at the stage of ideological doubt. Some of the basic beliefs of the group are questioned and even abandoned. Frequently these areas have included prayer life (personal and communal), poverty (simplicity of lifestyle), and apostolic works as a primary means of satisfaction and personal fulfillment.

Many congregations in the Western world have come through this phase; it was easily detectable (at least in hindsight) in much of what they were experiencing in the 1960s and 1970s. Anxiety about the issues mentioned above is no longer so pronounced and widespread. This does not mean that the problem has been solved. In fact, religious have not progressed; they have compromised. Poverty, prayer, and apostolates are still emotive issues for many communities and congregations. They tend to discuss them in a safe way. Ideological doubt still remains and has, in fact, intensified. Now religious doubt not only the issues, but also what might happen if they really tried to address them. The ability to cope, reform, and change is doubted.

Discussions, meetings, assemblies, and formation programs are some of the methods religious use to address this dilemma. I do not underestimate such noble projects, which have heightened awareness, and alerted religious to an internal malaise.

In a province or in a specific community, the stage of ideological doubt tends to surface in individual claims for freedom and autonomy at the price of shared group values, in an unwillingness to mobilize resources to address serious group issues (let authority handle the problem), in a lack of shared reflection, and in an unwillingness to discern about the future of the group. Even the assistance of outside facilitators may be fruitless at this stage, the dilemma often being that an enlightened leadership perceives a problem that the membership is unable or unwilling to acknowledge.

Reversing the Curve.   Why can't religious reverse the
curve at this stage and set in motion a new life-giving myth?
The re-creation of the myth can evolve from either the stages
of ethical or absolute doubt. In fact, the former seems to be
the crucial point of intervention to determine whether the
final outcome is one of extinction or revitalization. Can the
enterprise be salvaged at the stage of ideological doubt?
It is unlikely that the cumulative awareness of the group
is sufficiently coherent to address the impending decline.
At the ideological stage, there exists a general malaise, but
only the more intuitive and enlightened (usually a minority) can perceive its eventual outcome. Most members of
the group wonder what all the fuss is about and feel that
addressing the problem only exacerbates it. At the ethical
stage, the seriousness of the situation tends to be more apparent and there is a much greater chance of the group responding favorably and acknowledging that something must
be done.

It seems, therefore, that the stage of ideological doubt
must ripen into ethical doubt before it commands serious redress. Things have to deteriorate markedly before enough
people can comprehend that the situation is serious. The
group must lose touch with its life-giving myth or institutionalize the myth so that it has become an ideology that
inhibits rather than enhances growth. An enlightened leadership, therefore, acknowledging symptoms of the ideological
stage, seems to have no choice of action other than guiding
the group toward the ethical stage.

One thing is certain: the vitality curve cannot be reversed. Once the group goes beyond the point of "utopian
flaw," the only course is forward, which is downward.

There is no route to the reincarnation of the myth other
than through the vitality curve — at least to the point of
ethical doubt. One cannot short-circuit the earlier stages
of operational or ideological doubt and leap directly to a
new myth. Why not? Because the consciousness and will-
to-life necessary for the new dream does not exist within the
group. Nor does it seem possible that either an internal or
external agent can activate or generate this awareness. Only
the death-resurrection dynamic (without which the vitality

curve is meaningless, even in a secular context) can generate the consciousness appropriate to negotiate the various stages.

Ethical Doubt. Of all the breakdown stages, this one is most easily identified. When members begin to ask questions or express moral reservations — such as, "Is it right for us to be. . . living in big houses?. . . teaching in selective schools?. . . upholding old-style parochial structures?. . . " — then the group is moving into the stage of ethical doubt. In other words, members are questioning if the context in which they live the religious life is morally tenable. Can it stand up to the test of moral integrity?

These reservations are serious and involve deep questions of conscience. Provincial administrators often resolve them by allowing the proponents to assume an alternative form of ministry, often one of their own choice. It is a sensitive and caring response, but it fails to address the real issue. The real problem is not personal but structural; the longer it is left unattended the more problematic it becomes for a province or congregation, and specifically for a provincial administration.

Sometimes the ethical doubts are dismissed because those who question cannot present their objections in a cogent or convincing manner. Protestors can misjudge a situation and may even be deluded in their perceptions. However, it is also possible that one may have a genuine sense of something being deeply wrong without being able to name the reality. Usually the unease centers on the fact that the underlying moral values are perceived to be alien to the Christian message; for example, a religious-run school in which fees are so high that poor people cannot avail of the service. The province or congregation has implicitly (usually not deliberately) opted to exclude the poor, a stance for which there can be no Christian justification.

The resolution of ethical doubt may demand drastic action, such as closing down an enterprise. This may incur the disapproval of those deprived of a congregation's service and generate a lot of pressure from groups with vested interests. It may also cause a whole range of negative feelings from within the congregation. But action seems imperative, because not to act only exacerbates the apathy and unrest

that already prevails. How soon one should act is a matter
of discernment, but better to err on the side of "doing something" rather than on that of "waiting for the right moment."

How a province or congregation handles this stage largely determines whether or not the group will have to endure
the final stage of absolute doubt.

Absolute Doubt.   In this stage, the personnel shortage
bites so hard that houses have to be closed down and long-
established works are handed over to others. Members are
growing old and there are no vocations. Even where aspi-
rants are forthcoming, the group (especially its leadership)
realizes that it is inappropriate to accept them. Existing apostolates are handed over to lay people, except perhaps for a
few key leadership positions. Provision is made for older
and ailing members (especially in congregations of sisters).
A mixture of depression and resignation prevails. In this scenario, the group acknowledges, however begrudgingly, its
impending dissolution. There is an attempt (largely unconscious) to die with grace, peace, and dignity.

Other groups, probably a majority, will fight for survival.
Some members, usually a minority, perceive how critical
the situation is and propose drastic remedial action; this
initiative may also come from an enlightened leadership.
The group must radically change or otherwise face extinction. In the province generally business may go on as usual,
although it is fairly obvious that many members have neither heart nor feeling for what the province is attempting to
do. A high degree of fragmentation prevails, covertly if not
overtly.

The remedial action means the launching of experiments[2]
to reincarnate the founding charism (myth) and address the
urgent needs of today's world and not those of the past,
however valid past service and ministry might still be. This
usually means relocation of resources and personnel, which,
in turn, usually demands withdrawal from traditional apostolates.

It is very much a death and resurrection experience with
the classic resistances noted by Elisabeth Kübler-Ross.[3] Grief
and pain of separation has to be endured before the joy and
hope of resurrection (relocation) becomes possible. If a group

can face this transition together and enable and support each other through it, then it becomes a powerful experience of growth and new life for the whole province or congregation.

That is why it is desirable to confront the ethical doubt sooner rather than later. The longer a group continues in a doubting, questioning, and fragmenting atmosphere, mistrust and uneasiness grow and the more drained it becomes of life-giving energy. Visionaries move to the margins or, perhaps, leave all together; the more traditional members become defensive and uncooperative. Increasing numbers opt for a more individualistic lifestyle which gives a semblance of the security and affirmation they no longer feel within the province.

The eventual outcome of the decline may be the slow death of resignation or an explosion of negative energy. In the latter, the fragmentation becomes so pronounced and so obvious that members abandon the enterprise. Disagreements and feuds prevail, and projects are forced to close, possibly because of scandal or total mismanagement. A higher authority intervenes and the project is put into "receivership." The group becomes so stuck on the hill of Calvary that members cannot enter into the experience of resurrection. In the case of the death of resignation, it would appear that the group has chosen not to go to Calvary because they perceive it to be too painful; like most of the apostles, they run away — an observation with no judgmental intent, because even the apostles who ran away had much to offer to the emerging church.

In the history of religious life, we have few concrete examples of this outcome. They were so negative and so destructive that nobody chose to document them; in not a few cases, one suspects, nobody was left to record the demise.

Thus we complete the cycle. It may be the end of a province or of a whole congregation, but not of religious life. Inspired by the Spirit, new visionaries rise up and a fresh cycle starts all over again. The cycle of life and death and new life seems inherent to all living reality.

8

Refounding and Revitalization

Even if it is God's will for a congregation to die out,
until we can unequivocally read the writing on the wall,
we must fight on and not surrender. It is not for us to
commit congregational suicide.

— Gerald A. Arbuckle

An estimated 65–70 percent of families of religious have
faded into oblivion. Extinction seems to be the natural destiny for most orders and congregations. At one level this
need not surprise us since death is the final outcome of all
life forms. On the other hand, so many natural processes and
a great deal of human aspiration defy this sense of finality.
Plant and tree life reproduce in cyclic fashion. Humans live
on in their children and in their creative impact on civilization. From earliest times to the present day, there is a human
conviction, however vague, that our dead are not on another
planet or in another place, but close to us in a mysterious,
cosmic relationship.

The Christian concept of resurrection and the Hindu/
Buddhist concept of reincarnation are both theological articu-
lations of the primordial human conviction that in death life
is changed but not ended. In a similar vein, St. Paul challenges us with these words: "There is no change of mind
on God's part about the gifts he has made or of his choice"
(Rom 11:29). The giftedness, which is life in all its variety
and diversity, is intended for growth and expansion, not for
diminution and dissolution. In the final analysis, the will-to-
life and the will-to-meaning cannot be subverted.

There is also an abundance of historical and spiritual evidence to suggest that revitalization is the natural destiny of

all social phenomena, including religious orders and congregations. Once again, I wish to distinguish between religious life as a global, cultural, liminal movement and its many and varied expressions, explored in part one. Any of the expressions may die out — most have become extinct — but the phenomenon itself, because it is so fundamental to the human condition, cannot and will not fade away. Religious life is a permanent dimension of the human will-to-meaning. The Spirit of God at work in our world and in human hearts guarantees survival. However, it is a permanence characterized by growth, change, and alteration; only by becoming ever new can religious life maintain its traditional and permanent significance. This is one of the supreme paradoxes of all life forms.

The various expressions of religious life, therefore, cannot hope to survive unless they, too, are changing, renewing, adopting, along with the cultural and spiritual aspirations of each new era. And yet, for religious-life groups, survival is a more natural destiny than extinction simply because the wider phenomenon (religious life itself) cannot become extinct. In this chapter, I wish to examine revitalization which I believe is a possibility for every order and congregation; indeed, not just a possibility but a destiny, since God does not withdraw his gifts but instead offers to all the grace of being born anew.

Why, therefore, do so many groups decline and die? I believe the answer is quite simple: because they become so encrusted and fossilized in human institutions that they lose contact with their life-giving, spiritual source. Revitalization, therefore, means reconnecting with the "source," getting back to basics, reawakening the myth, and starting over again!

The revitalization process is more complex than we care to acknowledge;[1] in all situations, and at all times, it demands profound change in spirit, orientation, and structure. Cada and associates suggest three elements which are central to the revitalizing process: a transforming response to the signs of the times; a reappropriation of the founding charism; and a profound renewal of the life of prayer, faith, and centeredness in Christ.[2]

Revitalization and the Founding Charism

Revitalization initiates a new vitality curve. I wish to emphasize that it is a NEW one, and not the repetition of a former one. In the case of a province or congregation, this may mean a whole new vision, with new strategies, new lifestyle, even a new spirituality. How does this relate to the guidelines of the Second Vatican Council, which suggests a return to the spirit of the founder?

I consider this to be a very complex subject, the intricacies of which have been underestimated in the renewal taking place since the council. I am not even sure that the council fathers themselves (many of whom were not vowed religious) understood the implications of the guidelines they proposed.

Of central importance is the invitation to religious to return to the spirit of the founding person. Some religious interpreted this as a re-enactment (even a repetition) of what the founder did — for example, "Our foundress ministered to the sick in hospitals; therefore, working in hospitals must continue to be one of our primary works"; or "Our founder taught only boys; consequently, we cannot opt for coeducation."

Others understood the guidelines to mean a translating of the founding vision into the categories and concepts of today; for example, a particular devotion to the Blessed Virgin Mary, formerly expressed via specific prayers, devotions, and rituals focused on her, now becomes an internalization, personally and communally, of Mary's call to make Christ incarnate in the world of today. Apostolic options may remain largely unchanged; members consider the nature of apostolic involvement to be secondary, even irrelevant, since they assume that the apostolates are influenced and revitalized by the impact of the new spiritual vision. In this case, underlying assumptions need careful examination: members may genuinely believe that a renewal of spirit will automatically make effective a renewal of ministry and lifestyle, but the emphasis on spiritual renewal may be a subconscious way of avoiding the structural renewal where the real blockages to growth might lie. A tendency to overspiritualize is, and always has been, a perennial temptation for religious-life groups.

A third manner of interpretation acts on the discerned response to the question: "What would our founder or foundress wish us to do if he or she were alive today?" Many people feel that this question is misguided because the founding charism continues to live in the members and traditions of a congregation. Still, the underlying motives merit attention. Proponents of this view tend to perceive the founding person as one who was keenly aware of the needs of the time and responded appropriately to those needs. In this context, a return to the spirit of the founder means a reappropriation of those attitudes, perceptions, and values which determined and influenced the founder's options. The outcome of that process in the late twentieth and in the twenty-first century, however, may be totally different from that of former times. What the group now chooses to do may have little or no resemblance to what the founding person actually did.

In striving to reappropriate the spirit of the founder, the world being addressed is as important as the person addressing it. What seems unique about many founding persons is their ability to comprehend in depth the fundamental needs of the age, and their ability to respond in a creative way to those needs.

Reappropriating a charism in our time, therefore, has as much to do with "reading the signs of the times" as with understanding the vision of the founding person. Many congregations of the fifteenth and sixteenth centuries specialized in the education of youth. Formal education was practically non-existant, religious were often the pioneers in the field. But is this an urgent need of the late twentieth and the twenty-first century? Perhaps in the third world, but not in the first where education is readily available thanks to the pioneering work of religious. An urgent need of the present time is education in leisure as we face large-scale unemployment, and education in coping with the pace of change in contemporary life. And one wonders if these new educational needs can be met appropriately from within traditional structures often serving a consumerist and competitive rat-race!

Most congregations founded in the nineteenth century lent support to the foreign missionary endeavor. Once again, the scene has changed dramatically. We no longer evangelize simply to convert others to Christianity. We work for the development of the total person and the total culture. In *Evangelii Nuntiandi* a new missiological agenda is set: we ourselves must be evangelized by those we seek to evangelize. While theologians discuss the theological refinements of inter-Christian dialogue, a new wave of interfaith exchange is surfacing everywhere in the world. Indeed, it is only a few decades before Europe and the United States become mission territory. It is a vastly different vision from that espoused by many founding persons in the nineteenth century.

Finally, interpretation of spirituality causes problems for reappropriating a founding charism. Many founders of the nineteenth century employed a spiritual focus on the Sacred Heart, the Blessed Virgin Mary (under several titles), or the Holy Spirit, explaining the titles of many congregations from that time. Some admirable attempts have been made to transform those devotions into more holistic spiritual orientations for our time; for example, devotion to the Sacred Heart is no longer understood in terms of penance and reparation focusing on one biological organ, but with a more incarnational understanding resonating with the New Testament understanding of "heart." The total person, loved and redeemed by a "heart-felt" rather than a "heartless" God, is challenged to bring the same unconditional love and goodness to humanity.

The return to the spirit of the origins of orders and congregations has led to renewed research on the lives of founders and foundresses and a spate of writings, documentation, replicas, and sacred objects connected with them. In some ways this is an admirable pursuit, but it also contains many questionable elements. When one notices a contemporary convent dotted extensively with pictures, statues, and other holy objects relating to a foundress, one is forced to ask if the founding person is not in danger of being enthroned as a false God. There are, I think, many contemporary situations in religious life where the treatment of the founding person comes dangerously close to idolatry.

The Process of Revitalization

With these reflections on the nature of a founding charism, we return to our consideration of the task of revitalization, and thus complete our survey of the vitality curve. Revitalization involves the reappropriation of the founding myth in the light of the group's reflections on the contemporary signs of the times. In a sense, it is the original myth come alive again, but with a radically new look.

How do we know that the charism has been retained? A founding charism continues to live primarily in the members, not in writings, sacred objects, traditions, specific works, although these form part of the reality. A charism survives in the people who articulate the new myth and channel it into the belief and norm stages. They may employ neither the thought patterns nor conceptual ideas of the former model, but this does not mean that they have betrayed the founding charism. They have merely translated it into concepts and categories that respond to the contemporary situation.

Thus a new myth, a new dream, a new story, is born. Deep in their hearts, the members know it is right. This feeling won't arise from intellectual arrogance or from rationalizations, but from a deep rootedness in God's Word, along with a cherished and integrated awareness of the founding charism. Refounding and revitalization is a distinctly contemplative experience. Indeed, it is inconceivable that a group can recreate a myth without a spiritual foundation. Personal and structural conversion go hand in hand.

Revitalization may be initiated at different levels. Leadership teams are often acutely aware of this need but unsure about procedure. Where does one start? How do we go about it? How do we hope to bring all the members with us? Will it create more fragmentation and polarization within the province?

These are critical questions which are best addressed by exploring the questions themselves rather than seeking answers or solutions. The vitality curve is based on a

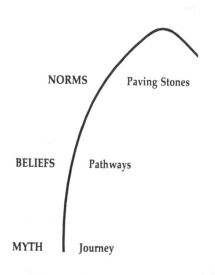

NORMS   Paving Stones

BELIEFS   Pathways

MYTH   Journey

death/resurrection dynamic for which there are no simple or easy answers. Why did Jesus have to die such a cruel and meaningless death before experiencing resurrection? And why did he have to die alone and abandoned by those on whom he staked so much? Why does the seed have to fall into the ground and die before producing new fruit? (cf. Jn 12:24).

I believe these questions are central to the more pragmatic concerns facing religious today. They have that koan-like quality found in Zen Buddhism. One needs to feel them in one's stomach and in the inner chambers of the heart. Only when religious sit long enough with those questions can they hope to attain the wisdom that enables them to adopt a fresh course of action.

At the Provincial Level

Revitalization at the province level demands a variety of strategies and approaches, keeping in mind these broad guidelines.

First, traditional orders and congregations in different parts of the world are likely to be at different stages on the vitality curve. In contemporary Europe many provinces and communities are operating at the levels of ideological and ethical doubt, and veering more toward the latter. However, communities of those same groupings in Asia and, more so, in Latin America, may be experiencing growth of the type depicted on the upward slant of the vitality curve.

A community in Latin America in which liberation theology is the dominant conceptual framework for lifestyle and ministry is likely to be at the stage of moving from the myth to the belief in a new life cycle. A community, region, or province anywhere in the third world, with increasing numbers of native vocations and a well-established lifestyle and apostolic outreach, is likely to be at the normative stage. A perennial danger for such a group is the urgency to consolidate; despite the influx of native vocations, the group is continuing to recruit more personnel from the home province. It may be more appropriate for the expatriate group to be thinking about withdrawal so that the native church can get on with its own task of evangelization.

Second, in those parts of a province where the downward slant is operative, there is a high probability that refounding persons are already beginning to surface.[3] Some will continue to operate within the congregation, even in a traditional capacity, but most are likely to move to the fringes. A perennial task for leadership is to identify these people and channel their vision and resources. Arbuckle suggests that they should be placed either in initial formation communities or in new ministerial experiments. He goes on to suggest that they should not be placed in authority or in leadership roles, especially in those of administration.

Along with refounding persons, there may also be refounding groups, members of congregations who have set up or wish to explore new models of living the vowed life. Sisters in the U.S.A. provide a number of such inspiring initiatives, many of which are unknown because of unresolved relationships with the Holy See (regarding constitutions in particular). Refounding experiments — alternative ways of living the vowed life in response to contemporary needs — are even more important than refounding persons. Without the context or opportunity for the experiment, the mythical vision of the refounding person may remain only a dream; in time, it comes to nothing. A congregation has good reason to rejoice in the fact that it has been blessed with refounding people (only a minority are likely to respond in this way), but it must waste no time in opening up new structural possibilities to ground the refounding vision. In short, it must create new wineskins for the new wine!

A third guideline suggests that members need to be informed and educated on the nature of revitalization. Because of the traditional, hierarchial nature of religious life, many members expect renewal to come from the top down. This is seldom the case. The initiative in the vast majority of instances, inside and outside the church, comes from the ground up. It is also appropriate that these initiatives, personal or collective, should be characterized by a sense of Marxist proletarianism, rebellious youthfulness, and disregard for law and structure; these are all consistent with mythic enthusiasm. In a climate of tolerance and forbearance, these traits will progressively diminish, not in the sense of being obliterated, but in the sense of being channeled into belief systems that will encapsulate the new vision.

Leadership in provinces and communities has the urgent and delicate task, not of attempting to reform the whole province as if somehow it was exclusively their task to do so, but of awakening, identifying, animating, and enabling refounding charisms. And a supreme challenge for the members of provinces is to allow and enable leadership to do that. If every domestic problem has to be referred to a higher authority, then we simply condemn people in leadership to being mere functionaries who will spend so much time and energy doing things (that the members should be doing for themselves) that there is no vitality left to dream, imagine, pray, discern, and redirect the province into new life.

The fourth guideline raises a question: Can we be sure that the revitalizing process will not cause further fragmentation? Social scientists suggest that a typical enterprise consists of three broad categories, with a degree of overlapping. The first category are those who believe in business as usual; they see no problem and believe that the group should continue doing what it always did. The voice of authority is very important for this group, and the more moderate members may be swayed by new ideas coming from the leadership. The second category are those at the opposite end of the scale, the "progressives," with varying degrees of openness to change and revitalization. The third category are those in between, the majority who tend to fluctuate toward one or the other of the above positions. In this category, one finds people who are very devoted to the outfit, who have worked hard and for long years. Precisely, because they have done this, they have never known any other reality and have had neither the time nor opportunity to become acquainted with other possibilities. But their minds and hearts are open, and, although they may initially be quite threatened by change, they can, with gentle and appropriate urging, make the transition.

It is widely held today among advocates of both spirituality and the social sciences that people can change, radically and dramatically, at any stage of the life cycle. I would strongly endorse this view, acknowledging that it is often possible only after the painful removal of blockages in counseling, psychotherapy, or spiritual direction. Religious owe it to each other to encourage, enable, and urge one another toward change; complacency and comfort are not valid options. Growth and change are inherent to the God-given destiny of religious and to their vocation as liminal, prophetic people.

In the end, however, every person's freedom is to be respected. If, after help and encouragement, people refuse to change, they have chosen to remain as they are. But they must not be allowed to hold back those who wish to move forward. How leadership within congregations choose to handle this dilemma is a sensitive issue on which it would be unwise to generalize. At any level of life — personal, familial, or collective — growth and change are always at work. In the past, they were largely taken for granted, but increasingly, they become the center-stage issues which will absorb a great deal of time and resources into the immediate future.

Refounding and Experimentation

To conclude our reflections on revitalization at the provincial level, I make the following general observations. It is unlikely that a refounding program can be activated simultaneously and with equal depth and intensity in all parts of a province. In fact, there seems to be very little historical evidence for programmed revitalization. The change is so dramatic that only a small proportion of any group is likely to adopt it.

Refounding experiments, at the mythic stage, operate on an elusive dynamic. A great deal of experimentation takes place and there tends to be a tremendous investment of time and energy. At the mythic stage, there are no limits to the group's vigor and enthusiasm, but the honeymoon experience cannot last forever. The refounding group must channel their new-found vision into appropriate structures.

Some refounding groups, reacting against the rigidity of former structures, mistakenly try to maintain the mythic values permanently; for example, "We wish our new-found community to remain superiorless and totally open to local needs as they arise." This is a prescription for anarchy, and the investment of time and energy needed to maintain this state unnecessarily long will eventually destroy the group. How long the mythic stage should last can only be determined by the discernment of the group itself, aided by members of the group, friends, and provincial leadership.

The mythic enthusiasm can also militate against the founding group's potential for the revitalization of the whole province. At this early stage, the experiment may be considered so wild and fanciful, so unorthodox and disorganized, as to alienate the more traditional elements of a province. This is more a problem for the province and its leadership than for the refounding group; it is never a good reason for toning down the experiment. Polarization may be avoided by attempting beforehand to educate the province on the nature of the experiment, although this admittedly can be difficult.

The mythic stage requires the abandonment of models perhaps still deeply cherished by most members of a province. To try and hold the two realities together and open up channels for some degree of cross-fertilization is a major task for provincial leadership. On the success or failure of this effort may hinge the death or revitalization of a whole province.

As the refounding group works through its new identity, progressively articulating its dream and stating its objectives, it moves into the belief stage. How soon this will happen can only be determined by the group itself; the skills necessary for it to happen are good communication, open sharing, and prayerful discernment. Factors that could prevent it from happening are excessive enthusiasm and vigorous activity which leave neither time nor energy for the reflection, sharing, and praying. The myth may also be suppressed by the unsympathetic stance of higher authorities within a specific congregation or within the church itself.

When the refounding group progresses to the normative stage, it is then approaching maturity; it has come of age. It is clear about its purpose and mission, and has achieved a degree of credibility in the province. Even the opponents realize that this has to be the way forward. There may still be quite a degree of polarization, but it is manageable and no longer poses a major threat to the unity and integrity of the province. The members of the refounding experiment are no longer out on a wing; they become part of the institutional fabric of the order or congregation.

The vitality curve incorporates some of the best insights of the social sciences, but it is essentially and profoundly a theological framework of birth-death-rebirth. At each stage the Spirit of God is at work, often calling us to places we would rather not go. Negotiating the cycle demands not one but many conversions, personal and structural. Along this rather precarious and paradoxical route are burial tombs; most of them remain sealed, but some are burst open again. Resurrection is always a possibility.

I believe religious have the choice of being remembered by an "open, empty tomb" or by a beautifully engraved tombstone. Which one is chosen depends on openness to the Spirit, who rekindles life even from dead bones:

> They keep saying: "Our bones are dry, our hope has gone; we are done for" . . . . The Lord Yahweh says this: I am now going to open your graves; I shall raise you from your graves, my people, and lead you back to the soil of Israel. And you will know that I am Yahweh, when I open your graves and raise you from your graves, my people, and put my spirit in you, and you revive, and I resettle you on your own soil. Then you will know that I, Yahweh, have spoken and done this . . . (Ez 37:11–14).

Conclusion to Part Two

In the Christian and Catholic tradition, a great deal has been written about religious life. Much of this material tends to be excessively spiritual and devotional in tone; a solid corpus of theological reflection on the religious state simply does not exist.

Despite a very rich historical and sociological tradition, there is also a dearth of written material on these aspects of the religious state. Consequently, the contents of part two might have been quite new to many readers. Undoubtedly, some will take offense and object to placing religious life under sociological scrutiny. But it is a social phenomenon (as well as spiritual) and, precisely because of its distinctive spiritual reason for being and its close liaison with the institutional church, it may need the challenge and correction of a social critique even more than an exclusively secular movement.

I have not intended to be dogmatic and inflexible about the historical and social considerations of this section. I readily acknowledge inadequate evidence, inconsistent conclusions, some generalizations, and unexamined alternative possibilities. These exist precisely because I find both the historical and sociological paradigms to be fascinating and inspiring. They open up many possibilities, indicate new ways of interpreting things we largely take for granted, enable us to learn from the failures and successes of the past, and, above all, pave the way for a future of hope, vision, and renewed vitality.

We are reminded by Marxists that context governs consciousness. So often in the past, particularly in the tendency toward entrenchment prevalent within Catholicism since the Council of Trent, we have contextualized religious life in a crippling, stultifying frame of reference. It is, I repeat, totally inappropriate to vision what is essentially a liminal, global reality in exclusively legal and devotional categories of any one religious denomination. The broad cultural and profound spiritual consciousness is in grave danger of being choked and stifled when restricted to any one institutional framework.

The renewal of religious life today has a very precise agenda: it is desperately trying to break out of the imprisonment of traditional institutional religiosity. Throughout the 1960s and 1970s it did quite well in that task; then came a period of clampdown (at least in the Catholic church), but that will not last. Historically, there is nothing to verify its timeliness, and, sociologically, it can be understood as a classic, institutional defense-mechanism. It will cause further pain and havoc within religious life, but for those who can look beyond the institutional tendency toward self-perpetuation, who can imbibe something of the hope and vision which history bequeaths us, then it is but a temporary crisis. Indeed, it is a minor one compared with some of the major hurdles that religious have encountered throughout the ages in negotiating the vitality curve.

The historical and sociological paradigms engender hope and new vision. Today, more than ever, we need the cumulative wisdom of our past to help us through the threshold of the present, launching us into a new future: the birth of the third millennium!

Part
THREE

The Living Context:
Enabling and Empowering

9

Community and Intimacy (Celibacy)

In social organization . . . our alternatives seem to be narrowing down to either an ant-heap, or else something resembling the Mystical Body of Christ.
— Gabriel Marcel

God is an intimacy in the flesh that otherwise is death.
— Sebastian Moore

Religious life, because of its inherent liminal nature, tends to shun social structures and veer toward an anonymous and marginalized space within the social fabric of society. This trend is particularly noticeable in the bedrock monastic tradition of all the major systems, with a strong tendency toward vagrancy, occupying remote places, and adopting an adversary stance against secular and sacred institutions. Even in its more institutionalized state, religious life seeks special status, as in the canonical exemption of the Christian tradition and the special political status of the monks in Thailand and Burma. Beyond these more apparent characteristics is an illusive and indefinable ambivalence arising from the fact that religious are "in the world but not of it."

Despite this social estrangement, religious comprise a very definite sociological unit. The monastery, convent, or commune is easily identified, and, despite all misgivings, acquires a concise institutional character. The wandering ascetic, too, tends to acquire a social identity, the assumption being that he or she belongs to a specific order or congregation.

Endemic to the religious life is a liminal tension between the secular and the sacred, the monastery and the world (or the church), the individual and the community. It is the complementarity between individual and community that concerns us specifically at the beginning of this chapter. More so in the East than in the West, the individual (wandering) ascetic is considered to be more heroic and perfected and, consequently, is deemed to be a more authentic witness to evangelical holiness.

The communitarian aspect is less well-known, but equally pervasive. The group consciousness, a sense of common exploration and shared pursuit for "union with the divine principle of order,"[1] is fundamental to religious life in its various cultural settings. The heroic hermit is the exception rather than the norm, although the solitary figure looms large and tends to hold pride of place in historical records and in popular hagiography. But the cultural impact of religious life, East and West, the means by which it has provided the counterculture so necessary for human and earthly growth, has been primarily that of a community-based movement.

What Is Community?

In the global context of the monastic/religious life, community has not one but many connotations. The concept of a group of people sharing a common lifestyle (in one physical setting), animated by a shared vision, is probably the most widespread. However, we have already noted alternative expressions, such as the Christian *lavra* and the Buddhist *avasa*, and we know of mixed monasteries in early Christian times.[2] In the Eastern tradition, binding commitment to a community has never been for life, as it has in the West. In the Hindu ashrams, most people stay for six to twelve months, but share fully in the life of the community; bhikkus (Buddhist monks) are free to leave whenever they feel called to another way of life. Finally, the monastic/religious life in all major traditions rarely portrays a sense of monopolizing community. There exists a strong consciousness of being part of a larger social entity, from which emerges forms of social outreach. Basilian monasticism in early Christian times and the Buddhist Theravada tradition of present-day Thailand vividly exemplify this orientation.

David Clark draws a distinction between community
of place and community of concern.[3] It is the experience of
many religious today to be "in communion" with quite a
number of significant others. Often, relationships with people
outside a community can be more intense than those within.
Mission demands greater mobility with increasing numbers
of religious living on their own[4] or in households of two or
three members, all of whom may not belong to the same
congregation.

It is in diverse settings of this nature that we need to remember that "community becomes a reality to be carried
in the heart rather than a place in which to live."[5] I cannot discern or dialogue in isolation. I need fellow pilgrims
whose insights, wisdom, and prayers enable me, with them,
to discover and rediscover the Lord's call in the renewed
awakenings of daily life. Religious communities do not automatically provide this climate for dialogue and discernment;
in many cases, traditional mores, roles, and expectations hinder and, at times, totally inhibit the openness, trust, and vul-
nerability needed for this deeper sharing. Consequently, it
becomes imperative to explore other forms of community, to
authenticate one's inspiration and vision, and to find the mutual support and affirmation if we are to witness fruitfully as
liminal and prophetic people.

I use the term "community" in a variety of senses: some
structured, others less so; some localized, others more universal; some belonging exclusively to one congregation, others accommodating people of different congregations, even
of various ways of life. Two features, however, permeate
all the different expressions: a strong sense of personal conviction (a sense of significance) on the part of those people
creating community, and a sense of solidarity with all those
who enter the experience. These form what many social scientists today consider to be the "poles" of genuine community: "It is only when people feel a sense of their own worth,
on the one hand, and the sense of being intimately part of
the group, on the other, that we can be sure that community
exists."[6]

These two dimensions — personal significance and group
solidarity — may be perceived as complementary aspects of

one reality. The evidence of culture and religious life suggests that we can only discover our true selves in community. The psychological, sociological, and anthropological aspects of this statement cannot be treated here — they would need a book on their own — but the theological considerations that follow will confirm the discoveries of the social sciences.

Community and Relatedness

In the experience of humanity, religion is as much a social as a theological phenomenon. From the time when our ancestors gathered around the fire (which was discovered some 600,000 years ago) down to the formation of formal religions some 4,000 years ago, the search for meaning became progressively one of shared exploration and dialogical discovery. The lone, individual inventor or explorer is very much a product of our recent past. The group consciousness is the context from which has emerged all the great discoveries of our race and culture; they may be internalized and articulated in one person's vision, but the dream is inherent to the group story and will only strike root if the group consciousness is sufficiently developed to receive it.

Consequently, we find in the major religions a strong social component intended to promote growth, cohesion, unity, and fellowship, based on love, care, and compassion. Sadly the component has a regrettable record of division, pain, and persecution. There are two dimensions to this social aspect: The human need for shared meaning and an innate socializing myth at the heart of all religious systems.

What do I mean by the "socializing myth"?[7] There is at the heart of all religions a sense of relatedness. A supreme being called God (by whatever name used in the different religious traditions) who does not merely exist but is forever seeking a reciprocal relationship with creatures and with creation as a whole. I believe this statement is consistent even with Buddhist thought in its pursuit of enlightenment. Indeed, it is no small coincidence that Buddhist literature uses the word "compassion" (karuna) more extensively than does Christianity.

This reciprocal relationship, which I suggest to be the essence of Godhead, Christians call the Trinity. In Hinduism, this relationship is called the triune figures of Vishnu, Shiva, and Shanti; in Buddhism, the doctrine of the three bodies (manifestations) of the Buddha, namely, the dharma-kaya (eternal dimension), nirmana-kaya (appearance body), and sambhoga-kaya (bliss body); in the Egyptian system, the cult of Isis, Serapis, and the divine child Horus; and in the Neoplatonic triplicate, the good, the intelligence, and the world soul.

It would appear we are dealing with an archetypal value system, explaining a very fundamental aspect of all life forms, namely, that life consists essentially of relatedness, relationships, interconnectedness, and interdependence. We encounter a profound truth that God is essentially related- ness; consequently, the Christian dogma of the Trinity is not really a theological jigsaw in which we try to fit three persons into one. The category of "person" may even be a barrier to our understanding of what the trinitarian relat- edness is about. Whatever categories we use, the Christian revelation is of a God whose deepest essence is love (related- ness) and that Christians can only know and serve that God by relating with others with "a love like his" (cf. Jn 15:9ff.).

I am not trying to impose the Christian concept of the Trinity on those of other religious persuasions, but am using the trinitarian model of relatedness to articulate a dimension which I perceive to be basic to all the monastic/religious systems of humanity. The Buddhist and Hindu pursuit of knowledge and the Christian pursuit of love are essentially the same thing; in fact, both words are used interchangeably in John's gospel.

It is this dimension of divine relatedness that provides the theological foundation for community in the monas- tic and religious life and gives priority to the community over the individual in the historical-cultural tradition of the vowed life. Being essentially liminal, it is the task of reli- gious community to embody and articulate those values that deeply concern human life — most fundamentally, the need to relate deeply and meaningfully with God, with people, with creation, and with life at large.

It is a quality of reciprocal interaction that elucidates the dual dimensions of personal significance (Father, Son, and Holy Spirit are separate and unique) and a sense of solidarity (without the others, no one person of the Trinity is capable of communicating with life at large). By the same token, religious life has, as its supreme norm, that personal growth, in and through relationships, which is the channel of human and divine unfolding most appropriate for human beings.

Much of what is written above is comprehensible in terms of family life and the nurturing, loving relationships we all need to achieve mature adulthood. What we have attempted is to take that family model onto a global, cultural, and spiritual level. However, it is not my intention to use the family as a starting point, because the family itself is only one (albeit the most extensive) articulation of the underlying global phenomenon that I wish to explore.

Kingdom and Community

In the Christian faith, the divine-human interaction finds its clearest cultural elucidation in what Jesus called the kingdom of God (kingdom of Heaven in Matthew's gospel). We may define the kingdom as the reign of godliness brought about by divine intervention, supremely embodied in the life and ministry of Jesus, but not identified exclusively with Christians. In other words, although the kingdom is uniquely expressed in Jesus (from the Christian point of view), Christians cannot claim that they belong to the kingdom in a way that excludes other believers or even non-believers.

The New Testament (especially the gospels) asserts quite categorically that the reign of God is not confined to any place or human realm, nor to any one historical epoch (cf. Mt 11:11, 13:47ff; Lk 6:20, 17:20–21), not even to the present earthly order (although it includes this). Neither does it belong to human beings to manipulate or control, although humans share intimately in its existence and are invited to foster its growth and development.

The kingdom is about the process of transformation. It seeks to establish a universe marked by "truth and life, holiness and grace, justice, love and peace," in the words of

the preface for the feast of Christ the King. The charter for
this undertaking is most clearly outlined in the Beatitudes
(Mt 5:1–12), characterized by a global sense of inclusiveness,
the pursuit of justice, and above all the establishment of
right relationships among all peoples and creatures with
divinity itself in its entire, cosmic wholeness.

By inclusiveness, I mean that everybody, irrespective
of social or economic status, is included; even the earth itself (cf. Mt 5:5) is apportioned a new role in the life of the
kingdom. The dominant world order, where the rich and
powerful succeed at the expense of the poor, is reversed; the
marginalized become not merely the focal point of care and
concern, but the catalysts who confront the powerful with
the challenge of change.

God's new reign in Christ is one marked by the pursuit
of justice, thus ensuring for all an equitable and righteous
distribution of the goods of the earth. Furthermore, building
bridges of unity, harmony, and reconciliation is inherent to
kingdom living, in the face of which warfare (of any type) is
totally alien to the Christian vision and a compromise with
the forces of evil.

All the beatitudes proclaim blessing and deliverance.
In the Old Testament, God is frequently portrayed as the
one who empowers the people, thus freeing them from the
bondage of slavery. The healing and forgiving ministry of
the New Testament provided even more poignant examples
for all who accept the invitation into the new reign which
Jesus came to inaugurate and establish.

"Be glad and rejoice . . ." predominates in the beatitudes.
Even in the face of adversity and persecution, the children
of the kingdom proffer hope and continually celebrate the
God who enables and empowers the people for the task of
building up and transforming the universe.

The church is intended to be a primary but not exclusive
expression, an earthly embodiment of this new relatedness
and at least in its infancy it seems to have achieved this
ideal:

> And all who shared the faith owned everything in com-
> mon; they sold their goods and possessions and dis-
> tributed the proceeds among themselves according to

what each one needed. Each day, with one heart, they regularly went to the Temple but met in their houses for the breaking of bread; they shared their food gladly and generously; they praised God and were looked up to by everyone. Day by day the Lord added to their community those destined to be saved (Acts 2:44–47).

The whole group of believers was united, heart and soul; no one claimed private ownership of any possessions, as everything they owned was held in common. . . . None of the members was ever in want, as all those who owned lands or houses would sell them, and bring the money from the sale of them, to present it to the apostles; it was then distributed to any who might be in need (Acts 4:32, 34–35).

The expanding church, as depicted in the Pauline writings, continues to articulate this vision.

As it emerged in early Christian times the church may be described as "the gathering together of the people for worship, service, and prophecy, proclaiming in word and deed the kingdom of God." The crucial element in this description is not that of worship, service, or prophecy but the gathering together.

The primary function of the church is that of gathering people together to relate as a community and thus become a microcosm of the kingdom. Worship, service, and prophecy are only meaningful if they help to create, maintain, and enhance the sense of community.

Because community is the essential nature of the church — indeed, a primordial dimension of the human search for meaning — then we can assume that the collective unconscious (to use Jung's term) will always encourage the existence of liminal groups embodying archetypal (communal) values. This, in fact, has always been the case and is likely always to be. Because the community dimension of the contemporary church is largely suppressed (by the institutional dimension), the communal archetype is quite volcanic, creating a ripple effect across the world.

What is surfacing in our day is a deep human desire to reconnect with a basic myth of human existence, one which seeks articulation and expression primarily in a church context — namely, the search for community. The church in every age and in every religion springs from community; the fundamental myth is essentially communal. In the Christian churches (and perhaps universally), the myth has lost its vibrancy and has become chocked by the "norms" of clericalism, parochialism, congregationalism, and denominationalism.[8] We are out of touch with our roots.

Paradoxically, the church has never fully lost touch with the underlying myth of community. It seems to have dominated Christian life and practice up to the beginning of the fourth century when, under the Emperor Constantine, Christians were allowed to practice their faith openly and publicly. Order, structure, and organization became important to the church in its efforts to leave an imprint on the prevailing culture, and it modeled itself on the dominant Roman institutions of the time.

It was a critical moment in the church's history. Although there were real possibilities to dialogue with the world, there was also a danger of conforming to the world. Precisely at this time (the beginning of the fourth century), the Christian monastic movement was born, largely as a protest against the growing institutionalization of the Christian message. In the eyes of early monks, the church had already modeled its life and mission very much on secular institutions. When Christianity was acknowledged as an "acceptable" religion by the Peace of Constantine in 313, the monks felt that the Christian vision (the original myth) was in danger of being absorbed by worldly standards. Therefore, they sought to recreate the myth with its original flavor and radicality.

Most historians do not acknowledge the counterculture dimension of the Christian monastic movement. Consequently they are unable to appreciate the nature and impact of communal movements which have arisen in almost every century of the church's history and have been viewed with scepticism. Even at the present time, the religious orders play something of an ambivalent role in the Christian church. They have lost virtually all semblance of a countercultural, communal, lay movement, being cherished more for what they do (function) than for what they are (symbol).

Toward an Inclusive Model

Community is central to any authentic form of religious/ monastic life. Religious are intended to be "experts in communion . . . witnesses and architects of the plan for unity."[9] The same document points out that this is no mere ecclesial task; the admonition is set in a distinctly global context. Consequently, religious must never consider community as something over which they have a monopoly, or something they live in a manner that is unique to their way of life. An inclusive model is the only one that can embrace, enable, affirm, and encourage human efforts at living in meaningful fellowship. The gift they have as experts in communion is one they continually offer to others.

Our reflections thus far point to a concept of community marked by (a) openness to all forms of human fellowship no matter how "secular" or transient; (b) a call to global and personal transformation through the promotion of kingdom values; (c) a new sense of ecumenicity, transcending not merely Christian divisions but also distinctions made in the name of religious allegiance; and (d) a commitment to the formation and development of relatedness at all levels of life.

Religious do not have a monopoly of this task. In today's world it is clear that many other groupings, such as the basic Christian communities of Latin America, carry out this mission with greater facility and conviction than many religious groups. Nonetheless, I submit that it remains the primary function of the monastic and religious life. When religious fail to undertake this challenge, other groups fill the vacuum, which alerts religious to the urgent renewal needed in orders and congregations.

An internal quality of life augments the prophetic and ministerial role of our communities. The life of a group will fail to radiate its liminal potential if members are not deeply united in their relatedness to one another and to the God who calls them into fellowship. Personal intimacy and prayerful discernment are two important elements of an authentic community.

Many religious today are struggling for a meaningful experience of community. Conflicting expectations, unresolved personal tensions, and excessive work are just some of the blockages to community growth. Nonetheless, there is an expanding awareness of the challenge and an openness and readiness to employ the expertise necessary to work through those things that hinder growth. This is often a painful process, more for female than male religious.

The Call to Celibacy

If the basic myth of the religious state is that of relatedness, mediated primarily through community, then celibacy becomes a central aspect of that experience. Buddhist and Hindu monks also vow celibacy, but without the lifelong commitment of Christianity. Islam, Judaism, and Sikhism, because of what they perceive to be the sacredness of procreation, have never had institutionalized celibacy, but all three systems have a mystical orientation with leanings toward a non-married status.

The justification for celibacy is a complex issue which I do not wish to treat in detail, but it merits consideration if we are to outgrow outdated myths. In the Christian tradition there have been three primary explanations: (a) ascetical detachment, so that a person may be totally devoted to prayer and the affairs of God; (b) moral perfection, an invitation to rise above the sinful and instinctual urges of the flesh through penance, sacrifice, and self-control; (c) sublimation, redirecting sexual energy to enhance the human potential for other forms of human and spiritual growth.

In all three explanations there are a number of underlying dualisms which prevailed in early Christian spirituality — for instance, man v. God, earth v. heaven, body v. soul, flesh v. spirit. The spiritual life was perceived to be a battle with the forces of evil which sought to ensnare the spiritual domain in the earthly, human, sinful condition. The ascetical life, therefore, was intended to create those conditions best suited to the release of the spirit or for the Buddhist attainment of enlightenment.

Dualistic thought patterns are a consequence of the hellenization of Christianity and of the religious life in particular.[10] Such thought patterns have surfaced in times when the Christian church was on the defensive against heresy;

consequently, they have been in predominance in the post-Reformation era, which dominated Catholic thought well into the twentieth century. Under the impact of the dualistic mindset, the more holistic, liminal, and prophetic elements of the vowed life have received scant attention.

A change in the understanding of celibacy began to emerge in the 1960s. Schneiders offers the following resume:

> Thus, for one writer, celibacy is a witness to the faithfulness of God; for another, it concretizes the hope dimension of the Christian enterprise by witnessing to the ecclesial incompleteness of the present dispensation; for another, it frees the celibate for universal availability; for another, it is rooted in a certain experience of God that renders marriage a psychological impossibility . . . for another, it is freedom for the one thing necessary . . . . "[11]

Gone are the heavy, negative, ascetical overtones. Inherent in each statement is a sense of vagueness and a tendency to generalize orientations that are quite consistent with the paradoxical nature of every liminal experience. If I were to fault these statements, it would be in the serious omission of the sense of relatedness. The celibacy depicted is still excessively spiritualized and disembodied. This is quite at variance with early Christian teaching on virginity (especially in the first and second century) and with the first elaborate treatment of celibacy by Clement of Alexandria written in the context and defense of Christian marriage.[12]

The more positive approach in the period immediately following the New Testament era suggests an exploration of the scriptural evidence itself. Within the scriptures there is a wide spectrum of understanding. Celibacy is alien to Israel's mentality and spirituality; it has, therefore, no basis in the Old Testament where marriage is seen as a natural obligation marked by the command to increase and multiply (Gn 1:28). While in the Old Testament, virginity prior to marriage was praised (Dt 22:14–29), virginity or celibacy as a permanent state in life was frowned upon because it posed a threat to the future of the Israelite nation.

The coming of Christ marks a departure. No longer does the kingdom of Israel, dependent for its survival on human

procreation, predominate; the sole concern now is the kingdom of God, where they neither marry nor are given in marriage (Mk 12:25; Lk 20:35). It is strange that this major shift
of emphasis receives so little attention in New Testament
times.

Non-marriage for the sake of the kingdom is a distinctive feature of the new dispensation. Equally new, however,
is the obligation of monogamous marriage. In the Old Testament, divorce was easy to obtain and in a sense, therefore,
marriage was polygamous rather than monogamous. This
close biblical relationship between marriage and celibacy
is frequently ignored by both married and celibate people,
much to the detriment of both states of life.

> A study of the understanding of celibacy ought to be
> preceded by some indication of the understanding of
> marriage, for these two christian ways of life cannot
> be studied separately. Christian marriage and christian
> celibacy are among the essential and complementary el-
> ements to the parable of the Kingdom of God which the
> Church is called upon to act in this world;. . . when the
> call to celibacy is too little heard, marriage gradually
> comes to be thought of as a reality of the purely natural
> order. . . when the vocation of celibacy is undervalued,
> so is that of marriage.[13]

In the New Testament we have two explicit references to
celibacy: Matthew 19:10–12 and 1 Corinthians 7:23–35. The
Matthean text is already well known:

> The disciples said to him: "If that is how things are be-
> tween husband and wife, it is advisable not to marry."
> But he replied, "It is not everyone who can accept what
> I have said, but only those to whom it is granted. There
> are eunuchs born so from their mother's womb, there
> are eunuchs made so by human agency, and there are
> eunuchs who have made themselves so for the sake
> of the kingdom of Heaven. Let anyone accept this
> who can."

It is generally accepted that this was an already existing saying which Matthew incorporated into his discussion on matrimony. Scholars differ on their interpretation
of Matthew's intent, but a significant number agree on the
interpretation that "eunuchs for the sake of the kingdom"

refers to those who have been separated from their spouses and do not remarry in obedience to God's word on the indissolubility of marriage.

We may never know for sure what Matthew had in mind, but an increasing number of exegetes agree that the original *sitz im leben* of the logion is to be sought in the fact that Christ himself, being unmarried and, therefore, defying conventional Jewish law and custom, was thereby insultingly dubbed as a eunuch.[14]

The words of Matthew 19:12 are not, as is frequently assumed, an exhortation to espouse celibacy. Such a proposition by Jesus would have been wasted on people who had come to regard the blessing of Genesis 1:28 (increase and multiply) as a divine command. The text is not exhortatory but declaratory ("there are eunuchs"), and the parting words ("Let anyone accept this who can") are not an exhortation to accept celibacy but an invitation to accept what has been said about it, namely, that it has happened, that it is a fact.

In this passage there is a further nuance with theological implications for religious celibacy. Concerning the verse, "And there are eunuchs who have made themselves so for the sake of the kingdom of Heaven," the original Greek text uses *dia*, translated in the RSV version, "for the sake of," indicating that celibacy has been chosen as a means to an end. But in standard New Testament Greek, *dia* with the accusative indicates the reason why something happens, and should, therefore, be translated, "on account of" or "because of" (as in Matthew 10:22 — hated because of the name). Taking this latter meaning, Matthew 19:12c reads: "And there are eunuchs who have made themselves so because of the kingdom of Heaven." Celibacy, in this case, is the consequence of something that has already taken place.

We come, therefore, to a new understanding of celibacy, aptly described by one of its strongest contemporary proponents:

> People...have been grasped by God's lordship so overwhelmingly as to be disposed of the capacity to commit themselves to anyone in marriage.... They are celibate because of an existential inability to choose to be otherwise.... In other words, the event of celibacy

> is intelligible as one that comes about within a major
> religious experience and as an existential repercussion
> to it. . . . And so in a manner of speaking, it is not the
> man who chooses his own celibacy; it is rather celibacy
> that chooses its own man in the act of happening to
> him.[15]

Against the theological background of the kingdom (understood as the new reign of God in the world), the call to celibacy assumes a whole new meaning. It becomes a valid option not merely at a theological level but also at a relational level that is inherent to our understanding of the kingdom: the new reign of God who is essentially a God of relatedness. The celibate state is a call or vocation to uphold archetypal values which transcend (but do not deny) the genital and procreative faculties in order to experience the deeper human/divine exchange of love and reciprocity. The celibate, therefore, remains a fully sexual person in tune with her or his sexual needs and those of others, but called to channel those sexual energies in a different way. It is not a superior vocation to that of the single or married person, but rather a complementary one in keeping with the celibate's liminal option.

Celibate Intimacy

Consecrated celibacy assumes a new ambience in our time, namely, the redemption of life-giving intimacy. This involves a growth in acceptance, warmth, closeness, and empathy with both God and people. For liminal witness, a celibacy out of tune with the human capacity for intimacy loses credibility. It must remain close to the longings of the human heart and articulate these in a manner that awakens and fulfills people's deepest desires. This demands a deep understanding of people; hence, the need for a community where the human capacity to give and receive love is articulated in verbal, bodily, and symbolic exchange.

The spiritual dimension, the loving relationship with God in prayer, meditation, and discernment, is of central importance but it must not become a substitute for the human dimension, as often happened in the past. It remains one of the supreme challenges of the celibate call to discover appropriate ways to exchange love and intimacy within communities. There is an emotional capacity in human beings which can only be nurtured by warmth, friendship, and tactility (touching, stroking, kissing); it is precisely when this dimension is neglected that sexual problems surface, that the need for genital gratification becomes inflated, in celibates and married people alike. A celibacy that denies basic human needs belies the incarnational dignity of human life, the supreme human and spiritual challenge of trinitarian (kingdom) love, and turns celibacy into an ascetical monstrosity.

Celibacy is a profoundly human reality and, potentially, a poignant social catalyst. It is a radical call to that intimacy which empowers us to love God and love one's neighbor as oneself (Mk 12:33), to forgive our enemies (Mt 5:44), to turn the other cheek (Mt 5:39), and above all, to be the recipients of that great gift promised by Jesus: life to the full.

Buddhism and Hinduism offer enlightenment, the path of knowledge, as the ultimate human destiny. Judaism and, to a lesser degree, Islam preaches righteousness: the path of right behavior; but Christianity is foremost a religion of love. Surely the time is ripe for Christians to salvage this message from the extremes of pharisaical legalism on the one hand, and devotional, sentimental virtuosity, on the other, and to make it what our trinitarian God always intended it to be, a dynamic, creative force in God's new reign of justice, love, and peace. Religious are intended to be the pioneers of such possibilities; such is the burden and privilege of their prophetic mission.

Making Sense Out of Celibacy

In the course of these reflections we have touched on a number of topics that merit closer consideration:

The Vocation to Celibacy: It is not uncommon for religious, undergoing some form of crisis or growth, to question their motives for being celibate. Frequently one encounters something of an existential vacuum often expressed in words like, "I just don't know why I am." Within this bewildering sentiment is a profound truth:

> If celibacy is to be right for those who make the decision for it, it will not be because it is right in itself but

> because they are right for it. And they are right for it
> if it has happened to them in the way it should. More
> precisely, it is the quality of the events from which
> the decision for celibacy emerges, not the quality of
> celibacy itself, that validates the quality of the decision
> for celibacy and celibacy itself.[16]

The choice for celibacy, therefore, is not really a choice. It is the consequence of a call that is essentially mystical and not capable of being understood outside the context of faith. It only makes sense to those who can accept that a new reign of God operates in the world and lures people into options and lifestyles that leave them with no choice other than respond affirmatively. Although essentially a faith experience, it does not have to be confined to the context of formal religion. Once we begin to experience the interconnectedness of life at the primordial, archetypal levels, old dualistic distinctions — sacred and secular, faith and irreligiosity — begin to break down. Religious are the people who must mediate this experience on behalf of the wider culture.

The Rationale of Celibacy: In the Western world, at least, we attribute great importance to rational explanations. If celibacy is the consequence of a larger vocational experience, then the recipient may have great difficulty in explaining this option. This leaves the celibate in a dilemma. If celibacy is a gift with implications for the wider culture — a liminal challenge, an archetypal value, a prophetic possibility — how can its meaning be communicated if it defies rationality? I do not underestimate the ambivalence a person can feel in confronting this question. Nonetheless, I don't think we can escape the fact that celibacy makes sense as a lived experience, not as something that can be rationally defended. A celibacy that makes perfect sense has not been explained; it has merely been explained away!

Religious should not be preoccupied with justifying celibacy. Their call is to witness to the love and relatedness of God because God's new reign has caught up with people. It is not an eschatological sign reminding us that our true home is in heaven; that is a theological cop-out! It is a sign that God's love has struck root in our earthly and human condition. A process of transformation is under way, and religious are invited to pioneer innovatively the possibilities that flow from it.

The Community Dimension: Celibacy is more than a mystical or ascetical phenomenon. Primarily, it is a gift given to persons for persons. Its origin is also personal: a God who relates interpersonally in the supreme relationship we call "Trinity." A celibacy whose primary function is the enhancement of love and intimacy must be grounded in the lived experience of a community. Only in this context can religious encounter each other as persons, interdependent and interrelated, their lives unfolding amid the daily mix of loneliness and alienation, joy and affirmation, tears and laughter. This is where we encounter the incarnate Christ, especially those deprived of love because of pain, poverty, or oppression.

Jean Vanier captures the mystery and delicacy, along with the pain and struggle, of sharing life in close encounter. When genuinely lived in an atmosphere of trust and openness, it leads to personal revelations that uncover hidden pain and exposes a vacuum that only love can fill. Only in this climate of trust and openness can our brokenness (which to varying degrees exists in all our lives) be made whole and our wounds healed. Thus, we have been loved into life!

There is nothing very dramatic about all this because it is a natural, inherent human propensity. It breaks through in a less inhibited manner in females than in males. It has to be worked at more in the celibate than in the married state where it has more spontaneous outlets. It is not absent in celibates, but there are barriers of cultural conditioning and moral prohibition. A public expression of intimacy between two celibates was frowned upon twenty years ago; thanks to more enlightened attitudes it is now more readily accepted.

It is at the level of local community that much remains to be done. Many religious today find more emotional satisfaction and growth in affectivity from sources outside rather than within their communities. This is a healthy development of the recent past, but it has risks and limitations. Some of the most important relationships we have with people outside our communities are often secretly withheld from those within. This creates an unhealthy dichotomy, just as it would for marriage and family life.

To redress the balance, religious need to undertake
a double task. Many religious today do not feel at home
in their local communities; assignments tend to be based
on the work a person is qualified to perform. Formation,
even in the recent past, has not enabled religious to share
their deeper feelings and aspirations. Sexuality is largely
a taboo subject, as indeed is anger, jealousy, and personal
animosities. A community which chooses, overtly or unconsciously, to leave these areas unexplored cannot hope to be
prophetic.

When religious begin to create an internal forum to articulate growth as emotional, sexual beings, then the relationships outside communities become sources for enriching
the growth taking place within. This interaction enhances the
community's potential to articulate archetypal values in a
manner that augments the community's growth and also that
of the people they seek to animate and inspire.

Historically, religious communities have tended to be
exclusively male or female. In the past twenty years, in the
Catholic tradition, some encouraging experiments of mixed
communities have been undertaken, and these offer hope for
the future. Celibacy as an archetypal value (instead of the
popular perception of a dominantly clerical issue) will only
come alive when lived in mixed communities. As celibates,
we remain fundamentally male and female, and the fullness
of life cannot be attained in an exclusively male or female
environment.

Solitude and Intimacy: For the first half of this century,
the relational dimension of celibacy was grossly neglected.
Little wonder there was such an exodus from religious life
in the 1960s; nor is it surprising to learn that some of the ensuing marriages have ended in either separation or divorce.
The affective dimension was so impoverished it could not
sustain a loving relationship either with God or with another
person.

My emphasis on the relational aspect is in no way intended to underestimate the need for solitude. This I would
understand to be the single most important complementary value to intimacy in both the celibate and married
states. For the celibate it entails something of the Lord's own

desire to leave the bustle of apostolic concern and go out to the mountain to spend the night in prayer (Mt 14:22–23; Mk 1:35, 6:46; Lk 5:16, 6:12ff., 9:18). This need for transcendence can only be satiated by contemplative discourse with the source of our being. In psychospiritual terms, we need space and time to come home to oneself, to tune in to the God within, the source of living water welling up in the heart.

Religious, especially sisters, give much attention to prayer and liturgy, often operating out of the conviction that an active spiritual life is all that matters. This approach tends to produce a spirituality of simplification. I advocate a spirituality of integration,[17] in which the experience of solitude is the context and opportunity to assimilate and integrate what God is saying to me in both my prayer life and in my interaction with others. It is the moment of holding together diverse experiences, with their possibilities and contradictions, while awaiting the birth of new insight, new intuition, new challenge, and a new sense of being called forth in the service of the kingdom.

Marriage and Celibacy: In the Christian tradition, especially since the time of St. Augustine, there has been a tendency to exalt the celibate over the married state, as is done in Hinduism and Buddhism. In all cases, the tendency seems to be fueled by a questionable asceticism.

On the other hand, all three systems positively affirm marriage, even more so in contemporary Hindu and Buddhist religious life than in the Christian form. In the Far East a young man's emotional maturity and suitability for marriage is gauged by the extent and quality of his stay at the Ashram or in a monastery. The monastic community is considered to be one of the best centers for maturation and readiness for the responsibilities of adult life.

In this Eastern experience we have a classic example of the religious community providing a liminal context for articulating archetypal values. But the experience also highlights the fact that celibacy and marriage are to be seen as complementary, not contradictory. The celibate strives to articulate and live out the same values which nurture love and growth in marriage. As complementary lifestyles, a celibate person or community can be immensely enriched by interaction with married people.

Let us name some of those values which enrich both the married and celibate states:

— A transcendent aspect is inherent to every mature relationship; without this, the functional purpose (for example, procreation in marriage) may become an end in itself and, consequently, an escape for subconscious or repressed feelings.

— The essence of human life and love is in giving rather than receiving; the celibate gives of one's life and love without seeking recognition or recompense. Indeed, these qualities are often more apparent in the dedicated and devoted parent than in the life of consecrated celibacy.

— There is a deep concern for the other as other, without any attempt to perceive the other to be for one's self-aggrandizement.

— There is need for restraint, detachment, and self-control if relationships are to be life giving. True friendship implies purifying suffering which also enhances growth and transformation. Thus an early Egyptian monk describes purity of heart in these words: "Remoteness from anger, friendliness toward enemies, peacefulness of disposition and sincere love for God and man."[18]

— Life and love are essentially gifts; all life comes from God and we are his agents in the continual growth of creation. Sexuality, too, is a gift for the unfolding of the kingdom on earth.

— Affective growth demands deep and sustained relationships, which cannot be limited by time or based mainly on the physical aspects of a specific relationship.

— In a world "permeated by unredeemed sex,"[19] celibacy provides a countercultural witness, a reminder that true freedom and liberation is to be found not in erotic license nor in sexual exploitation, but in interpersonal relationships marked by devotion and integrity.

These statements are attempts to express the inexpressible. They are intended to help the reader to concretize what otherwise might seem to be vague generalizations.

The Genital Dimension: Must the celibate experience exclude all forms of genital intimacy? This question, which is
often posed by contemporary religious, is an indication of
shifting sexual and cultural values. Premarital and extra-
marital sexual relations are largely taken for granted. The
disintegration of sexual mores, even the AIDS scare, has
not produced the Victorian prudishness predicted by the
prophets of doom. We are confronted with a new sexual
agenda with widespread personal, social, and cultural implications. As celibates, we must acknowledge this reality,
confront its impact on our lives, personally and communally,
and respond in a manner that befits our liminal, prophetic,
and consecrated calling.

In large measure, the so-called sexual revolution is the
product of a former era in which sexual repression seriously
impeded holistic human growth and development. A great
deal of guilt and shame centered on sex. The "new" sexual
ethic was intended to liberate people from fear and facilitate
sexual integration, but was so dominantly Freudian that it
exacerbated the inner battle with uncontrollable instinctual
drives. Self-control and sublimation became labels for a great
deal of repressed sexual energy.

It would be wrong to suggest that sexual liberalism is
merely the fruit of a repressive era. There is a strong and
definite correlation, but there is also a positive development
of immense cultural and personal impact which seems to be
poorly understood. Marilyn Ferguson, in her analysis of the
cultural evolution in today's world, claims that in the "new
age" relationships will be marked by breadth rather than by
depth.[20] I do not understand this to mean that loving relationships will be less intense or less exclusive, but rather an
assertion of what is already happening. People will seek love
and intimacy with a circle of people beyond the traditional
confines of spouse, family, and close associates.

This trend is already well established, negatively reap-
ing havoc on the exclusive nature of marital and family life
but positively opening the way toward a sense of the family of humanity in which the divine wish that "they all may
be one" can begin to take shape. There exists in today's
world an extensive desire for greater love and intimacy;

paradoxically, it was never so urgently needed. I suggest, therefore, that trends such as the extensive practice of extra-marital sexual relationships and the upsurge of homosexual intimacy are primarily symbolic gestures of a deeper human aspiration, namely the desire to broaden the parameters of love and intimacy. The gestures may not be entirely appropriate and there are negative and destructive repercussions but, nonetheless, the proposition merits serious consideration. Religious, in particular, because of their liminal and prophetic role, must sensitively discern what the Spirit is saying to their world through such trends.

In fact, this is happening, and out of the concern and experience arises the question: What might genital intimacy mean for those vowed to celibacy? If Ferguson is right in her perceptions of the emerging psycho-social nature of humanity, then at some point in the future our celibate archetypal values may incorporate appropriate forms of genital intimacy. As yet, we are not at that stage and I don't believe we can realize it by developing forms of genital celibacy. In a sense, this is what people like Bhagvan Rajneesh and Swami Muktananda (both of the Hindu monastic tradition) have attempted to do, with after-effects that discredit any potential for good existing in their vision of a new world order.

In contemporary writing on religious life, the subject of genitality surfaces frequently. This is not a mere incestuous preoccupation, but taken out of its broad cultural and archetypal context, it could easily become a fetishism, a form of narcissistic navel-gazing. With appropriate structures for dialogue and intimacy, relationships between religious must continue to be essentially non-genital.

We live in a world inundated with sexual preoccupation, an unhealthy situation that contributes to spiritual and psychological disintegration. Religious share this environment and their celibacy has a profound relevance as a countercultural challenge. But religious are human and subject to the weaknesses and allurements of the human condition; they, too, can become enslaved to drives which in their hearts they know inhibit love, growth, and human-spiritual development. These considerations challenge both their honesty and integrity; frequently they will need spiritual and pyschological expertise to negotiate, in a life-giving way, the challenges of their celibate vocation.

Celibacy and Community

I have deliberately examined celibacy and community in the same chapter. Consecrated celibacy is first and foremost an articulation and cultural embodiment of an archetypal human need for intimacy, a reciprocation of love in total self-giving, a mythical elucidation of the human desire for sexual integration (where they neither marry nor are given in marriage), a confirmation that restraint and abstinence are inherent to affective growth and maturity. At the deepest level of our being, we all share these ideals; precisely because we do, we need liminal groups to articulate and enculturate them for us. And it is inconceivable that these values can be lived out outside a concrete human community where people live, share, and grow in daily interaction.

The celibate vocation, therefore, has a distinctive theological and humanitarian ambience. Theologically, the celibate is lured into being a kingdom person; he or she is being called apart, not to the desert of ascetical torture, but to the barren virgin soil where the Sower has spread the seeds of transformation (cf. Mk 4:26–29). Sharing the pilgrim journey of all God's people, his or her location (liminality) is at those nerve centers where the seeds of transformation begin to sprout, where love transcends all barriers, where the creative voice forever re-echoes: "Behold, I make all things new" (Rv 21:5).

10
Listening in Order to Discern (Obedience)

Obedience began to appear with the growing need for fraternal communion among anchorites and semi-anchorites, and manifested itself fully in the first communities of Religious.... This characterizes the Religious community not only as a group-that-listens, but as a group-that-seeks.

— John M. Lozano

Our reflections on religious celibacy open up a whole new understanding of religious life, with the focus on relationships and intimacy rather than on asceticism and the emotional isolation of bygone days. Workshops and renewal courses, especially on personal growth and community interaction, have enabled religious to deal much more creatively with their sexuality.

Concerning the vow of obedience, there is a vast chasm between theory and practice. While many subscribe to a new model, focusing on participation, consultation, subsidiarity, and discernment, the practical outcome still tends to be functional and utilitarian. Many people insist on doing their own thing; provincials expend much time and energy persuading people to "take jobs"; community meetings aimed at reflection and discernment still bore people to tears. In many communities the co-responsibility has gone full circle, culminating with a superior who is entrusted with so much trivia that he or she has no time or energy to lead (that is, energize, enable, and empower). On top of that, in Catholic religious life, canon law insists that old authoritarian structures must be maintained, while in Eastern forms (especially

Buddhism and Hinduism) the guru tends to be treated like an inflated deity.

Breakdown of Patriarchy

There is a great urgency in addressing the outwardly structured and organized model, which underneath is riddled with contradictions, unresolved tensions, and drained energy. It is the one dimension of contemporary religious life that is seriously undermining its liminal, prophetic potential. While the religious state maintains and upholds a pyramid, authoritarian structure (ruling from the top down), it is inevitably supporting all systems of patriarchy that exploit and oppress. It continues to be perceived as a powerful institution against the powerless, the marginalized, and the impoverished to whom religious should be offering solidarity and hope. Because religious are so respectable we have been absorbed by the institutional church, and even sisters have become clerics in disguise.

The problem is further nuanced, which exacerbates its urgency.[1] The contemporary world has seen the breakdown of patriarchy, as evidenced in the 1960s and 1970s with the student revolts, in the build-up of trade unions in many Western nations, in the rise of feminism, and in the rise of consultative processes within professions. Presently, there are widespread tendencies to revert to patriarchy, to return power to the top, in the hope of achieving the illusive "law and order." It is happening in both church and state, although even some of the people supporting the return are uneasy about it. The entrenchment is a defensive reaction against a new consciousness and fresh strategies. The often chaotic movements of the 1960s and 1970s have not disappeared; they are being temporarily suppressed, and there is a great deal of anthropological and sociological evidence to suggest that these were merely the birthpangs of a new model of leadership and authority, a new paradigm to articulate the aspirations of our time.

If the breakdown of patriarchy is a feature of our age, signaling the end of autocratic leadership, then it must surely be inappropriate for religious to be living and operating by such a system. As a liminal, prophetic movement,

the role of religious would seem to be one of accompanying, affirming, and enabling those striving to create a more
participatory, communitarian form of authority and leadership. I am not suggesting this solely in terms of its cultural
appropriateness; it is also in keeping with the fundamental,
archetypal meaning of obedience.

The Power to Listen Attentively

The word "obedience" is derived from the Latin *obaudiere*, meaning to "listen attentively," which is the biblical
connotation. In the Old Testament, God speaks; the people
respond and repent (or refuse to repent). The covenantal
relationship is an ongoing dialogue between God and the
people. Obedience is not primarily a submission to laws,
whether of the old or new covenant. It is life lived with
alertness to the Spirit, an attentiveness to things that really
matter. This attitude is evident in Christ's own life, in his
continued awareness of and listening to God the Father
(cf. Jn 4:34, 5:30, 6:38, 17:4).

In this, the Christian tradition is one with the great traditions of the East. Superiors in religious life are practically
unknown in Hinduism or Buddhism. On the other hand,
the spiritual father or guru is central to the Hindu Ashrams,
the Buddhist Sangha, and the Sufi schools of Islam; his role,
however, is not administrative but spiritual. His task is to
enable and empower the novice and subsequently the monk
(although he is perceived to be much more autonomous), to
respond creatively to the divine will, to listen to life's call.
Over the centuries, the task of the spiritual guide tends to
fluctuate between extremes; at the present time, many of
these gurus in the East manipulate and exploit those entrusted to their care. In this regard, the Eastern monastic
systems have much to learn from the more developed communitarian obedience of the West.

Van Kaam pushes this argument even to the level of
animal behavior.

> Over the millennia, animals have coped and adapted so
> well that higher forms of animal life evolved continu-
> ously. Thus, it would seem that a necessary condition
> for survival and development of an animal species is

> the principle of listening to environmental events com-
> bined with the readiness to behave in accordance with
> the messages communicated in that listening. This ele-
> mentary guiding principle in animal life could be called
> an instinctive, organic obedience.[2]

Van Kaam goes on to suggest that these "fundamental biopsychological structures" underpin all three vows
and express an evolutionary and universal will-to-meaning,
detectable in higher animals and progressively developed
over millions of years of human evolution.[3] This is an inge-
nious thesis which, although propounded initially in 1966,
has never permeated contemporary understanding of religious life.

For the vow of obedience, the primary archetypal characteristic is respectful and attentive listening: to God, to others,
to life's circumstances, to nature, to the many "calls" of daily
living, and to respond in a manner that enhances growth. An
important dimension of this listening is to discern the patterns and relationships that enhance growth. This includes
the need for structures and even for hierarchies, but it also
includes that adaptability that has enabled species to survive
in the face of evolutionary changes. This latter, I suggest, is
what religious seek to articulate in the archetypal value system of religious obedience.

The reality we are exploring has nothing whatever to do
with submissiveness, permissions, assignments, roles, etc.
Our ambience is essentially contemplative, primarily a form
of searching and seeking, a pursuit that lends itself much
more naturally to collective and communal interaction. The
values being explored articulate the interconnectedness and
mutual interdependence of all life forms. We strive to listen
to a God who speaks in the diversity and complexity of a
continually unfolding universe; the Spirit awakens our inner
being but it is that same Spirit that "groans" in the heart of
creation (cf. Rom 8:22–23). The inner and outer, the spiritual
and secular, are essentially one.

The call to obedience, therefore, even for the solitary
monk, is fundamentally communal, in the sense that none
of us has a right to close our hearts or ears to what the Spirit
is saying. It is no longer appropriate to subject universal life

to the crude, manipulative mechanical paradigm of Newtonian science and Cartesian philosophy.[4] Dividing life into spiritual and secular categories, into political and ecclesiastical realms, into contemplative and apostolic witness, is the product of a consciousness that served us well in the past (some would dispute that) but has little to offer for the future. The lone person, the lone enterprise, can no longer suffice. Almost in spite of ourselves, we are drawn into the great communal shift to the future. We'll get there in each other's arms, or we won't get there at all!

Networking

This vision has important ramifications for religious persons and communities. Listening demands communication and interaction with other people within and outside our immediate communities, enterprises, and churches. It may be calling forth social and organizational structures that are new and unique in their ability to transcend old mechanical and dualistic divisions. Foremost among them are networks.

The social upheaval of the 1960s produced an important merger between the quest for collective social change and the yearning for individual personal growth. It led to the conviction that it is only in relationships that we find our true selves. Networking is an attempt to translate that conviction into practical action. It refers to people coming together, often in circumstances of powerlessness and deprivation, rediscovering their personal worth through the group interaction, but also generating the power to achieve collectively what they could not hope to accomplish individually. This is very much the experience of grassroot movements such as cooperatives and basic Christian communities.

Lipnack and Stamps describe a network as a web of free-standing participants cohering through shared values and interests.[5] There is no hierarchy in a network unless the group itself chooses to have one; everybody is on equal standing. Networks tend to arise not so much to address problems as to explore possibilities; the group becomes united around broadly shared aspirations. Because of its focus on the future it often poses a threat to dominant institutions whose concern tends to be more the demands of the present and the traditions of the past.

Networking also has the connotation of expanded horizons and, consequently, begins to link up with what today is called General Systems Theory. The theory suggests that in our contemporary world it is inappropriate to address any issue in the exclusive context of one particular discipline; in other words, we need to adopt a multi-disciplinary approach. In practice, this means that the contemporary doctor needs to be in addition to a medical practitioner, a spiritual healer, a psychologist, a counselor, and a sociologist. The old mechanical paradigm that perceived the human body as a machine and the doctor as a mechanic who makes an intervention at the point of illness is no longer adequate or appropriate. Some of the leading diseases of today's Western world are not the result of "mechanical deficiencies" but of defective relationships with life at many levels. We are dealing with a whole new paradigm.

What has this to do with the religious vow of obedience? In its call to listen attentively, the liminal person or group cannot hope to respond appropriately without linking up (networking) with other people, groups, or agencies. For example, in the contemporary pursuit of peace and justice, many groups work in relative isolation because of perceived denominational differences or political implications. The cause of peace and justice would be much more enhanced if these groups linked up; many groups would be confirmed in their mission and may discover whole new possibilities that would remain unexamined if they continued to work in isolation.

Networking is quite applicable to religious life. Catholic religious groups have been employing consultative persons or agencies to enable them to attain a better quality of communication and interaction at community meetings. This is a good example of networking, and most groups who initially felt quite threatened by the experiment now accept it enthusiastically. So far, these services have been employed to assist in deliberative processes, but few groups have used the approach for discernment purposes. This entails the more delicate and, at times, painful challenge of listening to those religious are called to serve, especially the alienated, marginalized and oppressed who often perceive religious as oppressors and will not hesitate to say so, if only they would be listened to.

Networking opens up vast unexplored arenas of possibility for all the religious vows. To some it is an exciting challenge, but to many religious it seems a betrayal of a long and sacred tradition.

Historical Background

What is this tradition, and how sacred, in fact, is it? I'd like to address that question by examining the historical evolution of the vow of obedience in the Christian heritage.

The concept of obedience that older religious have known is well expressed in the following excerpt written in 1950:

> The essence of obedience lies in submitting our will to the will of another person considered as superior. The Rule has force only as an expression of this, that is, the will of another person, namely the founder living on in his successors, or, rather, of the supreme authority for the time being of that religious family and of the whole Church, represented by the living pope. The religious always has something more than a dead letter before him: he has the living will of a superior.

This passage re-echoes sentiments that can be traced back to the fourth century, especially to the writings of John Cassian and the anonymous Rule of the Master. Despite their important influence on early monasticism, obedience, in practice, was exercised with restraint and sensitivity. We also know that the thinking on obedience varied considerably throughout the centuries, reverting to the more rigid and literal approach (outlined above) in the aftermath of the Counter Reformation. Many people are of the opinion that the Second Vatican Council changed this; but the following statement from *Perfectae Caritatis* (no.14) suggests otherwise:

> By their profession of obedience, Religious offer the full dedication of their own wills as a sacrifice of themselves to God.... Moved by the Holy Spirit, (they) subject themselves in faith to those who hold God's

place, their superiors. Through them they are led to
serve all their brothers and sisters in Christ. . . .

Many things may have changed in the aftermath of the
Second Vatican Council, but the theology of religious obedience is still couched in an archaic, ascetical, legalistic, and
paternalistic formula — the product of the authoritarian
structure of early Roman times. Religious obedience is theologically impoverished and continues to enmesh religious life
in structural frameworks and organizational practices that
are not merely inappropriate for our times but are, I suggest,
fundamentally un-Christian.

Few writers have addressed this issue as courageously
and thoroughly as John Lozano. Referring to the statement
from *Perfectae Caritatis*, he writes:

> It is useless to seek a New Testament basis for this
> kind of obedience. Although the entire New Testament
> speaks of obedience to the salvific will of God as the
> starting point of all Christian life, and although some
> texts recommend submission to Church ministers, there
> is no saying, either of Jesus or of the apostolic Church,
> recommending that one should submit freely to a hu-
> man authority as a special profession of evangelical life.
> Although Jesus was a celibate, thus illustrating in a con-
> crete manner a possible lifestyle, there is no event in
> Christ's life nor is there any text in which freely chosen
> submission to a human authority appears as a possible
> form of Christian existence. We can cite only the obe-
> dience of Jesus to the Father, which inspires all forms
> of Christian obedience but which is not by itself suf-
> ficient to establish Religious obedience. The transition
> from God to a human being as the immediate object of
> obedience remains to be explained.[6]

Referring specifically to submitting one's will to that of
another person, Lozano notes:

> Where monastic renunciation is spoken of, renuncia-
> tion of family and goods is pointed out but there is no
> mention of renouncing one's own will. . . . Candidates
> are expected to be docile. They were free to choose the
> spiritual advisor they wanted, but once they had made
> their choice they had to be open to instruction. This
> was docility (*docilitas, docibilitas*), the quality of being
> teachable. . . . The New Testament does not speak of

mortification of one's will, but of union with the salvific
will of the Father; not of hypotage (submission) but of
hypakoe (to be listening).[7]

Lozano goes on to show that there existed in early
monasticism discrepancy between some teachings on obedience of dubious Christian origin and the practice of obedience, especially in the monasteries of Pachomius and
Basil which tended to be wholesome and consultative. In its
origins, religious life knows of no superiors. The spiritual
father, who was the central person in the early monastic experience, may be considered the prototype of what today we
call the spiritual director, but not of a superior. In fact, the
superior's role seems to have emerged from that of what today we call the *bursar*, the person who oversaw the practical
and financial running of the early monastic groups. Subsequently, the Rule of the Master and Cassian's writings, both
advocating that the abbot in the monastery should be considered the equivalent of the bishop in the local church, laid the
foundations for what has become almost an unquestioned
theological and spiritual construct. Biblically and theologically, it is riddled with contradictions and, at the present
time, militates seriously against the liminal and prophetic
possibilities of the religious state.

The historical situation is more complex than outlined
above, but the analysis is intended to clarify the source and
nature of the problem. I believe the people who must confront it are religious themselves, not theologians or the hierarchical church. Moreover, in the spirit of liberation theology
and against the background of reading the signs of the times
in today's world, it seems that a new theology of vowed
obedience should arise from praxis (lived experience) rather
than from theoretical foundations.

Let us now turn to the Jesuit orientation on obedience,
often erroneously perceived to be blind and irrational. Many
congregations founded in the nineteenth century sought to
model their spirituality and lifestyle on the Jesuit tradition. It
is often assumed, therefore, that unquestioning allegiance
to the superior and to authority in general is a dominant
feature of the Ignatian heritage. This view is misleading, as
pointed out by Futrell.

> There has been a tendency to read too much theologi-
> cal assertion of some kind of special, quasi-sacramental
> presence of Christ in the superior into the expressions
> of Ignatius especially in the letters.... It is true that a
> tradition developed in Jesuit spirituality which asserted
> much more of a special presence of Christ in the supe-
> rior than appears in the vocabulary of Ignatius.[8]

Futrell, along with a number of contemporary writers, carefully distinguishes between the original Ignatian teaching and the subsequent accretions which suppress rather than develop the original communitarian vision. As with all the outstanding founders and foundresses in the history of religious life, we find a tendency in the church to tame and structure the original mythic vision, characterized by flexibility, variety, and humanitarian concern. Perhaps one day we'll learn from the mistakes of the past!

In many communities and in all the major religious traditions, there are people listening, sharing, and discerning, often struggling to comprehend what God is saying to our world. From the depth and diversity of that experience we can extrapolate the ingredients of a new theology. For the remainder of this chapter I wish to explore how we, in the Christian tradition, can set about that task.

What Is Discernment?

The term "discernment" encapsulates the scope and profundity of religious obedience as it is now coming to be understood. There are three stages to the process of discernment: *perceiving* (attending to, listening, understanding, comprehending, attaining insight); *distinguishing* (exploring options and alternatives, differentiating); and *choosing* (opting for courses leading to appropriate action). The process incorporates intellectual, affective, and deliberative skills, but it is primarily spiritual and intuitive. It is based on a wisdom that comes from within, rich in feeling and imagination, centered more in the heart than in the head.[9]

Before examining each of the three stages, I offer a few observations on the relationship of personal and communal discernment. In popular usage we speak of people discerning their vocation; we tend to envisage this as an individual exercise whereby the person, having sought advice, now quietly and prayerfully tries to figure out what God is asking. The spiritual exercises of St. Ignatius and much of the tradition of Jesuit spirituality uphold this orientation (although some scholars such as Futrell would argue that Ignatius himself favored communal discernment). This understanding (the pursuit of individual holiness) predominated in post-Reformation times and largely eroded the communal values of the Christian life, especially in the nineteenth century and in the first half of the twentieth century.

The individualistic approach was not as widespread in the early church as popular hagiography would lead us to believe.[10] Discernment sought to identify the motivating or animating spirit; this was usually done in prayer and reflection, in dialogue with the spiritual father. Without using the word, many of the early monastic communities (especially those of Basil and Pachomius), resolved issues and reached decisions through communal reflection, discussion, and agreement based on consensus. In the great Eastern traditions the pursuit of individual liberation has always prevailed, again with the spiritual master (guru) playing a key role. Only in recent times, notably in those Indian ashrams where Hindus and Christians share life, has discernment in its fuller sense begun to operate.

In the bedrock tradition of Christian religious life, discernment holds a prominent place. It took the intuitive genius of people like Pachomius, Basil, Francis, and Ignatius to realize that it needs to be both personal and communal to realize its fullness. In a sense, it cannot be communally effective unless pursued by people who themselves are in tune with life. On the other hand, the communal context seems essential to enhance the personal capacity to discern, check out its orientations, and enable and empower one toward life-giving action. Without the communal dimension, individual holiness may fail to bear fruit in appropriate apostolic action; only at this level does it relate to and connect with the wider ambience of life and thus is saved from the Jansenistic individualism that bedeviled Christianity in the post-Reformation period. The personal and communal are mutually enriching complementary dimensions without which human life cannot hope to be holistic or integrated.

We will now proceed to examine the three stages of the discerning process.

Perceiving: Perception is something we largely take for granted and grossly underestimate. We see, hear, feel, detect, learn, and absorb many things every day, but our way of and capacity for perceiving is colored by upbringing, education, and cultural conditioning. Most of us assume that what we see and hear around us is objective reality, yet we all have experienced the conflicting views of two people observing the same phenomenon. Perhaps reality is not as simple as we perceive it to be. And how do we handle the understanding that perception *determines* what we see; in other words, our perception is a way of controlling our environment.

It is at this first level that we may have to undergo the greatest conversion. When I begin to share my reflections and experiences with another, I begin to glimpse new possibilities and unsuspected nuances (I am assuming communication is taking place in a climate of trust, openness, and mutual interaction). At times, my strongest convictions and clearest ideas can contain paradoxes and prejudices I scarcely suspected; and what I thought I perfectly understood is no longer the full truth because of a fresh insight which may come from the wisdom of age or the innocence of youth. With good reason, therefore, John Shea writes:

> Every person has a faith, a set of presuppositions which are tested out in everyday life. If this foundational structure is too constricted or self-centered, a crippling lifestyle develops. Attitudes and behaviors become destructive of both self and community. The depth of sin, therefore, is not in the destructive activity itself but in the consciousness which encourages and validates that activity.[11]

When a religious community of six people gathers to discern about a new apostolate, their major hurdle may be this first level, that of perception. There may be a whole array of underlying and unspoken fears, regrets, nostalgia, anger, but fortunately skills can be learned to negotiate these feelings.

Uprooting and relocation may offer exciting possibilities to some members, but also apprehensions which may threaten the identity of other members. There is a whole range of new apostolic possibilities, only one or a few of which can be chosen. Some groups won't even consider a range of possibilities, assuming that the choice must be education because that is what the congregation always has done; it may be difficult to unearth the underlying perceptions here. Finally, there is the basic concern: what is *God* asking *religious* to *be* and to *do* in *today's world*? That is the consideration that may tie in knots the whole discerning process because in all probability members will have different perceptions and assumptions about each of the italicized words.

Thus, we begin to glimpse something of the delicacy and tediousness of the first stage, and the immense trust and good will necessary for a successful negotiation of the stage. Skills such as good communication and sharing at a feeling level are imperative. Verbal communication, however, is not as liberating or as expressive as we frequently presume. A more artistic form that sets free the imagination and the capacity to dream can be a great deal more enriching and cohesive for the discerning group. Usually this demands gentle and sensitive handling on the part of the leader (animator). An outside facilitator, which may be a member of the congregation from another community, can be immensely helpful.

An occupational hazard for a religious group is the tendency to overspiritualize. Listening attentively to the ordinary exigencies of life is a central part of the discerning process. We must also acknowledge the evil in the world and understand it for what it often is: goodness turned inside out. Frequently, we examine trends in moralistic and judgmental ways that inhibit any hope of perceiving their deeper meaning. It is good to remember that a trend (no matter how evil it may seem) is a process of people struggling to meet their needs. We need to unlock the nature of their struggle and the needs they are striving to meet. Then we will be capable of an authentic response.

Background information is frequently neglected because members are overworked and can't find the time to gather it.

In many religious communities, the value of reading, prayer, and reflection tends to be underestimated. Without intellectual input and spiritual assimilation, religious fail to bring to the discerning process an enlightened attitude and a receptive disposition that are inherent to all genuine dialogue. The richness and immense potential of communal discernment will only surface in a community in which all members are genuinely and deeply seeking out the Lord's will for themselves and for the community in the context of the contemporary church and world.

Distinguishing: Distinguishing refers to the process of examining our perceptions in the light of kingdom (gospel) values: What factors in the trends we have perceived are alien to the growth and dignity of people and the universe, and what underlying values need to be cultivated and nurtured? This is a key question for the second stage. Consequently, in examining a trend such as unemployment, we note its negative effects on unemployed people, on their homes, families, and relationships. We may be less willing to look critically at the oppressive political and economic structures that make unemployment a stigma in the first place, but that consideration is all important if we are to evaluate an issue like unemployment in the context of kingdom justice and liberation.

In the distinguishing stage, we interpret the problem and dream alternative possibilities. Our enthusiasm for what could be done is dissipated soon after by our powerlessness. At this juncture, the solidarity and support of the community becomes all important. Kingdom people, although frail like all creatures, must not capitulate to apathy and fear. Religious must continue to dream, imagine, and create alternative ways to move forward; that is their supreme prophetic task. If they shy away from it, they defeat the reason for their existence, diminish themselves, and betray the treasure they hold on behalf of the people.

Religious readily acknowledge their weakness and limitations, but this is not an excuse for abandoning the exploration of a new vision, and it most certainly does not justify the conclusion that we simply continue doing what we have always done. One of the supreme paradoxes of

the New Testament is that our greatest strength comes from
weakness; when our plans come to nothing, when our
dreams seem incapable of getting anywhere, then we become
highly creative. This may be the moment when we break
out of our narrow perceptual mold and begin to network
with other pilgrims who share the same helplessness. This is
when the prophetic exploration of alternatives (chapter four)
becomes all important.

In the distinguishing stage, therefore, the "real" confronts
the "ideal," and we inevitably find ourselves drawn into
that poverty which is the condition for creativity. This is the
sphere in which we are called to explore the appropriateness
of righteous anger, protest, and political involvement. What
did Jesus do to proclaim the kingdom, and, in the light of
his example, what are we called to do in the church and
world of our day? With that question we are launched into
the next stage.

Choosing: Good ideas do not bring about reform, although with Vico we agree that there is nothing as powerful
as an idea whose time has come. When the stages of perception and distinguishing have been traversed, ideas sponta-
neously lead to action. What is significant at this stage is the
value system that unites the group. The prophetic values of
love, peace, justice, and right relationships lead to the exploration of apostolic options. Choices will have to be made,
and in the process long-established and cherished traditional
works might have to be abandoned. Lifestyle and even personal behavior may also have to alter.

The choice to act follows quite naturally from the two
previous stages; indeed, the whole process of discernment
would be meaningless if it did not culminate in some form
of action. Now that the choice is made, the implementation
process, although it may only involve one or a few members
of the group, needs the support of the entire community.
The new undertaking will need ongoing evaluation and
renewed discernment in response to each new call of the
creative Spirit. This is what the discerning listening we call
"obedience" is about.

Where does the superior of a community fit into this scenario? Does it mean that the superior has become unessential

and that the community has taken over his or her duties? The focus is definitely on the community and not on the superior as a focal point for the group or as one who mediates God's will for them. But it doesn't mean that the superior has become unessential. Even in groups which initially choose to be a superiorless community, the tendency to assign specific duties to members quickly emerges and, in not a few cases, one member is delegated with overall responsibility for the group's life and mission. It's a natural tendency.

In the discerning group, the superior, in fact, has quite an exalted role, depending on the person's skills and abilities. The superior of the discerning community may be compared to the captain who animates and motivates from within the field of play. He or she gathers the team to discern, perhaps by refusing to make decisions for them. The superior need not chair the meetings; ideally the chair should rotate. Encouraging people to do their homework and providing important relevant information that enhances the discerning process is very much a superior's task. The superior, therefore, is very much a confrere among confreres, one who enables and empowers, affirms and encourages, and, at the end, rejoices with his or her colleagues that together they made it.

The superior's role thus is not diminished, but recast with dignity and grace in the long-standing, life-giving role of the spiritual father or mother, a tradition that has an expansive and sacred history in the religious/monastic systems of all the major religions.

This quality of leadership best arises from within a group itself, and, consequently, it is desirable that a superior is selected by a local community when possible. The recent trend of providing special courses and workshops for superiors should not detract from the more urgent need to train all members in those skills of awareness and participation that encourage leadership from within. In this way the religious community mirrors the liminal, prophetic potential which should characterize it in a unique way.

Conclusion

In many spheres of life today, institutions are crumbling and traditional authority structures no longer hold sway. Over the past twenty years, we have experienced renewed efforts at asserting leadership from the group up (as opposed to the top down). A transition is taking place as we move away from pyramid-like authority structures to systems of "people-power" in which leadership rests in the center, with everybody at the same level.

This new orientation, still in its infancy and chaotically expressed at times, is a great deal more friendly to kingdom values and to liminal, prophetic mission than the old style authority with which the church still has strong associations. The new model is inclusive in its ambience; relatedness and interconnections are important; love is the unifying force; justice and equality for all are primary values.

Religious should be in the frontline, pioneering this new model. Their failure to do so not only aligns them with the "powerful" who often oppress and "lord it over them," but condemns religious to a futility in which they lack the luster and freshness that challenges the wider culture and makes them feel irrelevant and problematic even to themselves.

Addressing the authority question is a real double-edged sword for contemporary religious. They are so closely aligned with the institutional church, yet, deep in their hearts, many of them know that it is hypocrisy to continue upholding a system that is theologically spurious and culturally problematic. Meanwhile, their past rises up, reminding them of their failure, but alerting them to those deep biblical roots and life-giving historical traditions that challenge them to be obedient in a new way: listening and responding to the Spirit who awakens in their hearts and in the world the call to become a new people centered on the one Spirit who unites all things in Christ.

11
Resources for Sharing and Caring (Poverty)

Religious Life must reinterpret its vow of poverty, moving away from an interior, private and ascetical meaning to one of public commitment to solidarity with the economically poor and socially downtrodden.
— Leonardo Boff

It is bewildering that all the major religions treat the world with a mixture of scorn and indifference. Buddhism probably heads the list with its belief that all created reality, including humans, is a mere illusion; enlightenment alone is real. The main challenge for Buddhists and Hindus alike is to break the cycle of suffering by withdrawing from the world and eventually escaping into the spiritual (heavenly) state of Nirvana.

Hinduism actually doesn't go quite that far! The great Hindu scholar and statesman, Radhakrishna (1888–1975), is quick to point out that maya (meaning illusion) has a creative as well as an illusory nuance. In that understanding, Hinduism comes close to Christianity. It, too, has advocated a distinctly adversary stance toward the created order, but because of its incarnational dimension has rarely given this teaching the literal application of other major religious systems.

Islam, probably the most theistic religion of all, adopts a rather neutral attitude to the created order. As long as people confess the oneness of God, it matters little how they relate with creation and the cosmos. Of all the major religions, Taoism is probably the most creation-centered, acknowledging and respecting the divine imprint and adopting an attitude of respect and devotion for all life forms.

159

It's evident how religious life came to adopt an orientation of abandoning, denying, even hating the world. We do not find this negative approach to the world in prehistoric religion; moreover, the founders of major religious systems — Buddha, Confucius, Jesus, and Muhammed — never advocated this stance and were deeply immersed in the human and earthly reality. In the negative attitude toward the world, we are dealing with a powerful myth and unexamined ideology that has caused immense pain and suffering to humanity by encouraging sloth and indifference. Some ridiculous and neurotic behavior in the so-called pursuit of holiness has resulted.

A Call to Stewardship

It is against this background that we examine the vow of poverty and strive to understand its evolution and development. Archetypally, it is the easiest of the three vows to comprehend in the sense that the dominant underlying values — sharing, simplicity, ecological stewardship, care and concern for the created order — resonate deeply within all people and have a strong contemporary appeal in a world continually living under the shadow of nuclear annihilation. On the other hand, it presents a value system which poses a huge threat to the dominant institutions of the Western world and to the security and well-being of those who work within them. As a liminal value system, the vow of poverty (which should be renamed a vow for responsible stewardship) challenges all people to live simply, that is, uncluttered by excess baggage for personal comfort and aggrandizement; to share generously their time, talents, and resources; to espouse fully the call to be stewards (not masters) of creation; to respect the natural ecological processes of our universe; to denounce and confront the injustices that polarize peoples and undermine human dignity.

In its deepest meaning, the vow of poverty acknowledges before God that humans are stewards of creation. We own nothing — we have no rights whatsoever over the created order — and yet we share everything. Creation provides us with ample resources and possibilities so that the billions of the earth's population can live in dignity and happiness. We know painfully well that this is not the case; hence, the need to foster those archetypal values in more radical and creative ways.

Contemporary writers on religious life are keen to stress the global context of this vow.[1] Some religious point out that this new emphasis comes dangerously close to being "consecrated communism" rather than consecrated poverty. The religious vow of poverty, in its liminal prophetic aspect, has definite, unambiguous political orientations. Simplicity and justice cannot be lived out without reference to the ruling powers, their policies and activities. Praying for the poor and talking about their poverty is mere sham and hypocrisy unless accompanied by action to alleviate their pain and suffering. In practice, this means a readiness to network with others involved in social action, a sense of solidarity with the poor themselves, and a readiness to contest the oppressive forces that impoverish and degrade human beings and the earth we all inhabit.

Liberating the Poor

This, too, is the message of Jesus, one that most religious comfortably ignore. We begin our reflections on the Christian dimension with Christ's own preferential option for the poor. Quoting the prophet Isaiah, Jesus says in Luke 4:18–19:

> "The Spirit of the Lord is on me,
> for he has anointed me
> to bring the good news to the afflicted.
> He has sent me to proclaim liberty to captives,
> sight to the blind,
> to let the oppressed go free,
> to proclaim a year of favor from the Lord."

God's new reign (the kingdom) inaugurated by Jesus is one of liberation for new life. Freedom from pain, sickness, oppression, poverty, and deprivation are the consequences, mandated and activated by Jesus in his own ministry. Nowhere in the New Testament does Jesus condone or advocate that people should be poor. Poverty is an evil, something to be got rid of.

Of the twenty-four references to the poor in the New Testament twenty-one relate to those who are materially

162

deprived. But they have profound spiritual implications. Not alone is Jesus inaugurating a new reign of godliness (goodness) in the world but he is choosing to do it primarily in and through the poor. On this point the biblical scholar J. Dupont writes:

> The reason for their privilege should not be sought in their spiritual attitudes, but in the way God exercises his kingship. The poor are blessed, not because they are better than others or are better prepared to receive the Kingdom, but because he wants to make his Kingdom a dazzling manifestation of his justice and love for the poor, for those who suffer any kind of affliction. The privilege of the poor has its theological basis in God. It is an error to place it in the moral attitudes of the poor, which makes us spiritualize their poverty. The poverty of those to whom Jesus announced the Good News is centered in a wretched human condition, which makes the poor victims of hunger and oppression. Poverty is an evil; and, precisely, for this reason, the sufferings and privations of the poor appear as a challenge to the royal justice of God. Thus God has decided to put an end to it all.[2]

The poor, therefore are declared blessed (Mt 5:3ff.; Lk 6:20ff.) not because they are poor but because they are the recipients of God's new reign inaugurated in and by Jesus. It is through the deprived, suffering, and marginalized that Jesus gives concrete expression to his liberating mission; without these people the radical nature of God's new reign would remain undisclosed. While the message of Jesus is for all people, its power and creativity are most potently demonstrated in the ministry to the poor and the hope and freedom awakened in the poor as they experience liberation. Consequently, when Jesus is approached for confirmation that his message is real and authentic he responds:

> "Go back and tell John what you have seen and heard; the blind see again, the lame walk, those suffering from virulent skin-diseases are cleansed, and the deaf hear, the dead are raised to life, the good news is proclaimed to the poor; and blessed is anyone who does not find me a cause of falling" (Lk 7:22–23; Mt 11:4–6).

In both the Lukan and Matthean texts there follows this statement: "I tell you, of all the children born to women, there is no greater than John; yet the least in the kingdom of God is greater than he" (Lk 7:28; Mt 11:11). In other words, the recipients of God's new reign are the living proof that God in Jesus has entered our world and inaugurated a process of transformation that will only culminate when the kingdom comes in its fullness.

Preferential Option for the Poor

Few statements cause such consternation in religious life today as the "preferential option for the poor." It is clear that the statement is really about a preferential option for the kingdom of God, and in the light of observations made in earlier chapters, it means an option for communitarian, liminal, and prophetic structures that will activate and promote justice and well-being for the poor in our world. The poor we refer to includes all those who feel deprived of meaning, dignity, and purpose in their lives. These include the materially poor, victims of injustice, the marginalized and rejected, unemployed people, refugees, people suffering sickness or pain, the aged (and, at times, the young), and rich people who feel an inner emptiness (for example, Zacchaeus). We have the poor with us no matter where we live; undoubtedly, their presence is much more pronounced and their cry much more acute in the Southern hemisphere of our earth.

The preferential option is the contemporary call to engage with the poor so that we can evangelize one another and thus become recipients of God's new reign. It is not a question of making the poor rich nor enabling them to become Western technocrats. Nor is it a case of religious *doing* something for the poor; that is often only manipulation which leads to exploitation.

Religious are called to an evangelical task of befriending (inter-relating with), of activating a process that enables the poor to procure the basic requirements to live in dignity and self-respect. It involves a giving of ourselves, our time, our resources; more importantly, it demands a form of solidarity with the poor and frequently a call to protest against the forces of injustice and oppression. Throughout that process the "givers" become the "receivers"; we receive something of the fullness of the kingdom, activated by the Spirit in our relationship with the poor. Our hearts are changed and we see anew; often we are healed by those we seek to heal. The gospel comes freshly alive as we strive to share it with others.

The preferential option is problematic for many religious because deep within they know it is stating something important and that there is a price to be paid for the option. The lifestyle of religious has become comfortable and secure. They live out of an ideology called "poverty" by cluttering their lives with petty, legalistic, and pecuniary trimmings. The word itself, which we consider to be so sacred, doesn't even exist in the New Testament (all references are to "the poor"). The preferential option challenges that sacred, comfortable idol; it calls our bluff and painfully exposes a value system religious should be vociferously contesting. It gets religious back to their roots, to the basic prophetic call of religious life.

The significance of the preferential option varies from one continent to another and in various cultural and geographical settings. Enabling people to survive and live with some degree of sanity and dignity is a major task in much of the Southern hemisphere. Many groupings, including a substantial number of religious, make invaluable contributions in this area. Where religious are weak is in their prophetic call to denounce and disown the forces of oppression that exist with equal ferocity in both the North and South. Religious brothers or sisters in an American high school, which adopts a curriculum that leads young people into work related to arms production, are themselves oppressors by upholding the forces of oppression in our world. In many ways, religious are pioneering projects which make the rich richer and, consequently, the poor poorer.

What Leonardo Boff calls "the spirit of acquisitiveness" is deeply ingrained in the competitiveness religious often foster in the name of excellence. It is a devious and dangerous orientation which contradicts many of the fundamental values we seek to espouse in our vow of poverty.

> In the poor, we see the inhumanity and injustice of
> poverty and the evil and indignity of wealth. Let us re-
> alize that one causes the other. The cause of poverty is
> not lack of opportunity, laziness nor lack of motivation
> to work but lies in unjust relationships, in unbounded
> acquisitiveness, in despoiling and robbing, in fraud, in
> extortion and in the exploitation of one person by an-
> other. This is the spirit that gives rise to rich and poor.[3]

The history of Christian religious life highlights the perennial dangers of excessive wealth. Indeed, there is no historical epoch of decline and decay (within religious life) without an accompanying accumulation of wealth, property, and prestige. In a desperate attempt to obviate this temptation, the Cistercians in the late twelfth and early thirteenth centuries built all their monasteries on wasteland, far from towns and cities. To keep the conversi (lay-brothers) occupied they set about reforming and cultivating the wastelands, and within one hundred years they were surrounded by some of the finest and richest terrains in Europe. The Taize community in France provides us with a prescription which may be the only genuinely evangelical response to this dilemma, namely provisionality. This means that a religious group doesn't root itself in any one place; the group is always ready to move on, especially if its prophetic role is in danger of being undermined.

The concept of provisionality as articulated by the Taize community is well portrayed in an event of the mid 1970s. In 1974, some 60,000 people came to Taize for the Council of Youth. A local speculator, perceiving Taize to be a future place of pilgrimage, set about building a hotel near the monastery. On hearing of the plan, the monks informed him that if the project went ahead, the monastery of Taize would cease to exist and all the monks would choose to live elsewhere. The enterprise was abandoned.

This example merits closer examination. So many religious congregations would endorse such a project because it would increase their clientele and range of influence. Christian religious carry a pastoral attitude which smacks of old-style conversion rather than genuine evangelization. In the name of christianizing our culture, we often adopt strategies and structures which become millstones around our necks, destroying not only our liminal credibility but also our potential to announce the good news of the kingdom.

So congregations today find themselves in a dilemma. They are surrounded by massive buildings which cost a fortune to maintain and encumbered with rich properties from which they cannot disaffiliate because of conditions laid down by well-meaning but misguided benefactors. The houses in which they live, although often simple and austere within, militate seriously against their potential to be a liminal, prophetic presence in today's world.

Their apostolates, too, create problems for their sense of poverty. They cannot run a major educational, social, or medical institution without accumulating property and resources. The whole project may be in deep financial debt, but the image projected is what nullifies the possibility for witness. Moreover, such institutions lure people into living comfortably, at a standard of living enjoyed by the middle classes of society. It is difficult to run a private school without being seen as upholding the value system of the selective group we minister to.

Consequently, a real ministry to the poor links up the structural, institutional, and apostolic choices inherent to that ministry. That is why the preferential option causes so much unease. Constitutions treat of the subject, but, in fact, it impinges on all aspects of the mission and lifestyle of religious. Life is made into a soul-searching experience, one that can become extremely disturbing. Implicit in this experience is the awareness, however confusedly expressed, that it is only in a real ministry to the poor that religious will be able to live the vow of poverty authentically.

Strategies for Renewal

Where and how do we begin? Do we close down the big houses, sell off the rich properties, and move from traditional apostolates? How do we even attempt to analyze our situation without ending up at loggerheads? It is a daunting prospect, but one that all congregations today feel obliged to confront.

The following observations are meant to aid the discerning process:

A New Understanding. We need to transcend the narrow, utilitarian context of understanding the vow of poverty. The amount of money I have and the things I am allowed to possess or not possess can become infantile preoccupations which often cause abuse.

In its primary meaning the vow of poverty is about our relatedness to the created order, our sense of stewardship, care, responsibility, and work. It articulates a deep, human aspiration that all people live in harmony and justice, sharing equally the goods of creation and treating with gentleness and respect the earth from which we receive life and sustenance. Against this background the task of religious readily becomes one of contestation against the many forces at work today damaging and even destroying creation while also exploiting people in a highly competitive and consumerist market. In a sense, therefore, the vow of poverty, like the other vows, becomes a pursuit of humanitarian concern, of relationships marked by justice and equality.

Without this profound theological and creation-centered context, the vow of poverty, instead of being a potent force for incarnational goodness, will tend to become an ideological obsession of people occupying a false and sheltered utopia. Religious life was never intended to be that. To the degree that it regresses into that comfortable ghetto, it loses touch not merely with the people it is intended to serve, but also with the Spirit of God who invigorates it in the first place.

Poverty and Mission. Disposability, or availability for mission and service, is considered to be an important aspect of religious life today. There is still a tendency to think of mission as something pre-existing and obvious to everybody. There are unexamined assumptions that lead us to believe that mission is essentially stable and static.

In fact, mission is quite indefinite at times. Moreover, we can no longer assume that it is exclusively a church or even a religious issue. Indeed, any dimension of mission or service that becomes the exclusive focus of the church, with a tendency to juxtapose the sacred and secular, must

be considered suspect. Life is one; dualisms are human constructs which frequently lead to bigotry, sectarianism, and
idolatry.

The vow of poverty implies a readiness to network with
all those seeking the good of humanity. The poverty experience here is often the simple admission that religious don't
have all the answers or the humble acknowledgment that
"secular" organizations can empower them into mission in
a way they could never do on their own. This observation is
closely related to the distinction between the inclusive and
exclusive understanding of community outlined in chapter
nine. The inclusive interaction not only enhances apostolic
possibilities but also may conscientize religious anew in
their commitment to vowed poverty. Relating these observations to the Latin American experience of religious life,
Cussianovich makes some pertinent observations:

> Many Religious men and women are now living as
> members of Christian communities made up of the
> common people. There they are simply militants along-
> side other militants. Far from draining our Religious
> communities of meaning these experiences are en-
> abling us to view our Religious communities calmly
> and hopefully, though not without serious questions.
> Many would like our Religious communities to pos-
> sess the simplicity and the apostolic vitality we find in
> the people's communities. The lifestyle of militant peas-
> ants and workers shows us that there are simpler ways
> of being Religious in the very midst of the people. We
> cannot help wonder if the canonically recognized form
> of Religious Life has not met its match in the vitalized
> community life and the fraternal experience of the com-
> mon people and their Church.
>   The people's communities do not claim to monop-
> olize certain charisms that have dropped straight out
> of heaven. They do not dwell on ways of winning
> over the "influential" people in society and the church
> so that these people will protect their organizations.
> Their annals do not narrate the shrewd ability of their
> founders to win ecclesiastical or papal approval of their
> constitutions and rules. The Christian lifestyle of these
> grassroots communities raises serious questions about
> the solemnity and complexity of our monumental insti-
> tutions. The church of the people is already arising as a
> sign of liberation out of these militant communities. It is

not arising out of our high-sounding institutions, which
are often more preoccupied with completing picture-
galleries of saints from other centuries. Is it possible
that once again the Lord is throwing the wise and powerful into confusion?[4]

Peace and Justice. Working for peace and justice has
become a primary task for many religious in the Southern
hemisphere and is becoming increasingly important for orders and congregations in the Western world (cf. chapter
twelve). It tends to center on voluntary groups of lay and religious who set out to address local issues, such as housing,
unemployment, women's rights, ethnic minorities, improving
people's lot, and lobbying political powers to respond more
favorably.

For most religious this is still a spare-time activity, even
in parts of the third world. The political ramifications sit un-
easily with most religious, especially in the Catholic tradition
where the dualistic distinction between church and state still
militates against prophetic witness. The fact that religious
feel called into this quality of witness is a sign of the times,
signifying new orientations for the future of the vowed life.
The ensuing interaction with the deprivation and suffering of
others often has profound repercussions for the mission and
lifestyle of an individual or an entire group.

New Apostolic Orientations. In religious life today, there
is a shift in orientation from apostolates based in our own
institutions toward ones based in the larger community.
Instead of bringing in the people to where we are, we go
to where the people are. Religious never planned this development. It transpired over a period of time and would
seem to be one of the ways in which the Spirit of God is
leading religious forward. I would suggest, therefore, that
field-based ministries should take preference to congregation-
based ones, even if it means closing down a long-established
enterprise.

The Context of Poverty. Discussing the poverty issue in
isolation is futile and usually counterproductive. Lifestyle
and apostolate are intimately linked; one cannot be explored
without the other. As liminal, prophetic groups, religious
are not called to be simple, sharing, and ecologically-minded

just for ourselves. We reflect these values primarily in our
dealings (relatedness) with people in real-life situations.

Sometimes religious encounter contradictions, often
missing the paradox underlying them. Work, for instance,
was often not salaried or remunerated in the past. Consequently, religious relied on charity, donations, and monies
collected through various forms of propaganda work. Today,
most religious are salaried, yet quite a lot of propaganda
exists with highly sophisticated strategies, frequently justified in the name of missionary maintenance and training for
ministry.

Such practices seriously militate against our liminality
and our prophetic option for the poor and marginalized.
Only when religious venture into the insecurity and financial uncertainty of so many in today's world, only when
they earn their daily bread alongside those who struggle to
make ends meet, can religious become genuinely authentic
in their call to radical stewardship. It is not my contention
that religious only utilize what they earn from daily work,
because clearly the identification of "work" with "money" is
a value system that is no longer adequate for post-industrial
civilization.

Small Communities.   Another dominant trend of the recent past, especially among sisters, is the transition from
big houses to small communities. In large measure, this
has arisen from an unease with the impersonalism of the
big houses. In the 1960s and 1970s many of these small
communities, which also adopted a very provocative lifestyle, came to nothing. Those established since 1980 have
endured more and tend to be more creative in apostolic orientation, simple in lifestyle, and close in relationships. One is
reminded of Van Breeman:

> "What do I see? I see a small band of people who re-
> ally want to follow Christ with their whole heart. We
> find them in communities everywhere. They will be
> liked by the people because they will be one with them.
> They have a mystery which they carry within them-
> selves and to which they witness. And they are happy
> in doing so. The people living that radical, incompre-
> hensible life radiate joy and they do 'refer' to God. I
> believe that this is the mission of Religious Life today."[5]

This, too, seems to be the emerging vision in the Hindu tradition — the small ashram: simple, intimate, prayerful, a symbol of life and hope for those who come and stay, and a liminal challenge to the wider culture.

Individualism. A tendency toward doing one's own thing is a strong feature in religious life today and in the recent past. In a sense, it is one of the most unexplored phenomenon of contemporary culture. I do not wish to exonerate all religious (and their number is increasing) who pursue an individualistic approach to lifestyle and apostolate, but they often articulate possibilities for the future of religious life that are worthy of consideration.

There are some who go it alone because they are loners by nature or because they find the group context oppressive in some way. There are others, the majority I would suggest, who feel they can live better as religious by adopting an approach other than that available within a specific congregation. Many people in this latter category may be the "hidden prophets" of orders and congregations. In them, the Spirit may be calling forth something fresh and new. Whether or not the rest of the congregation is intended to follow can only be determined from prayer and discernment. The more popular trend to dismiss and criticize such people rather than reflect and discern on their orientations arises more from the self-righteousness of the rich and powerful rather than from the prayerfulness of the poor in spirit.

The Contemplative Dimension. Finally, and following on the last point, is the biblical notion of the "poor in spirit." Matthew 5:3 refers to those who need God to alleviate the emptiness that no human agency can fill. In our human condition, we all share this plight; we can expend a great deal of time and effort trying to fill this vacuum with the "things that pass away." Consequently, we need to hear the daily call to "walk humbly with our God."

In the past, there has been a tendency to over-spiritualize the poor in spirit, leading to excessive individualistic piety, on the one hand, and to infantile dispossession of material goods, on the other. The "poor in spirit" has an unfortunate connotation of weakness, deprivation, and humiliation. In its broader sense the phrase has a distinctive tone of energy, passion, and sensitivity.

The poor in spirit, because they are disposed to God's love and wisdom, are those who can listen most compassionately to the God who suffers in the brokenness of humanity and the earth. They are open to being evangelized by the poor of the world. In and through the poor they perceive God not merely suffering, but mysteriously celebrating the pain and groaning of all life for the liberation of the kingdom (cf. Rom 8:22ff.). This prayerful awareness often leads to the desire to be in solidarity with the poor, to live geographically and culturally close to them, or, at least, to live a life of simplicity and sharing that affirms the poor in their struggle for a more meaningful and dignified life.

The contemplative dimension, therefore, is no mere passive devotional sentiment. It is compassion (suffering with) in the best biblical sense.

> Only the willingness to suffer can conquer suffering in the world. Compassion destroys suffering by suffering with and on behalf of those who suffer. A sympathy with the poor that is unwilling to share their sufferings would be a useless emotion. One cannot share the blessings of the poor unless one is willing to share their sufferings.[6]

Religious face a double challenge in revitalizing their vowed commitment: the living out of their poverty demands a new context, and this, to varying degrees, demands a readiness to part with old customs, archaic structures, and outdated institutions. But more important is the conversion of mind and heart to become poor in spirit, and thus attain the sensitivity and inner strength to let go of the old and assume the new. As Boff reminds us, *both* elements are essential to the transformation we seek to make possible for ourselves and for the world:

> Both these meanings of poverty, although different, are essential and imply each other.... On the one hand, a commitment to eliminate poverty (oppression) without an attitude of poverty (humility) would not be true justice and liberation for the poor. On the other hand, poverty (humility) without a commitment to

eliminate poverty (oppression) would be no more than
a mysticization of the gospel meaning of poverty, and
a refined way of carrying on the beautiful discourses of
the rich about poverty.[7]

Conclusion

On the poverty question, religious have had a great deal
of rhetoric, some action, but, as yet, no real breakthrough.
It continues to be one of the most sensitive and explosive
issues confronting them. It will continue to demand their
attention because, individually and collectively, they perceive
that it touches the deepest meaning of their lives.

Above all, they need to affirm and encourage each other
to persevere in their painful exploration. The preferential
option for the poor is the articulation of a profound biblical myth that for Jesus culminated on the cross of Calvary.
Religious, his followers in the *sequela Christi*, cannot expect
to have it soft or easy. Their vocation invites and enables
them to follow the path that he and they have chosen: the
unfolding of the kingdom, which is the central context of
the religious life. At times, it may be as gentle and graceful
as the sprouting seed, but it can also be the lonely search of
the shepherd seeking out the lost sheep. It can be a struggle
marked by pain and even violence. The poverty of religious
is, in fact, the inner resourcefulness that can hold together
all the different dimensions of life and, with God's help and
grace, bring them to fruition.

Conclusion to Part Three

The three vows of the religious state articulate some of the deepest values pertaining to human life at the levels of possession, affectivity, and power. But as Schneiders indicates, they also articulate a set of cultural values which tend to be channeled into the fields of economics, social life, and politics.[8] There is an important global as well as social and personal context to the vowed life.

As an archetypal value system, religious life must continually re-examine and redefine its relationship with people and with the universe. It is not a privileged call for the selected few who can claim special access to perfection and salvation. The value system of the vowed life has profound ramifications for culture; without this liminal transparency, life loses much of its profundity and potential for relatedness.

A fresh understanding of the vows demands a new language to articulate a new vision. For a start, I suggest we speak of "vows for" rather than "vows of"; instead of chastity/celibacy, obedience, and poverty, I suggest we speak of intimacy, receptivity, and stewardship. These terms captivate much more poignantly the archetypal value system in which the emphasis is on a new order of creation, the kingdom.

This new order is marked by a new quality of relatedness with (a) our fellow human beings, personally, communally, and globally (intimacy); (b) the creative energies at work in our universe, divine and human, which merit our listening attentiveness, discernment, and response (receptivity); and (c) the goods of creation entrusted to our care for the well-being and growth of all life forms, human and earthly (stewardship).

When we connect with these archetypal values and strive to redesign their institutional context, we cannot escape the sense of interconnectedness that characterizes all life in the universe. Traditional dualisms, segregating one state of life from another (God v. man, heaven v. earth) and scientific paradigms (based on cause-and-effect) break down completely. The essential unity and progressive realization of harmony and convergence must become the main thrust of those called to liminal and prophetic ministry.

The values inherent in the three vows are those to which all people aspire. Religious merely embody and ground them in a more explicit way. Their vocation and mission is essentially lay (as it was in the Christian tradition up to the twelfth century), not clerical. Their liminal space is not in heaven but on earth. Their prophetic task is not a prescription for perfection to attain the hereafter, but a commitment to re-create intimate, just, and caring relationships, as a permanent reminder that God's kingdom has come and continues to bring about the transformation of heaven on earth.

Part
FOUR

Approaching the Twenty-First Century!

12
Justice That Liberates

The active and effective commitment of our members to social justice is going to continue to shake up Religious congregations as nothing else except contemplation itself can shake them up.

— Sandra Schneiders

The traditional image of religious life is essentially that of a long journey inward to contemplative union with God. Accordingly, the aspirant was separated from the world and schooled in a discipline and devotion that discounted the things of earth so that the mind and heart could concentrate on the things of heaven. Even within the sacred building there was the enclosure, from which laypeople were barred. Monastery and marketplace were worlds apart, the former, the royal road to perfection; the latter, the less-worthy path of worldly cares and concerns.

How such a dualistic and spurious theology of religious life ever emerged, at least within the Christian tradition with its emphasis on incarnation and liberation, remains one of the great puzzles of history. Fortunately, the practice never quite matched the theory. Even in the most anti-worldly phase of Christian history (post-Reformation times), religious women and men lived and worked in the heart of the world, gracing humanity with compassionate care and striving to create a culture marked by love and justice.

The justice issue is not entirely new to religious. In the world today, there is a new economic and political agenda, demanding novel and creative strategies. Religious are striving to respond as they have often done before. In the past, the quality of response tended to be that of initiating apostolic projects which, in time, proved to be eminently suitable to a more just and caring society. These tended to be educational and health-care facilities, refugee centers, social services, commercial and agricultural agencies, and a vast variety of voluntary outreaches for the poor and marginalized. Projects of this nature are known to have flourished in all the major religious-life systems, and are yet another cross-cultural feature we share in common. In the Christian tradition, this orientation seems to be more pronounced and consistent over time.

In the latter half of the twentieth century, the justice issue became much more focused and demanded more attention. The wasted, tortured bodies of little children became a powerful visual symbol for the millions deprived of food in a world where 15 percent of the people control 85 percent of the wealth and where 30 percent eat more food in one day than the remaining 70 percent would consume in a whole month. Meanwhile, we learn of massive hoarding of resources in food mountains and wine lakes to maintain a Western economy based on greed and self-aggrandizement. We also know of billions of U.S. dollars spent on arms that could destroy humanity several times over. Eventually, the diabolical global scene of gross manipulation, pollution, greed, and exploitation has turned out to be a festering sore endemic to Western civilization itself. The world order is wrong because we live unjustly and sinfully within our own nations, often within our own households. Justice becomes not merely a global issue but a primary evangelical option for personal and social redress.

Justice as an Evangelical Option

In 1966, a strange event happened in Vietnam: six monks burned themselves to death. It was a powerfully symbolic gesture of protest against the desecration of human life in a war-ravaged nation. Few people understood its logic but it touched the hearts of millions and marked the beginning of a new sense of justice as an evangelical option. It was no longer adequate to talk or preach about justice; praxis became the new strategy — the action that speaks louder than words.

Since the 1970s the pursuit of justice has been a primary concern of religious in the Christian tradition. It is no longer viewed as an extra option, but as an orientation in the history and charism of every order and congregation, a characteristic that determines the credibility of religious life in today's world. It was highly appropriate, therefore, that in 1981, the Holy See issued a new and creative challenge to religious to review their life and charism in the light of these four concerns: a) The option for the poor and for justice in our time; b) social activities and works of religious; c) involvement in the working world; and d) direct participation in politics.[1]

In this document, we are reminded that: "The themes of a gospel liberation founded on the Kingdom of God should be very familiar to Religious."[2] Consequently, " . . . the prophetic nature of Religious Life requires that Religious embody the Church in her desire to give herself completely to the radical demands of the beatitudes."[3] Religious are encouraged to engage actively with all those who are struggling " . . . to overcome everything that condemns them to remain on the margin of life"[4] and to provide a voice, a conscience, and a commitment for the voiceless and marginalized.

The task of creating a new social order calls forth " . . . new forms of solidarity and involvement."[5] Religious are encouraged to work closely with laity, participate actively in secular employment, especially in the pursuit of justice and human rights, and become actively involved in trade unions.[6] Since politics touches every aspect of human life and welfare, religious must be politically alert and, in exceptional circumstances, may become directly involved in political activity.[7]

There is no realm of human life considered to be exempt from the conscientization and reform envisaged in the liberation of God's new reign. The kingdom is about right and just relationships — at the human, earthly, and spiritual levels. It demands conditions appropriate to live out these relationships which so often are hindered by oppressive regimes, exploitative political and economic systems, lack of basic resources, unfair distribution of wealth and knowledge, and attitudes based on ignorance or prejudice.

The unjust forces are often complex and global in nature. People feel powerless and at the mercy of those who rule their lives often in devious and sinister ways. Gone are the days when we encourage people to bear the cross of injustice in solidarity with the suffering Christ. The only cross that makes sense to contemporary human beings is the sweat and toil, the word and action, that courageously and persever-ingly sets out to eradicate from our earth all that oppresses and alienates. There is no issue too big to be addressed, nor is there any institutional context (including that of party pol-itics) that can be considered external to religious.

Action for Justice

The creation of a better world and a new social order is endemic to the universal charism of religious life, and to the particular charism of each congregation. It stands out more clearly in some traditions than in others, but I would wish to suggest that it is a dominant undercurrent of all au-thentic forms of the vowed life. In Christian history, we can observe this orientation in the bedrock tradition of Cappado-cia and Egypt, and in early Benedictinism which, despite its explicit contemplative charism, became a powerful and timely reform movement in the early middle ages. An ori-entation toward a new social order can also be found in the great Franciscan charism of the thirteenth century, and in the many apostolic endeavors of the sixteenth and seventeenth centuries when religious became the voice and social cata-lysts for the marginalized masses.

In the bedrock tradition of every order and congregation, and in all the great non-Christian traditions, the preferential option for the poor, the desire to set aright the injustices that cause pain and suffering, emerges as a dominant motif. The Christian tradition is unique in so far as it tends to trans-late the ideal into practical action — much more consistently than the non-Christian forms. The justice of the Christian gospel is not an ideal to be prayed for, but a new way of liv-ing in relatedness that people make possible for one another.

The appropriate starting point, therefore, is action, not merely conscientization. Founders and foundresses did not talk about the victims of injustice; they did something to relieve their plight. They built schools, opened hospitals, and organized social services. A major dilemma facing many religious today is that our apostolates no longer reach the poor, deprived, and marginalized. Religious live with a very painful contradiction that they can no longer rationalize in the name of servicing the "poor in spirit." Attempts to resolve this predicament by missioning a small group into a deprived area, or opening a community in a housing estate, has only exacerbated the awareness of the double (and dubious) standards of religious. Amid the flux and confusion, they must acknowledge that change is taking place, and they are being thrust into the evangelical option they find so hard to confront.

In this regard, sisters are far ahead of male religious. Sandra Schneiders claims that social justice is the major concern of religious women in the U.S.A. today.[8] Untrammeled by the clerical trappings of parochial or diocesan institutions, women religious, being spiritually more sensitive to the signs of the times, can respond more readily to the urgent needs of the world. In this capacity, religious women are not merely exploring new ways of being religious but are giving birth to a new and vibrant theology of the religious life itself.

Practical action for justice and equality is the appropriate starting point. This may involve the courageous and painful transition from the security and comfort of a traditional apostolate to the risky and vulnerable presence among the poor and marginalized. Less dramatic, but often meaningful, is to network with people and organizations who are struggling with justice issues. Sooner or later this involvement will force religious to examine the discrepancy that may exist between their lifestyle and their apostolic option for the poor.

> The witness of Religious for justice in the world, however, implies for themselves in particular, a constant review of their life options, their use of goods and their manner of relating, because the one who dares to speak to others about justice must above all be just in the eyes of others.[9]

Action for justice is itself the most powerful means of conscientization. Through experience, one becomes aware of the evil forces that divide and alienate; indeed, one can be disturbingly jolted into the awareness that religious often augment the forces of injustice and oppression. The awareness that comes from praxis carries an aura of credibility that all the learned rhetoric on earth cannot convey.

Action also spawns its own hope and promise. The cruelest pain of any injustice is the stigma it can create for people: unemployed people feel ashamed to admit that they are out of work; the debtor doesn't know where to turn for support and understanding; the homosexual is scared lest his parents find out; the divorcee feels lonely and rejected; the hungry person wonders where the next meal will come from. Whatever the situation, it can be a lonely, frightening world. Any move to break down the personal and social isolation is a breakthrough, a ray of light, a glimmer of hope.

Confronting Unjust Structures

Injustice and oppression have bedeviled the world for quite a long time. The forces of evil today are probably no more acute than at any stage in past history. The difference is that we now know that we have both the wisdom and resources to rectify the wrongs in our world. We have enough food to feed all the billions of Mother Earth's citizens; the basic problem is that the resources are not shared equally. Scientifically and spiritually, more people realize that the earth is not an object to be exploited or polluted but a living creature whose health and well-being affects the quality of our lives for better or for worse. Competitive bargaining, political and economic, causes divisions and imbalances that degrade all life forms. Cooperation and shared stewardship are the only values that will create a sane and sustainable society. Our Western world view — with the machine as the basic working model, the brainchild of Newtonian science and Cartesian philosophy — is no longer appropriate for our emerging, holistic world view.[10] Our tendency to mechanize and compartmentalize — the nation, the institution, or the person — undermines and exploits all that is wholesome and unifying in the divine plan of creation.

There has been a tendency in Christianity to focus on right and just relationships on the assumption that reform and renewal begins "at home," that it originates in the heart of each person. Catholicism, therefore, has developed a morality that tends to be quite individualistic with the focus on the person and the family. The righteousness which begets justice has been largely ignored at the social, economic, and political levels. It is assumed, simplistically and naively, that there must be peace and integration in the person and in the home before righteousness can reign in the nation and in the world.

Today, we understand universal life as all of a piece. It is no longer a cause and effect world, but one of interdependence where everything (and everybody) influences and is influenced by everything else. Without a meaningful cosmos there can be no meaningful personhood. If the Aborigines in Australia are oppressed, we are all the victims of oppression. The ozone layer in the upper stratosphere is in danger of being damaged permanently, posing a huge threat to future life on the planet, not so much by major industrial pollutants, but by the accumulation of aerosol cans and refrigerators that ordinary folk carelessly discard. Everything is connected and interdependent. All life forms have rights and duties. In contemporary morality, the cosmos is as sacred as the person or the family; each has a right to a just and caring coexistence; "The needs of the planet are the needs of the person . . . the rights of the person are the rights of the planet."[11]

The prophetic call to justice is a great deal more than fulfilling moral duties arising from religious allegiance. There are global, ecological, economic, political, social, and personal dimensions, all of which must be recognized and integrated into our justice ministry.

Global.   With the promulgation of *Gaudium et Spes*, the Second Vatican Council made a significant shift of emphasis from a dominantly European church to one of and for the world. A similar transition seems to have been taking place in all religions over the past twenty years. We perceive the world differently today, not as an evil place to be ignored or abandoned, but as the arena of God's wisdom and revelation, to be loved and nurtured.

Aided by the social and physical sciences, we experience our world afresh. It is becoming painfully clear that the rapid and intensive technology of the industrial era, while bringing immense good, has left us with a trail of ecological disaster. We humans have stepped outside of reality; no longer can we handle and manipulate the earth as if it were a machine, because it obviously isn't. Instead we are dealing with something of a living organism,[12] with an intricate self-organizing propensity[13] and a divinely inherited blueprint[14] that demands an attitude of mystical admiration rather than technological interference.

If they are to fulfill their prophetic role in today's holistic world, religious must become the frontliners of this new consciousness. This holistic and ecological sensitivity is the most powerful force for justice that exists at the present time. And it transcends many traditional and fragmentary barriers of creed, race, and color. Our search for a new earth — marked by justice and equality — is one of the most potent unifying forces in the hearts and minds of today's people.

Ecological. Any attempt to update the vow of poverty which ignores ecological concerns is doomed to failure. We humans are the stewards of creation. We have been entrusted with a fragile planet, richly endowed with life-giving energy, but also needing a reciprocal tenderness marked by care and compassion.

The Hindu and Buddhist retreat to the forest is an archetypal statement of our bond with Mother Earth. It is an attempt to return to the primordial womb, where all is natural and harmonious. The Christian flight to the desert probably embodies a similar sentiment, congealed in the ascetical myth. The call of religious to live simply and in a readiness to share everything is a prophetic expression of ecological interdependence. Most religious in today's world are (and always have been) vegetarian, not for ascetical reasons, but for aesthetic ones: we strive to live in harmony with our planet, causing as little pain and destruction as possible to any other life form.

For religious, there are some profound ramifications to
this holistic vision which they are only beginning to explore.
It is my conviction that the outcome will largely determine
whether or not religious become credible prophetic people
in tomorrow's world. How they relate to the earth will affect
their relatedness to people.

Economic.   Money is the great idolatry of our age. We
use it in manifold ways to exploit and control the world.
By so doing, we fragment the world. Everything, even human beings, is priced, in terms of wages, benefits, taxes,
allowances, or insurance. These things, which were intended
to unite and interconnect people, have come to alienate and
divide them from one another and from creation.

The most flagrant sin of injustice at the present time is
the inequity of a small percentage of humanity having excessive wealth and that an estimated 70 percent of the world's
people scarcely know what money is. Prophetic contestation
must make this immoral dinosaur its main target of attack.
The fact that the problem is global and complex must not
deter religious. Their line of redress can be threefold:

1)   They must confront the subtle and, at times, blatant
injustices of their own way of life. How and where they in-
vest money, how they dispense of their assets, how they
acquire wealth, and why they retain apostolates with a bias
towards the rich (and the consequent exclusion of the poor)
— these are just some of the obvious contradictions that seriously militate against the prophetic liminality of religious.

2)   In every nation today, there are voluntary agencies
addressing global issues of poverty and injustice. Religious
need to network more openly and courageously with these
organizations, join in their protests, and add weight to their
contestation. Because churches often do not endorse what
these groups stand for, political and economic forces often
dismiss the organizations as freakish and unrepresentative
of real people. Religious must be quite unambiguous in their
stance for justice and support all who are struggling for a
more equitable economic order.

3)   There are some creative alternatives to mainline economic strategies. Chief among these are cooperative endeavors in which people are paid according to need and work

is not measured in terms of wages. Any attempts to break
the vicious competitive cycle of traditional economics merit
support. Indeed, it may well be an apostolic prerogative for
religious in the twenty-first century to pioneer and launch
such initiatives.

Political. Politics touch every aspect of human and
earthly life. Political institutions have a powerful influence
on our fortunes, and no other institution of human inven-
tion is more likely to wield power unjustly. Never before in
much of the rest of the world has religion and politics been
so rigidly segregated as in the West — another outcome of
our dualistic, mechanical consciousness from which our universal well-being has little to gain.

Attempts to create a more just and equitable society,
where people can live in the liberation and power of God's
kingdom, cannot be divorced from political concerns. Preach-
ing justice is futile in a system whose infrastructure is essentially unjust; we must confront the system itself either
through dialogue, protest, or possibly direct involvement
in the political institutions. Frequently the benefits we feel
people are entitled to can best be acquired by working from
within rather than from outside the system. Far from being
a task devoid of spiritual content, participation in politics
seems to be a highly appropriate avenue to foster those values of justice, love, and peace proclaimed in the Christian
gospel.

The option for political involvement has other prophetic
possibilities, much more demanding in terms of discernment and commitment. There is the reform of political systems themselves. Most Western nations are governed by
an outdated, irrelevant capitalistic myth which artificially
segregates the rulers and the ruled, maintaining an archaic
hierarchical structure and a parliamentarian procedure no
longer capable of addressing the diversity of human needs in
today's world.

In the Catholic church, there is both concern and tension
regarding political tendencies, especially in South America.
From the perspective of the Latin American church, the bot-
tom line seems to be that the church can no longer endorse
the value system of the existing political structures. Rather

than strive to reform what is perceived to be a corrupt system, there is a strong orientation toward socialist govern-
ments with obvious links to Marxism. There are risks in this
orientation, but it merits our attention and respect as one of
the most creative and prophetic initiatives of a church addressing the political agenda in the contemporary world.

If prophetic ministry is to make sense today, religious
must take seriously the political scenario of the times;
structural contestation (and conversion) becomes the main
orientation of their ministry. It is a first encouraging step
to see that the Roman document "Religious and Human
Promotion" allows for this development, despite obvious
reservations.

Social.   By nature, we humans are social creatures. In
traditional Western society, the family and the workplace
have been the chief outlets for our social interaction with one
another and with the wider environment. Today, both these
institutions are changing profoundly and, in many cases, no
longer serve to articulate social needs or aspirations. Family
breakdown, particularly the nuclear family, has become
quite extensive, and the traditional workplace is quickly
disappearing. Millions of people are being left with feelings
of uselessness, alienation, and despair.

The social arena of the contemporary world, especially in
the West, is ripe for the exploration of creative and prophetic
alternatives. Marital relationships need new support structures to negotiate the varying demands of an unfolding relationship. Mutual growth rather than fidelity seems to be
the dominant value of meaningful relationships. The family
unit itself also needs new avenues to explore and resolve the
tensions and strains incurred by modern living. Because we
tend to perceive the family as a divinely bestowed institution
we hesitate to address its growth and evolution with the insights of history and of the social sciences. Again, we seem
to fall foul to a dualistic world view that is of little use in a
holistic age.

Unemployment is one of the great social and political
issues of our time. Politicians continue the futile struggle
of trying to arrest job losses and continue to make the spurious claim that more jobs can be found. It takes no great

wisdom to realize that unemployment is the fruit of modern technology and the first symptom of a leisure-based society. It is in fact the first realization of the goal which the industrial revolution set out to achieve. Educating and preparing people to adjust to and live in a leisure-based society is not utopian; today, it is a supreme prophetic duty and one that religious are slow to acknowledge and foster. In this endeavor, there is a new justice issue, namely the need to redirect political and educational resources for the enlightenment and rehabilitation of those alienated because of unemployment.

A third social issue of our time — indeed, one of the most creative forces of our age — is feminism. The injustices wrought against women and taken for granted for so long are already well known and need no further elaboration.[15] For women religious in particular, this is a ministry of immense importance. Apart from the U.S.A., women religious have been rather slow to network with women's groups and support a movement that has much to offer to the church and world of the present and the future.

Personal. The twentieth century, more than any other epoch of human history, has advanced the cause of human rights. Ironically, this progress has been matched (and marred) by some of the greatest barbarity humanity has ever known, exemplified in the mindless massacres of Hiroshima and Nagasaki. All people subscribe to the value and dignity of the human person but our ability to integrate that ideal into the social and political fabric of society is far from perfect. Even nations that overtly champion human rights, such as the U.S.A., sometimes covertly limit people's freedom and impede human growth and development. Classic examples are the monitoring of conscientious objectors to United States arms policies and to anti-communist propaganda that justifies interference in the affairs of other nations.

Many nations pride themselves in their legal systems upholding a person's innocence until proven guilty. Undoubtedly, legal justice, operating through the courts and tribunals, serves us well by bringing wrong-doers to justice and also by safeguarding the good name and integrity of innocent parties. Nonetheless, the legal and criminal systems of most nations fail to address the most crucial issue of all: rehabilitation of offenders. Most of our prisons are archaic, bureaucratic institutions which offer little or nothing to heal the inner and outer pain of those who rebel against common polity.

As we approach the twenty-first century, we need to cultivate a fresh sense of both rights and duties. We need to hold in balance the double awareness of human dignity and cosmic wholesomeness (holiness). People are precious, sacred, and special, but so is every other life form, including the planet itself. There is a holistic justice which seeks to respect and maintain everything in the complexity and diversity of creation. We humans are not the masters of the universe; we are the stewards of creation. Our rights and duties do not set us apart or above the rest, but within the complex web of cosmic relationships. Our capacity to relate as responsible stewards must motivate all our attempts to act in the name of justice and righteousness.

When we discover anew the sacredness of universal life, then we will rediscover our own value and worth as human beings. No longer can we assume that the universe is made specially for us; the universe can exist and flourish without us as it did for millions of years before humanity began to evolve. It is a sobering reminder that every life form on earth, including the planet itself, can get along without humans, whereas we need all other forms to survive meaningfully on earth. In the end, it is not our rights that are of primary importance but our duties, particularly our call to be stewards who will care gently, tenderly, and sensitively for the delicate planet we inhabit.

The Painful Conversion

In the light of these reflections, we can reconsider the Catholic church's call to religious to " . . . accelerate in others that conversion of mentality and outlook which will make the reform of economic, social and political structures authentic and stable, and place them in the service of a more just and peaceful coexistence."[16] How can religious enable others to assume this conversion if they themselves are not converted? How can they preach and advocate social justice if the institutions they maintain are themselves unjust, overtly or covertly?

The call to be champions of justice is a disturbing issue for contemporary religious. Deep in their hearts, they acknowledge that this is fundamentally what their lives are about. They can be neither prophetic nor liminal while they maintain the comfort of their middle-class status and the security of their traditional institutions. Movement to a new quality of life means big sacrifices, ones that will be a great deal more painful than the renowned asceticism of bygone days. But on that painful transition hinges the death or revival of religious in the twenty-first century.

Religious can glean some hope and encouragement from those who have already adopted this orientation. In many communities, there are creative individuals who quietly reach out to others within or outside a mainline apostolate. Of greater significance is the move to small communities; for many congregations the move to the small house, while generating a measure of jealousy and antagonism, is a creative initiative of hope and promise. Not only does it activate a more authentic option for justice but it reassures the entire group that the painful transition can be made, at least to some degree.

Universally, too, the Christian churches adopt justice issues with greater courage and boldness of vision. In the third world, in particular, the churches are prepared to confront the political institutions they once felt obliged to support and defend. The Latin American church in particular, in its profound commitment to gospel liberation, awakens the conscience of all who profess the evangelical option for justice and freedom; from that fountain of fermenting hope, we borrow the following passage, which serves to conclude the reflections of this chapter.

> Paying attention to the cry for justice, dignity, humanity and fellowship from those who suffer, we can and must hear the inescapable call to conversion that comes to us from them. To evangelize is to take up the cause of Christ and to make his liberating person present in what we are and what we do, through a concrete practice that involves total liberation. To evangelize is to

be converted, not through intellectual attempts to justify everything in order to leave the situation as it is,
but through an urgent change of attitude, and even a
change of position within the social structure. Evange-
lizing will thus be an action that liberates people. . . .
Christ Jesus finds, in our commitment, his second coming as liberator.

. . . Religious Life, in a world where so many people
and so many Gospel values remain in bondage, can be
a sign of joy, of hope, and of true liberation, so that no
one need be depressed or disheartened by the power of
social evil or by the ability of the prevailing system to
balance its contradictions.[17]

13

From Asceticism to Aestheticism

We are on the edge of a new era, and we don't know how to be reborn. . . . The entire understanding of what it means to be human must be enlarged.

— Sam Keen

Christianity records many epic tales of spiritual heroism of men and women whose pursuit of holiness challenged the very limits of human endurance. Every century has had its share of ascetic devotees, but some of our best known records come from early Christian times. Of this original epoch, the historian Lecky writes:

> There is, perhaps, no phase in the moral history of mankind of a deeper or more painful interest than this ascetic epidemic. A hideous, sordid and emaciated maniac, without knowledge, without patriotism, without natural affection, passing his life in a long routine of useless and atrocious self torture, and quailing before the ghastly phantoms of his delirious brain, had become the ideal of the nations which had known the writings of Plato and Cicero and the lives of Socrates and Cato.[1]

This quotation is quite unique for a number of reasons. It offers a type of critique very much at variance with the majority of spiritual writers who tend to admire and exalt the early Christian ascetics. Yet, it articulates a response that is widely held but rarely committed to writing, one which tends to dismiss ascetical behavior rather than attempt to assess it. The quotation is accurate and truthful, yet totally misses the essential message. Lecky judges by externals and misses the internal core of truth which I hope to unravel in this chapter.

The Ascetical Story

Ascetical behavior is closely aligned with the religious and monastic life in all the major religious traditions. It is one of the more obvious areas in which a great deal is held in common. The main features include: forsaking the secular world, fasting, penance and mortification, celibacy, solitude and prayer, and confrontation with demonic powers (more pronounced in the Christian tradition). The ascetical story, recorded with outstanding feats of accomplishment, tends to be told with awe and admiration. The ascetic tends to be projected as a model of holiness, one to be admired and emulated.

Asceticism is essentially a story, not a set of facts or achievements. It is a gripping story, deep-rooted in the psyche, transcending culture, race, and religion. It is a mythic story that seeks to convey deep fears, hopes, and aspirations. And contrary to popular opinion it is a narrative about life in its fullness, in its wholeness, and not the denial of life as we are often led to believe.

To clarify what I mean by asceticism as a story, I make two initial observations. First, in all religious traditions, the separation of the ascetic from the mainstream of society may be understood as a liminal, primordial period of maturation so that the person can return to the mainstream and contribute more effectively to the development of life and culture. In early Christian tradition, the monk does not leave the world in order to abandon it, but to return better equipped to confront the forces of evil that undermine a holistic human and earthly existence. The classic example is that of St. Anthony of Egypt. And this leads to my second important observation.

St. Anthony became famous mainly because of his biography written by St. Athanasius. It depicts a man of valor and endurance in continuous conflict with demonic powers, which he succeeds in controlling because of his unceasing prayer and extreme austerities. We are left with an image of a world infested with evil forces against which only the very heroic can hope to be victorious.

When we read the letters of St. Anthony,[2] we have a completely different picture. There are virtually no references to interaction with evil forces nor to extremes of self-denial and asceticism. We quickly identify a man so deeply imbued with love of God that his heart reaches out to others in compassion and concern. Even as a desert recluse, the hermits flock to him for advice and spiritual support. After some twenty years he returns to the "world," even more deeply in tune with this apostolic task.

> The picture that is given us of Anthony, as he emerged from his solitude, is in no way of an ascetic emaciated by asceticism that is its own end: it is that of a man calmed, brought into equilibrium, in whom everything human has become, as it were, transparent to the Spirit, docile to his influence.[3]

Why these two opposing renditions? How can we be sure that one is true and the other false? I would like to suggest that both are true at a level in which the simple dualistic category of truth v. falsity breaks down. There is the truth of story (St. Athanasius) and the truth of fact (St. Anthony). How do we reconcile these?

Hagiography is the name we give to that branch of spiritual writing which records the events and times of holy and saintly people. Inevitably, it is always colored by the culture of its time. When St. Athanasius wrote the life of St. Anthony it was assumed that every saintly person attained eminent holiness as a result of successfully conquering evil forces, within and without, through extreme penance and incessant prayer. Consequently, every person who gained a reputation for holiness was attributed with certain qualities and experiences irrespective of whether he or she experienced them or not.

In contemporary hagiography a writer is likely to be much more "scientific," and will only record verifiable facts. This was not the case in the time of St. Athanasius, nor indeed for a long time after as Cusack (1976) notes in his study on the biography of St. Benedict by Pope St. Gregory the Great.[4] This is not to say that these early spiritual writers were unscientific or superficial. They wrote out of a contemporary consciousness of humanity of their time. They told a story in a way that generated meaning, but which clearly needs to be re-translated if it is to continue to bear meaning for the contemporary world.[5]

I do not wish to suggest that all the heroic accounts are spurious and not true to fact. Nor do I wish to exonerate ascetical behavior in general. There have been many deviations. Ascetics have often been "loners" who exaggerated individualism; hence the supreme wisdom of St. Basil who sought to institutionalize ascetical trends in a communitarian context.

The Aesthetic Option

Our task for the remainder of this chapter is to get behind the stories, the popular tales of heroic deeds, and discern something of the deeper message of holiness and transformation. This will enable us to grasp more clearly what the call to liminality is about. As we pursue the journey of "interiority," we begin to realize that aestheticism rather than asceticism is the fundamental spiritual discipline espoused by the great ascetics in all the spiritual traditions of humanity.

Contrary to popular perception, asceticism is much in vogue today, not in the austerities of bygone days but in the strivings and aspirations for which I apply the term "aestheticism." The word aesthetic — which means appreciating beauty, order, and harmony — is derived from the Greek verb, *aisthanomai*, meaning to perceive, to understand holistically, to comprehend in depth and totality. The person of aesthetic disposition goes beyond externals to the deeper harmony, purpose, and meaning. The aesthetic outlook is essentially mystical: everything is precious and sacred within the cosmic ambience of life. Consequently, the development of the aesthetic consciousness is a requirement of that spiritual transformation to which all people aspire and on whose behalf it is articulated by liminal persons and groups.

Contemporary aestheticism is articulated in the yearning for a more just and equitable society, for a world marked by greater unity and harmony, for an environment whose beauty and variety needs to be safeguarded and restored, for an economic order of cooperation rather than competition, for a human community where sacredness and dignity is deeply cherished. In striving to achieve these ideals, we have rejected the asceticism of the past, but have not yet worked out an aestheticism of the future. This seems to be one of the major challenges facing religious as they approach the twenty-first century.

There is something distinctly new about this task and, yet, I believe it is nothing other than a rearticulation of the basic myth of traditional asceticism. The ascetical ideals of ancient times, because they touch primordial aspirations of humanity, remain valid and serve as a starting point for the aesthetic exploration in this chapter. We proceed to review some of the key concepts and ideas of ascetical spirituality. That exploration will suggest the main tenets of the contemporary aesthetical pursuit.

The Desert

In the history of religions, the words "desert" and "wilderness" are used interchangeably. The dominant motif is not that of social isolation or personal mortification but one of a nomadic pilgrimage culminating in the discovery (revelation) of the one true God of monotheism. Consequently, we find many references to the desert/wilderness in the Christian, Judaic, and Islamic traditions, but not in the great Eastern religions. In Hinduism and Buddhism, the ascetic withdraws, not to the desert but to the forest; although the geographical setting and spiritual experience denoted by both terms seems quite similar there are distinctive nuances.

In its primary meaning, therefore, the desert is a "place" (experience) of wandering in search of one's true identity (home), and the end result is perceived to be the discovery of the one true God. Consequently, in the Old Testament, we note the apparently contradictory themes. On the one hand, the desert is the locus of banishment and rejection (Gn 4:11–16, 21:9–15), the place of infidelity (Ex 17:7) and false worship (Ex 20), a state of primeval chaos (Dt 32:10) inhabited by all types of wild and dangerous creatures. On the other hand, the desert is portrayed as a place of apprenticeship and self-knowledge, leading to the discovery of one's true self. At a more evolved stage it becomes the focal point

of God's revelation of the betrothal of Israel to Yahweh, of
the offer of the alliance (covenant) and of the law that brings
revelation. According to Talmon, the love theme between
God and the wandering Israelite people, which dominates
the Exodus account, disappears thereafter and the desert
seems to take on a more negative and ascetical connotation.[6]

In the New Testament, the coming of the Messiah is
announced by John the Baptist (a wandering ascetic), not
in the populous places but in the desert of Judea. For Jesus
himself, the uninhabited place is where nothing separates
him from God which he seeks when he wants to escape the
crowds (Mt 14:13, Mk 1:45, Lk 4:42). Even the temptation
story of forty days may be interpreted in this light.

Throughout the Old and New Testaments, the double
themes of pilgrimage in search of truth and discovery of
truth (the true God, God's will, etc.) persist. The desert experience is essentially a withdrawal from the thoroughfare
of life to discover (or rediscover) in reflection and prayer the
deeper meaning of existence. The underlying assumption is
that the lone wanderer returns to the mainstream and brings
renewed vitality to bear upon daily life. This latter is clearly
indicated (in action rather than in word) in the life of Jesus
himself and is the focal point of contention in the Islamic
tradition. Muslims have always opposed the individualistic
mysticism that keeps the ascetic in the desert and inhibits his
or her return to serving God and humanity in the world.

It is from Judaism that we Christians seem to inherit a
tendency to glorify the desert and set it in opposition to
the world. The Jews maintained that the last and decisive
age of salvation would begin with the Messiah appearing
in the desert. Consequently, many messianic movements of
early Christian times and the original strands of Christian
monasticism adopted the wilderness as the ideal place to
anticipate the end of the world. This eschatological motif,
which underlies practices such as fasting, sexual continence,
and flagellation (adopted by Peter Damien in the Middle
Ages), strongly influenced the Christian monastic movement.
Moreover, the ideological opposition of desert and city, the
tendency to do no work (cf. 2 Thes 3:6ff.), and even a trend
to part company with the sacramental life of the church are

all influenced by this myth of the messianic age commencing in the desert.

I do not wish to suggest that messianic leanings were the only deviation in early monasticism. There also existed an admiration of martyrdom, prevalent in the pre-Constantinian era before Christianity was accepted as the official religion of the empire in 313. In the absence of blood-martyrdom, ascetics now sought what came to be known as white-martyrdom — the life of mortification and solitude in the desert. Many ascetics in post-Constantinian times felt that the church had succumbed to the forces of evil in the world. Since the desert (in popular mythology) was perceived to be the homestead of evil spirits, the ascetics went into the desert to do battle with these destructive influences.

These observations highlight how complex a notion the desert wilderness is in monastic history. There are several cultural and mythological strands often camouflaging sincere and genuine spiritual yearnings. Briefly, I wish to outline what I perceive to be the deeper spiritual aspirations of desert spirituality:

1. An archetypal desire to get to the heart of the matter, to encounter authentically and experience as fully as possible "God," the source and depth of my being.

2. By nature, humans are pilgrims and the desire to express and articulate our restless search is liminally elucidated in the love of the desert.

3. The desire for purity, described in an oft-quoted Buddhist text — "Remoteness from anger, friendliness towards enemies, peacefulness of disposition, and sincere love of God and man" — is expressed in several forms. This is essentially a life-giving concept which is often falsely portrayed as anticipation of the end of the world or a preoccupation with "saving my soul." In the purer desert tradition, the desired purification is a preparation for reinsertion into society as a more transparent vehicle of divine goodness, as exemplified in the life of St. Anthony of Egypt.

4. The primordial wish to do battle with the forces of evil arises from a profound desire to rid the world of destructive tendencies so that human life can be more wholesome and integrated. In our own day, the evil forces are

essentially social and political rather than mythological, and include such things as the North/South divide, torture, oppression, consumerism, nuclear arsenal, pollution, etc. The desert of the twentieth century is the world (Western civilization in particular) and not the wilderness.

5.   The "desert within," the interior desire to grow and to be wise, to learn and to love, is a universally shared experience.

> Solitude allows man to discover, and so to face, all the obscure forces that he bears within himself. . . . Seen in this light . . . the strange devilries described by ancient monasticism should neither disconcert us nor deceive us. They are simply the translation made by the popular imagination of a truth of faith, which is certainly one of the most profound truths of the Gospel.[7]

Every person, at some stage in life, goes through a process of inner purification. It may be encapsulated in one particular experience of spiritual search or psychological readjustment after sickness or breakdown. It may be found in less dramatic but frequently occurring episodes of darkness, search, and enlightenment in daily life.

6.   Underlying all desert spirituality is an archetypal notion of a wilderness transformed: a land flowing with milk and honey (Ex 3:8, 13:5), a land rich in water and vegetation (Is 43:18–19), the *desertum floribus vernans* (St. Jerome), or the barren places nurturing the hungry masses.[8] This same notion is beautifully captured in the words of a contemporary monk, quoted by Roszak:

> Everyone is called to be a monk today; everyone undergoes the desert experience, like it or not. The call is general. The Western world is undergoing a deep spiritual experience, and, so far, not doing too well.
>
> It is this time of chaos, this desert scene, this time of disintegration, that can be a grace. The ancient monks who went out into the desert found just this experience. Everything they had known, believed in, had confidence in, fell apart in that wilderness. Faced with the onslaught of chaos, they were tempted to despair, for they found the faith they had was too weak to sustain so great a demonic upsurge. Yet, in their distress they prayed for faith and faith was given them.

> If anything is needed in this hour, it is [people] who
> know their way around in the desert,. . . who can un-
> derstand what is going on there, can interpret it and
> manage with it. To be a monk in this time, then, is
> really to be the [person] of the hour. No [one] in the
> Church is more necessary, more useful. The desert is
> the monk's world, and today the world is a desert.[9]

The desert is not a place or a body of ascetical practices
and ideals. It is a deeply personal search and pilgrimage, but
also an archetypal, global aspiration for wholeness, integration, depth, solitude, purification, and unity. It is very much
an all-embracing, generic concept, not with the traditional
connotation of separation from the world, but rather inser-
tion at the heart of the world to bring about transformation.

Unceasing Prayer

In the monastic traditions of both East and West, contemplative intimacy with God is a central pursuit. Long hours
— often sleepless nights — are devoted to unbroken communication with the divine. Silence and solitude become
the conditions best suited to this endeavor. In the Christian tradition, the goal is described as union with the divine,
while the Hindu and Buddhist version is the achievement of
ultimate bliss, called Nirvana.

The focus on personal salvation, or enlightenment, is
inescapable, but nonetheless misses the essential point. The
true goal of unceasing prayer is one of self-realization as
a creature whose true destiny is one of self-transcendence.
It is a "letting go" of all the material and cultural props in
order to realize that in God alone we find our true selves.
It is a stripping of the false ego in order to rediscover the
true self.

In its deepest sense, it is not a selfish, introspective pursuit for personal perfection. There are social, cultural, and
even global repercussions. Unceasing prayer is not intended
to lead away from the world, but to see everything anew in
the divine, creative plan, and discern one's true role (call)
within that plan. Today, we use the term "discernment"
rather than "unceasing prayer" to denote that process of divine, intuitive sensitivity that leads to individuation (finding

my true self amid the diverse reality of creation) rather than
perfected individualism (escaping into personal salvation).

Fascination with the mystery of God, which is also the
mystery of life, is a recurring theme in all strands of the
religious and monastic life. There is a strong tendency in
mystical and spiritual literature to depict that fascination
as a highly sophisticated, individualistic pursuit for specialists endowed with the grace of perfection. Thus, there has
emerged in all traditions a tendency to differentiate the perfected from the sinners; the latter look to the former to earn
"merit" on their behalf. People in the Far East shower their
monks with quantities of food and material goods, most of
which are never used. In the West, we assign our contemplatives to enclosures where they can intercede on our behalf.

These developments are deviations based on misunder-
standings of the ascetical pursuit of holiness. The person
devoted to unceasing prayer is graced not with the ascetical power to escape the world of sin and suffering, but with
the aesthetical potential to enhance the transformation of
creation by striving to tune in to the divine creative energy
which animates and enlivens all that exists. The person of
unceasing prayer is not doing something "on our behalf,"
but serves as a liminal reminder of what all of us should be
striving to do.

Unceasing prayer, therefore, is not for the distant, barren
deserts of bygone days, but for the desert experiences of the
contemporary world. Its focus is action rather than words.
It includes all genuine efforts to bring God's healing, love,
compassion, and hope to the brokenness of modern life.
It seeks to discern God's will for his pilgrim people in the
world of today, and strives to empower people to transcend
the powerlessness and pain experienced in the struggle to
live and to survive. It moves beyond ascetical withdrawal
to aesthetical involvement, enabling people to rediscover
meaning and purpose and ultimate fulfillment, which God
alone makes possible.

In recent years much has been written on the distinction
between monastic and apostolic spirituality.[10] We still seem
to be immersed in dualistic thinking and fail to create the
more holistic vision we need for the twenty-first century.

Specific times for prayer and selected prayer styles will remain important, but most urgently needed is a new approach whereby we encounter God (who is simultaneously active and contemplative) in the heart of the world. I wish to suggest that the greatest achievement of the ascetics was not what they accomplished in the desert but the transforming power they brought to bear upon the world of their day. Their fame is not in ascetical achievement, but in aesthetical transformation — personal and cultural. Instead of admiring their ascetical heroism let us strive to emulate their aesthetical testimony to growth and wholeness.

Fasting

Abstention from food, whether partial or total, seems to be a characteristic of all major religions. Primitive peoples believed that demonic forces entered the body with the reception of food, a conviction held by many Greek thinkers in pre-Christian times; for example, Abarias, Epimenides, Pythagoras, Herodotus and Iamblichus.[11] This belief is closely connected with ritual purity and finds echoes in the Christian practice today of fasting prior to the reception of Holy Communion, a custom which in the early church extended to the sacraments of baptism and holy orders.

Among the Eastern traditions, Hindu and Jain ascetics fasted while on pilgrimage (as did Muslims) and in preparation for certain festivals. In classical Chinese religious practice, ritual fasting preceded the time of sacrifice. Taoism advocates "fasting of the heart" (purity of intention, attitude, outlook) rather than bodily forms. Confucians fast in preparation for the worship of ancestral spirits. Orthodox Buddhist monks fast from noon until the following morning, while the liberal ones fast and confess sins four times per month.

In Islam, the ninth month, Ramadan, is one of rigorous fasting between dawn and sunset. Some stricter Muslims fast on Mondays and Thursdays and on pilgrimages. Sufis recommend fasting for the purpose of communing with the divine (a practice for which there are many precedents in ancient religions).

Fasting prepared people for the reception of divine power to utter prophecy. It was in Montanism that the practice of fasting in connection with prophetic gifts became of greatest importance. Fasting was also considered important for the correct perception of the divine will in dreams and visions, a view expressed by Tertullian in early Christian times.

In the Christian tradition, fasting only became widespread with the rise of monasticism in the fourth century. The New Testament is extremely reticent on the subject.

> According to Mt 4:1ff and Lk 4:1ff, Jesus began his public life with a forty days fast in the desert, but as Mark's older account (1:12ff) shows, Matthew's and Luke's stylized version of a forty days' fast designates the beginning of Jesus' work as that of a prophet. It is probably a motif taken over from Ex 34:28 and 1 Kg 19:8; nor can we find any pronouncement of Jesus on fasting in Mk 9:29, for *kai nesteia* is an insertion in later manuscripts. It is only in Mt 6:17 that it becomes clear that Jesus valued fasting as a personal expression of piety: "thy father... will reward thee." Jesus also seems to have observed the prescribed collective fasts; otherwise, Mk 2:18, which is the most instructive statement on his attitude towards fasting, would be incomprehensible: fasting has nothing to do with the metanoia which must follow the arrival of the kingdom of God in his person, but it is a sign of mourning to mark the departure of the "bridegroom." Jesus' sovereign attitude towards fasting corresponds with the rare mentions of the observance of fasting by the very early Church (only in Acts 13:2f and 14:23; mention of fasting in Acts 10:30 and 1 Cor 7:5 was inserted in later manuscripts).[12]

Jesus left no definite guidelines on fasting, and as if to make up for the absence of a clear statement in the New Testament, the apocryphal literature (especially The Gospel of Peter and The Acts of Thomas) and the works of ecclesiastical writers such as Clement of Alexandria, St. Gregory Nazianzen, and Eusebius of Caesarea make abundant references to the necessity of fasting. Despite the popularity of the practice in the early church, it was never given official approval. In fact, the teaching on fasting, advocated by the Encratites and Gnostics, was condemned by the Council of

Ancyra in 314 (canon 14). The Shepherd of Hermas reflects
the continual fear of church leaders concerning excessive
practices:

> Here is the fast you must keep for God: do not commit
> any wicked deed in your life and serve the Lord with
> a pure heart; keep his commandments by walking ac-
> cording to his directives and do not let any evil desire
> enter your heart; have faith in God. If you do this, and
> fear him, and refrain from every evil act, you will live
> to God. And by doing this you will perform a fast that
> is great and acceptable to God.

The history of early monasticism records many instances
of long and excessive fasting. Once again, the popular im-
pression scarcely does justice to the historical facts. We
know that the anchorites of Egypt were frequently visited
by friends who also provided some food — dates, herbs, and
berries. The following account of monastic diet leads one to
believe that the Egyptian monks and hermits were men of
moderation, and insofar as excesses did occur, they were the
exception rather than the norm:

> ...some of the hermits dwelling at a distance from
> the main body were served with a ration (of bread)
> sufficient for six months. According to Cassian, the
> daily allowance of the normal monk was two loaves,
> each weighing half a pound. On fast days this was
> cut down by fifty per cent. The use of wine was not
> interdicted, although many thought and said that it was
> ill adapted to the digestive apparatus of monks; "two
> cupfuls, but never three," was the motto of Sisoes....
> Some lived entirely on fruit and vegetables; in fact,
> Theodotus had a theory that abstinence from bread
> reduced and quietened one's physical vibrations. Honey
> was a great favorite. Mostly they cooked their food,
> although one mail-clad warrior advised a brother who
> asked him for advice to eat grass, wear grass and sleep
> on grass. The cook at Tabenna had no sinecure. Into
> the daily salad he poured forty flasks of oil. At Nitria,
> the bread-making kept seven bakers hard at it all the
> time. There were doctors here as well, also confectioners
> and wine merchants.... In Anthony's monastery seven
> monks were detailed for the daily duty of scaring the
> birds from the date-palms.[13]

St. Basil in Cappadocia discouraged all forms of extreme asceticism and insisted that his monks avail themselves of all bodily sustenance necessary to work well:

> We should make use of fasting and eating in a fashion appropriate to piety; in order that we may fast when God's commandment must be accomplished by fasting, and when again the commandment of God demands food to strengthen the body, that we may eat not as gluttons, but as God's workmen.[14]

Later monastic tradition from Benedict to the present time has retained this balance and moderation, and any deviation has never won wide support. But there is more than "moderation" and "balance" in the tradition of fasting. There is an underlying value system, much in vogue in the contemporary world. Overtly, fasting means abstinence from food, but inherently it entails a process of detachment: restraint and moderation in the use of earthly goods, respect for nature and its life-giving nourishment (hence, the tendency towards vegetarianism which prevails in all monastic systems), inner purification by a modest consumption of food, and a desire not to exploit nature solely for one's own end. Ecological, aesthetic, and ascetical considerations are all entwined in the archetypal value system we call fasting.

Ever since the emaciated bodies and drooping limbs of starving children were displayed on Western television screens in the 1960s, we have adopted a different attitude to fasting. It no longer seemed appropriate to abstain from food purely for spiritual or ascetical reasons. Fasting became a symbol of solidarity with the starving people of the earth; and frequently fasting became a public act of protest against the exploitation and consumerism of rich nations of the West. Fasting came to symbolize the need for restraint at many levels, especially in the exploitation of ecological resources and in the injustices caused by consumerism and the greed resulting from the human urge to master and control. Stewardship of the earth and its giftedness became the new aesthetical value, cryptically worded in the slogan: "Live simply so that others may simply live."

In more recent times, the "fasting archetype" has erupted again in the West. With increasing evidence to suggest that many illnesses are related to diet, there is a new tendency towards vegetarianism and restraint in the use of food. There is also an increasing awareness of food quality and grave concern in some quarters about the potential damage of preservatives, additives, and inappropriate methods of cooking. At a purely secular level, fasting (in the sense of restraint and abstinence) has become quite fashionable. Is this yet another example in which the old distinctions between sacred and secular have broken down, and aesthetic intuition is outpacing ascetical obligation?

Food is a form of energy, a life line connecting us with the creative energies of the cosmos. Our attitudes to it affect not merely our bodily and mental health but our spiritual consciousness as well. In our world today, both the waste and abuse of food have reached disgusting proportions. A huge percentage of humanity is grossly out of tune with the creative and nurturing energies of the cosmos — some because of no food, others because of overabundance. International political action is urgently required to address this ungodly imbalance. But political consciousness must be rekindled and that is the task of liminal people and groups. Religious must once again reinvoke the fasting archetypal value system and articulate its meaning anew for the "starving" peoples of the earth. Personal ascetical acts of fasting aimed at individual spiritual growth are an insult to our creative God, as long as his incarnate Son continues to be gluttoned or starved in the people of our world.

Sexual Continence

In all forms of the monastic and religious life, a celibate lifestyle is deemed most appropriate for the quality of commitment envisaged in the vowed life. Even in Islam, where all "religious" are expected to marry (and most do), and in the Zen Buddhist tradition which consists largely of married monks, service in the monastery must always be given primary consideration over duties pertaining to spouse and family. In the spiritual writings of both these traditions, and also in the literary accounts of prehistoric shamanism, one finds frequent references to mystical marriage with angels or with some other heavenly creatures, indicating an archetypal desire towards the celibate value system.

It is legitimate, therefore, to state that all the major religious-life movements consider sexual continence to be the most conducive state for contemplative intimacy with the divine. It is this positive motif, rather than later ascetical attitudes which denounce sexuality as unclean and ungodly, which dominates the religious-life tradition. Sexual continence is primarily concerned with the exclusivity of the ascetic's relationship with God, not with ascetical self-discipline, nor with preparation for the Lord's second coming (eschatological motif).

This primary focus on the special nature of the divine-human relationship is the key to understanding virginity in early Christian times. In Syria, the celibate state is expressed in the concept *ihidavuta* (consecrated singleness) embracing three elements of consecration: (a) singleness by leaving family and not marrying; (b) singlemindedness (single in heart); and (c) united to Christ, the single One (*ihidava*), whom the consecrated ascetics put on in a special way.

Although the celibate state was considered superior to marriage, the Syriac exaltation of celibacy never involved a denunciation of marriage. Neither did it consider marriage to be in any way evil or sinful, a view widely held at the time by groups such as the Encratites, Manichaeans, and Montanists. The Syriac ascetics cherished celibacy for its own inherent value, as one can detect from these inspiring words of Aphraates:

> For those who obtain this portion there awaits a great reward, because it is in our freedom that we bring it to fulfillment, and not in slavery or under the compulsion of any commandment; for we are not forced thereto under law. Its model and type we find in Scripture. And we can see in the triumphant the likeness of angels; on earth it is acquired as a gift. This is a possession which, if lost, cannot be recovered, nor can one obtain it for money. The one who has and loses it cannot find it again; the one who does not have it can never race to pick it. Love my beloved, this charism (maohabtc: gift) which is unique in the whole world.[15]

The Syrian understanding of celibacy does not seem to have influenced posterity as extensively as one would have wished. There is good reason to believe that it became institutionalized in the monasticism of St. Basil, but it never gained the same popularity in the West.

Celibacy was not assumed for sacrificial or ascetical reasons. The context is a great deal more mystical and holistic, based on the aesthetical fascination with the divine rather than ascetical self-immolation (or perfection). The sexual energies are channeled not into the procreative relationship but into an incarnational encounter (what the virgins called "spiritual marriage") which is life giving for the human partner herself but also for the recipients of her spiritual and pastoral care.[16]

In today's world, celibacy as a life-giving, positive option is not easily communicated. It is not entirely the fault of an antagonistic, pleasure-centered culture. As we indicated in chapter nine, the manner and mode in which celibacy is lived sells short its deeper, liminal, and archetypal meaning. We need to rediscover, re-appropriate, and re-express the intimate rather than the ascetical dimension. If our celibacy does not bind us into a deeper love for God and for people, then it fails in its primary archetypal function to challenge people into a deeper, more respectful, restrained, and self-giving love. How urgent and relevant this vision is for our times!

Conflict With Demons

Early Christianity had an acute awareness of satanic powers in the world, and superstition was rampant.[17] Perhaps the oppressive nature of life at that time led to the conviction that the forces of evil were responsible for political unrest and religious persecution. The hermit and monk, in fleeing to remote places, had no intention of betraying or deserting the world. Rather, they understood themselves to be improving the quality of life by enduring combat with evil forces and thus, to some extent, controlling and withholding the ultimate catastrophe.

How real was this combat? How do we interpret the animal-like figures that attacked St. Anthony? Few people today accept this account as factual; yet, one feels uneasy in reducing these stories to pure imagination. Chitty asks the question: "Did the forms of Egyptian animal gods along the walls of tombs, occupied by the hermits, suggest the shape of the attackers?"[18] It is possible and, indeed, likely that they did. Thus in the intensity of a personal struggle, the ascetic records his or her experience in terms of the images provided by local surroundings, suggesting one possible explanation that preserves the element of a personal search along with its mysterious elements and gives credibility to the ancient record.

In the great Eastern traditions, encounter with evil forces is largely absent. The "forest" is not an evil or frightening place. In fact, the typical image is that of serenity and peace amid the enthrallment of nature. The ascetic has withdrawn to be in solitude with God, with nature, with self, and not in isolation with mythical evil forces.

These two traditions are stating complementary rather than contradictory truths. The East tends to underestimate evil, especially in its social context; the West has tended to glorify personal pain and suffering. In today's world, we cannot hope for peace and contentment until we first confront the "evil demons," both real and imaginary. Such forces include the massive injustices that divide our world, pollute the earth, exploit our God-given resources, and alienate people from creation and from each other. These realities create imaginary (compensatory) "demons," such as the lust for power, pleasure, and property.

Our vowed life is our conflict with the forces of evil. By living radically and archetypally we proffer alternatives to the oppressive status quo; we confront those values which undermine human dignity and erode human meaning. What we need to address is the means we use to achieve this. No longer is it adequate to assume the vowed life as an ascetical, holy, or special vocation. Our liminal space is not a blueprint for ascetical achievement but for critical and energizing action. As with the great St. Francis, perhaps the time has come again to shift religious life from the monastery to the marketplace. Our vowed life is not so much about the ascetical growth of spirituality as about the aesthetical that

God seeks to activate in our world through all those committed to his kingdom and its values.

Conclusion

Paradox is the universal law of growth and development. The way of the truth is not that of progress, but of return. The Christian gospel is unique in its description of this paradox: "We live in the world, but not of it" (Jn 17:14–19); "the last will be first, and the first last" (Mt 19:30); "he who loses his life will find it" (Mt 10:39). This effort to grapple with the incomprehensibility of mystery finds expression in all the religious systems and any effort to bypass the inexpressible nature of this paradox inevitably results in an unhealthy dualism. Thus every mystical/ascetical system speaks of a contrast, always perilously verging on a dualistic dichotomy which many scholars insist does not belong to the more authentic strands of Christian asceticism. We note this division in the maya v. saccidananda of Hinduism, the distinction between *purisha* and *prakriti* in the art of Yoga and the Yin-Yang of Taoism.[19] Eastern religions seem to be able to express this mysterious paradox with greater subtlety than Christian writers have yet succeeded in doing.

What we have attempted to do in this chapter is to delineate the underlying myth of traditional Christian acesis. In that process, we have not dismissed or explained away the real essence of asceticism, but have rediscovered archetypal values which transcend traditional categories and offer fresh possibilities to restate the goals of ascetical behavior.

Concepts such as the desert experience, unceasing prayer, fasting, sexual continence, conflict with demons, and worldly detachment are not much in vogue today. Their language is alien to contemporary culture. Yet, we need to re-examine and re-express these ideals because in their essential nature, they articulate not ascetical feats for the spiritually agile but aesthetic aspirations that transcend time and culture. They embrace values which seem to be eminently appropriate for the holistic vision of life that, in all probability, will characterize the twenty-first century.

14

New Ecumenical Horizons

The tragedy is that the Church in trying to avoid error has often been afraid to explore truth.
— Herbert Slade

In 1987, Ronald Reagan, President of the U.S.A., and Mikhail Gorbachev, Secretary General of the U.S.S.R., signed a treaty agreeing to cut short-range, strategic nuclear weapons. Apart from being an unique gesture of peace and goodwill, it was an event nuanced with subtleties, not least among them being the fact that the two leaders actually signed the agreement before negotiating the terms of its implementation.

The treaty was not so much the culmination of a process as the launching of a fresh initiative for a new world order. It was essentially a new way of bargaining and negotiating: begin with the ideal and work toward its realization. It is not entirely new; indeed, its philosophical basis was outlined by the French philosopher Gaston Berger in the 1950s.

Prospective methodology (as Berger called it) is profoundly Christian in its orientation. Christianity can be perceived as a pilgrim journey toward attaining the fullness of life we call the "kingdom of God," an ideal already articulated in the New Testament and embodied in the life and ministry of Jesus. As a methodology, it is creative and liberating and transcends many of the artificial and superficial barriers that inhibit growth and progress at all levels of life.

Activating New Possibilities

Throughout this chapter, I wish to adopt the prospective approach to explore future ecumenical horizons for the religious life. This unprecedented stance is consistent with

212

the liminal and prophetic nature of the religious state. In practice, it could mean allowing intercommunion between Christians of different denominations while theologians continue to work out a theological basis. In the case of interfaith dialogue, it would allow for creating participative forms of prayer, worship, and mutual interaction while dialogue continues to explore the ramifications of these practical experiments.

Before elaborating on this proposal, we need to reflect on why religious should concern themselves with ecumenical and interfaith questions and what this involvement may mean for their own ecclesial identity. Despite universal trends of secularization and declining religious practice in the West, religion continues to be a powerful cultural force. Indeed, its impact on people's lives is often more pronounced in the so-called "new religions" than in those of more traditional loyalties.[1] Religious adherence is often used to differentiate and segregate; seldom do we hear of religion(s) being used to unite people and bring them into some new experience of fellowship and togetherness. People strongly devoted to their own particular belief tend to disregard other systems or even dismiss them as being inferior. Whatever our religious persuasion, we must all bow our heads in shame at the amount of bloodshed and divisiveness that religion has caused and continues to create even among devotees of the same faith (for example, Sikhism and Islam).

A neutral observer cannot but notice how divisive religious belief can be. Even Hinduism, the great religion of tolerance and respect, is culpable. Few people are happy with this state of affairs, and there are admirable attempts to understand and appreciate differing views and practices. Nor must we ignore the progress of the recent past. Christian ecumenical dialogue began to blossom a mere thirty years ago after some four hundred years of isolation and separation. The interfaith dialogue is a more recent phenomenon, unheard of in many parts of the world before the 1970s.

The fact that both developments are of recent origin is often a limp excuse for not moving too quickly. There tends to be a great deal of reticence and caution in ecumenical and interfaith experimentation. Meanwhile, we tend to forget that millions of people all over the world are abandoning formal religion, sometimes opting for the "new religions," but frequently drifting into religious indifference. The Christian ecumenical dialogue, with a flare of hope and promise in the early 1960s, has lost much of its vitality; it has become something of an academic, theological preoccupation. The interfaith exchange has a much more creative ambience once adherents of various traditions begin to trust and affirm one another.

This is the global scenario in which contemporary religious are invited to respond in a liminal, prophetic capacity. The divisiveness of different religions is a crucial issue for the twenty-first century. In a world yearning for peace and unity, traditional religions with divisive undercurrents will fail to command allegiance or respect. More importantly, the search for spirituality, especially for "the God-within," is breaking loose from formal religious systems and surfacing not only in some spurious experiments, but also in movements with creative possibilities. The traditional distinction between the sacred and the secular is rapidly disappearing as an increasing number of seekers discover (or rediscover) God in scientific pursuit, ecological concern, working for justice, promoting peace, and creating "alternatives" that enhance life and meaning.

The old model of all religions is breaking down, despite the fact that the major systems command the nominal allegiance of millions. And it is not leading to a new religion as some people, such as followers of the Bahai faith, claim. The contemporary search is not for a new religion, but for that which underpins all religion, namely, spirituality. Belief in God and in God's relationship to humanity has been a part of human history for an estimated 70,000 years. Formal religions have existed for about 4,500 years, a mere 6 percent of humanity's spiritual evolution. The systems have served us well, responding to that level of consciousness appropriate for agricultural and industrial civilizations. But today humanity is evolving into a new psychic consciousness with the focus on information, knowledge, mind, interiority, and spirit. We need a new spiritual vision for our future on planet earth and we need catalysts to activate the possibilities.

Religious are intended to be cultural catalysts: frontier people with prophetic vision. Our close association with formal religions should place us in a privileged position to respond to the present challenge. From within the reality we should be capable of deeper perception, a more thorough understanding, and greater clarity of conviction for the future; thus we could energize for change! Unfortunately, our history binds us so closely to institutional religion, that often we are culturally and spiritually incapacitated. Our liminality has been eroded and usurped.

But there is always hope! Visionaries arise from unexpected sources and some of the great upsurges in Christian religious life have been in congregations and groups that initially seemed extinct.[2] What many of our congregations need today is a new challenge, relevant to the times, awakening hope in our divided world. Many religious foundations today incorporate the ecumenical/interfaith dimension. Taize is an outstanding example. Worthy of mention too are the great East-West monastic conferences of Bangkok (1968), at which Thomas Merton died, Bangalore (1973), and Sri Lanka (1980). The achievements of those gatherings bear fruit in an expanding interfaith monastic dialogue under the auspices of A.I.M. (Aide Inter Monasteres) in Paris-Vanves, France.

From Caution to Exploration

The ecumenical undercurrent of twentieth-century religious life has yet to flower and blossom. Awkwardly and cautiously, religious have explored a few safe openings and many have not even attempted that much. Religious who move in the ecumenical/interfaith arena realize that some of the most creative and pioneering experiments largely ignore or dismiss orthodox positions; for example, there are many Christian ecumenical groups who practice intercommunion in "free" church contexts. We are equally aware that by and large the Christian churches still consider Hindus, Buddhists, and Muslims as "pagans" to be converted. Evangelization may be the formal statement of intent, but conversion is inescapably the hidden agenda.

If religious wish to bring their global charism to bear upon the ecumenical/interfaith arena, they need to explore a new agenda. I suggest beginning with the world, not with the different religions and certainly not with the various Christian churches where many religious live and work today. By starting with the wider ambience, we connect more readily with what unites people. We are all citizens of the universe, sons and daughters of Mother Earth. The gift of creation, which we all share, has immense potential to bind and unite people. How we treat the earth and its life forms, and how we cooperate with one another or fail to do so, are considerations that engender a sense of equality, cooperation, peace, and justice. Before we invoke formal religion, we are in tune with the values of the Beatitudes.

Fox explores the immense potential of creation-centered spirituality for a rediscovery and revitalization of personal and communal faith.[3] People who become immersed in ecological matters cannot escape the mystery of the universe. Like our prehistoric ancestors, we encounter the Creator in the arena of the most creative activity, namely in creation itself. Devotion to the earth, the well-being of our planet, and the growth and promotion of ecology remains a potent and largely unexplored reservoir of spiritual sensitivity and religious sentiment. It is also a seedbed for ecumenical and interfaith dialogue. When we begin with formal religions, we veer toward theological diatribe, often of an academic and divisive nature. But when we begin with our common bond to Mother Earth, we are connecting with those creative energies which bind us to one another and to the source of all life. Theological, religious distinctions fade into the background; we become united in our concern for the future of the planet.

It is from that level of sharing common archetypal values that we build and unite. All religions are fundamentally one, not in the sense that they attach different names to the one God, but in the human and earthly value system that underpins all systems. Nothing seems more opposed than the Christian idea of afterlife (in heaven, hell, or purgatory) and the Buddhist/Hindu idea of reincarnation (awaiting the eventual release into Nirvana). We emphasize the differences, but what about the common elements, the shared conviction that humans are destined for eternal glory or enlightenment. Even in this apparently irreconcilable issue, there is a large measure of agreement — not in the respective dogmatic positions, but in the underlying values and aspirations.

How Important Are Differences?

In a world yearning for unity and peace, it seems to be a futile and fruitless exercise for religions to be probing their differences. It is a travesty that we are educated and conditioned into exploring religious allegiance in terms of what separates and divides us. We are all familiar with statements such as, "Catholics believe in...but Protestants don't"; "The Jews consider their Sabbath to be superior to..."; "In Christianity alone is revelation complete." Why the competition, self-righteousness, better-than-thou attitude? It seems facile, even infantile, in a world which — to paraphrase St. Paul — groans for that freedom and tolerance which should characterize all who believe in God.

I do not wish to underestimate the differences, nor am I unaware of the fear of being misunderstood in a multi-faith country such as Britain or the U.S.A. Those involved in interfaith dialogue emphasize the importance of understanding and respecting the differences; this generates the tolerance and trust that makes possible a deeper interchange. I fully endorse this approach but I also feel we must begin to explore a whole new orientation to the global and ecological "ecumenicity" of our times. The "fear of being misunderstood" is the product of an insular, mechanical consciousness that divides the earth into continents, continents into nations; that categorizes believers into Jews, Buddhists, Christians, Hindus, etc. That consciousness has outlived its usefulness; it is inappropriate, indeed, counterproductive for an emerging holistic age. To continue to emphasize differences only exacerbates the divisions and distinctions that already create massive injustice and exploitation, especially in the North/South divide. The alternative is not a bland, undifferentiated mass, as critics are quick to suggest. Our pursuit is for that unity which underlies and permeates the essential diversity of life on our planet.

I use the term "ecumenicity" to describe that quality of interchange which I believe to be a fundamental desire of our holistic age. It includes both the Christian ecumenical dialogue and the interfaith exploration. And it embraces the efforts of our age to rediscover spirituality, often in an ecological context. Even those we dismiss as non-religious, especially those we label "atheist" and "agnostic," can contribute richly to our exploration.

This is virgin soil for religious of both East and West, and threatening territory for many of the official churches. This perceived threat has surfaced many times in the Roman Catholic church's aspiration to retain parochial structures. Could it be that the parish is an old wineskin no longer capable of containing the new wine of ecumenicity? Perhaps the church of the future will be that of basic communities and not that of parochial or diocesan structures.

Such questions must become the daily agenda of monks and religious if they wish to contribute liminally and prophetically to the new ecumenicity. The agenda is vast and open-ended because that is the nature of life in the contemporary world. It is also deeply personal and distinctively communal. The time is ripe with creative possibilities and for new initiatives that may well give religious life itself a whole new future.

A New Agenda for the Religious

First, there is the challenge of conversion for religious themselves. We cannot hope to address religious questions until we undergo a conversion toward the world. It takes time to shed the anti-worldly stance that has dominated religious life for centuries. We must learn anew to listen to the world, even allow ourselves to be converted by it, especially by its current desire for peace, harmony, and justice. This conversion also involves a readiness to accommodate diversity and "pluriformity," to reject the simplification which prizes the spiritual over the secular and the divine over the human, but to seek the integration that can hold together all aspects of the created order. Perhaps most difficult of all, we must transcend dogmatism which safeguards truths often at the cost of undermining the truth's potential to bind and unite people in creative dialogue.

Religious cannot hope to activate conversion in other people and in the leadership of our churches until they take seriously the conversion process. It is not a once-for-all task to be accomplished but an ongoing program of listening, reflecting, and discerning. It is a process of opening up to the newly emerging world of our time with its pain and struggle, its problems and possibilities, and, above all, its profound desire to realize anew the family of humanity.

The second major task facing religious is one of conscientization. Monasteries and convents often shield religious from the real world and consequently close their minds to questions and aspirations of the people they represent. Not only do we need to undergo a change of mind and heart (conversion), but we need to be re-educated on what is happening in the church and world of our time.[4]

There remains the more precarious challenge of conscientizing the church of which religious are a part. As a prophetic dimension of the church, religious must assume this daunting task. A church without a "counter-culture" tends to become immersed in its institutions and bureaucracy. Many of the major religions in today's world suffer this predilection. The "new religions" enunciate this, not just in word but in action; unfortunately, the churches tend to respond with the oft-repeated response: they withdraw further into defensive institutionalization, thus creating the divisive polarization with which we are all too familiar today.

Conscientization seeks to enable people to break out of their narrow conceptual boundaries to rediscover the God of history and the church at the heart of the world. It helps people understand the nature of polarization and engages them in the struggle to rise above pettiness and defensive attitudes. It seeks to transcend the dichotomies and dualisms of models which have outlived their usefulness, helping people adjust to the new vision of holism and integration. Many people are already attempting this renewal program; the seed is already fermenting. Perhaps the real challenge for religious is not to feel that they must monopolize the task

(the attitude often adopted in the past), but that they must
network and thus expand what is already being attempted
at a grass-roots level. And we don't have to be experts; what
we need above all is the wisdom that comes from within,
that activates the possibilities and enables us to discover the
resources appropriate to open up hearts and minds to a new
vision for the future of humanity.

A third task is that of exploring the spiritual undercurrents of our time. This demands both analysis and discernment. Above and beyond the practice or non-practice of
religion is a "sense of the holy" (to use Otto's phrase) which
is quite volatile in today's world. At its basic level we may
identify this sense with the "search for meaning" which every person pursues (often subconsciously), thus obliging us
to conclude that every person is spiritual at the core of his or
her being.

People articulate their spiritual thirst in a variety of
ways, frequently outside rather than within formal religions.
It seems liminally and prophetically appropriate that religious should acknowledge and affirm these extra-ecclesial
endeavors, strive to discern their purpose and evolution, and
communicate their findings to the churches and to the wider
culture.

The churches tend to dismiss, ignore, and oppose many
of these developments. This often leads to alienation and
breaks the ground for the divisions and schisms the churches
try to avoid. Dialogue is the supreme tool for unity and mutual enrichment. In the new ecumenicity, the first challenge
for religious is not dialogue with interfaith or interChris-
tian folks, but with those people and groups who traverse
a lone spiritual path, seeking an alternative church, or perhaps trying to found a new religion. They may also be the
more earthly type who reconnect with their spiritual depth
through ecology, economics, science, or psychology. Whatever their starting point, they are involved in a spiritual encounter and often don't know where to turn to find the next
appropriate niche. The Hindu ashrams have always opened
their doors and hearts to these seekers; Taize has responded
with similar receptivity. Perhaps the time is ripe for all religious communities to address this challenge.

Our fourth challenge is the more thorny issue of ecumenicity itself. Taize is a landmark in Christian ecumenical dialogue, not because it talks about ecumenism, but because it lives it through the international, interdenominational character of the monastery itself. To achieve an ecumenical breakthrough that will demolish old animosities and generate new bonds of friendship and fellowship needs inspiring models. Religious, with their long tradition of community living, are uniquely endowed to initiate such experiments. The concept of temporary monasticism, with a long history in Hinduism and Buddhism, could be one useful working model.

The experiment need not be based within religious communities, nor does it have to be that of a residential group. Its focus can be any aspect of lifestyle, worship, or service that helps to bind people together and breaks down former differences. This suggestion is consistent with the liminal and prophetic nature of religious life and in tune with the broad scope of the Catholic church's orientation.

> [There is need] to devise new ingenious and courageous ecclesial experiments under the inspiration of the Holy Spirit.... A responsiveness rich in creative initiative is eminently compatible with the charismatic nature of Religious Life.[5]

The Catholic church (and the Christian churches in general) adopts an ecumenical stance of permitting ecumenical services (especially of a sacramental nature) only after theological agreement. Consequently, ecumenical dialogue has become an ecclesiastical issue for the informed few and has lost touch with the masses who have either abandoned the churches completely or experiment and explore in extra-ecclesial contexts. It is imperative that the churches allow experimentation, and theologize in the light of that experience. And women and men religious seem eminently suited for that pioneering work.

Our fifth consideration is that of interfaith experimentation. For Christians in general and for Catholics in particular, this subject raises huge theological questions, such as: "If we have the fullness of divine revelation, how do we bring this to bear on our interchange with other faiths?" Knitter is just one of a number of contemporary theologians who addresses this question in a lucid and tactful way.[6] The perceived exclusiveness of the Christian position evolved from a limited understanding of the Jewish notion of the "Chosen People" (which contemporary Judaism does not understand in an exclusive fashion). This led to the extreme Catholic stance, "Outside the church there is no salvation." Today Catholics understand the Christian church as the living community set up by the particular Jesus to celebrate the fullness of life embodied in the universal Christ. Our Christian faith, therefore, contains a "fullness" that in the past we used to monopolize others, but today we see as the resource within which we can acknowledge and accommodate all the other religious systems. We feel challenged, therefore, to reach out to others in a spirit of mutual dialogue, no longer threatened by the old fears of pagan infiltration because we feel secure in the fullness of our own truth.

"Fullness of revelation" does not become a tool for conversion, assuming that all others have only a partial grasp of the truth, but rather an openness to "cross-fertilization" or "cross-evangelization," so that we Christians can realize the diversity of truth inherent in our own tradition. In other words, that experience of the Christian revelation which focuses on the universal Christ (rather than on the particular Jesus) can only be fully and appropriately experienced through the interaction with other faiths (and, perhaps, with non-believers). Catholics will want to know if this is official church teaching. The answer is yes.[7]

In practical terms, what does this mean? How far do we go in meeting the other party? First, it is important to assert, and most ecumenists would agree, that interfaith dialogue strengthens rather than weakens one's own allegiance, because one begins to experience one's faith as a potential for new encounters and not as an exclusive ideology that cuts one off from the wider, energizing experience of life. One is reminded of Panikkar's challenging remark:

> Western Christian tradition seems to be exhausted. . . .
> Only by cross-fertilization and mutual fecundation
> may the present state of affairs be overcome: only by

stepping over present cultural and philosophical boundaries can Christian life again become creative and
dynamic.[8]

The interchange can also awaken a desire to experience
another person's belief system by embracing it temporarily
or permanently. Knitter deals with this subject in a balanced
and delicate way, encouraging us to move beyond the negative perceptions of betrayal and denial to the more positive
view of entering a holistic exploration of truth and life.[9] In
this context, he frequently adopts Lonergan's remark that
we no longer pursue truth as a search for certainty but as a
pursuit of understanding.

We are left with a more tantalizing question, one of immediate importance for many Christian missionary congregations in places such as Africa and Latin America: "What
approach do we adopt to missionary work?" Do we hold
on to our traditional policy of baptizing large numbers into
Christianity? May we dialogue with tribal religions and
meet them half way? And how do we balance developmen-
tal skills with evangelization? Any order or congregation
committed to the new ecumenicity has an onerous task in
addressing these questions. Apart from the theological and
cultural nuances, they often arise in contexts with long-
established traditions and pastoral practices and with roles
and expectations that are difficult to change.

Yet, a new missionary theology is emerging, and quite
appropriately it is ecumenical in the breadth and depth of
our present considerations.[10] Dialogue is not a question of
meeting people half way; nor is it one of enculturation in
the restrictive sense of accommodating local custom when
and where possible. It means an encounter in trust and love
between two parties coming from positions of strength and
conviction and, therefore, not feeling threatened or fearful
of the reciprocity which they (rightly) expect to be mutually
enriching. Once we rise above the ideological perceptions
and the narrow limited horizons of sectarianism, then interfaith dialogue is not only possible but seems to be an
eminently appropriate realm for that oneness of humanity
which paves the way for a world of equality, justice, love,
and peace.

Our sixth and final consideration is the liaison with existing ecumenical endeavors. Whenever and wherever humans strive to build bridges of life-giving fellowship, religious can offer a supportive presence. Their depth of community living and prayerful discernment can enhance the attempts in today's world to build community and to discern, in small groups, what God is asking of people and of our world. Religious can also contribute to the ongoing theological debate and initiate programs to translate the ideas into ecumenical action.

Religious and the Institutional Church

We have already touched on how religious may relate with the hierarchical church on ecumenical and interfaith issues. To date, religious have attempted very little in this sphere, apart from the Christian-Marxist dialogue in Latin America. First, let me briefly address the accusation that religious sometimes act and think as if they were outside of, or superior to, the church. The tension, I suggest, is not one relating to church but to kingdom. Many times in this book, I have noted that the archetypal values of the religious state are primarily kingdom values with an ambience larger than the church. Second, the prophetic witness in its biblical sense cannot be interpreted as belonging to the church in an exclusive way. These are serious theological issues which must be addressed before religious and the hierarchy can hope to dialogue meaningfully.

Who initiates the dialogue? One would like to think that the channels are always open; the blockages, I suggest, tend to be ideational at the theological and theoretical levels. There is a widespread and unquestioned perception among clerics and laity that religious are pseudo-clerics with specific functions of ministry and service within the church. A little knowledge of history will reveal how naive, superficial, and utilitarian this view is. Religious are first and foremost lay people, and all the major religious traditions distinguish between the function of the priest and that of the religious. There also exists in all the major religions a definite tendency, although blurred and unclear, to perceive religious to be outside or on the margins of formal institutions. Finally, the functional roles assumed by religious are dominant in Christianity and Islam (and in both cases at variance with the primary perceived purpose) but not in the other major systems.

There is a great deal of ignorance and misunderstanding about religious life. I believe that religious are to blame for this unfortunate situation. Either because of anti-worldly trends in their respective traditions (alienating them from the dominant culture) or excessive functionalism (whereby they become absorbed by the dominant culture), religious fail to convey the true nature of their vocation. In many cases, they are so closely aligned to the institutional church that they become incapable of engendering creative alternatives which keep the church fresh and new, under the Spirit's divine inspiration.

Breaking out of this institutional mold in which religious life is legislated in every detail will not be easy; differences of opinion seem inevitable. There is also a growing aware-ness — in Christian circles at least — that there are creative and appropriate forms of disobedience and dissent.[11] Resis-tance to the "royal consciousness" is an important dimen-sion of prophetic witness. This option is not without pain or contradiction, nor is it easily negotiated within a religious community or congregation. Moreover, it should only be adopted after other options have been explored.

Returning to our ecumenical considerations, it seems important that religious adopt positive rather than nega-tive orientations. There is a huge qualitative difference and a vastly creative ambience between the statement: "We are refusing to baptize children just for the sake of increasing numbers" and "We opt to explore alternative ways of being church for those who feel alienated." The "option for alterna-tives" has a distinctly prophetic flavor, and it would seem to be a challenging and creative context in which to explore the new ecumenicity.

Conclusion

The explorations of the present chapter are designed to be reflections for religious moving into the twenty-first century. It is very much a vision of possibilities, not a false idealism nor an unreal utopia because the one world which underpins these reflections is already unfolding. People of every race, creed, and color are caught up in this new dream; people are being drawn together by a new magnetic force.

Churches and nations are largely oblivious to the new movement. They are too preoccupied with survival and the maintenance of their elaborate institutions. The structures of both church and state are becoming increasingly cumbersome and costly. They wish to serve people and their real needs, but people are beginning to lose faith and are already looking elsewhere. Grassroots movements with a focus on economics, politics, spirituality, industry (for example, co-operatives), technology, and ecology are cropping up all over the place. Things are changing.

What we are experiencing is a double communal myth: at the macro and micro levels. The desire for a universal world order is matched by an unconscious (but potentially powerful) locally based sense of cooperation rather than competition, and networking rather than the cut-throat contentions of multi-nationals, nations, religions, and churches. It is a double aspiration of autonomy and community. The earth and all its individual parts has a right to exist (autonomy), but that is only possible through co-existence and mutual interdependence (community).

The agenda for religious life — if it is to make sense in the twenty-first century — is no less global and ambitious. Religious are bridge builders for one humanity. As prophetic people they help to dissolve (and perhaps destroy) everything that militates against peace and reconciliation. As liminal people, they proffer a new vision, a dream of hope and unity. On that double front religious allow neither church nor state to hinder them in making their contribution to the future of civilization.

15

On Monks and Atoms!

All matter is created out of some imperceptible substra-
tum . . . nothingness, unimaginable, undetectable. But it
is a peculiar form of nothingness out of which all matter
is created.

— Paul Dirac

In medieval Europe, the monastery was the powerhouse
of cultural progress. Apart from being a center of spiritual
vitality, it provided the impetus for learning, agricultural development, and commercial trading. Monasteries procured
shelter for refugees and solace for the sick and the poor.
The monks contributed to the political structure and stabil-
ity which enabled Europe to survive the breakdown of the
Roman empire. The monastery and the "world" had quite a
remarkable affinity.

But monasticism paid a price! Power, property, and corruption left a trail of destruction and disillusionment. The
Cluny and Cistercian reforms were attempts to recapture
something of the golden age, but they had only limited success. Nonetheless, the monastic phenomenon continued to
grow and flourish with its moments of cultural influence and
its never-ceasing commitment to the interior life of prayer
and contemplation.

The monastic endeavor has rarely recaptured the glory of
medieval times. The absorption in "secular" affairs seems to
have created an exaggerated sense of caution, exemplified in
the attempts of the early Cistercians to locate their monasteries far away from the thoroughfare of life. The withdrawal
to seclusion and basing of prayer and contemplation within
the monastery or convent has deprived both the world and
monasticism of the enrichment coming from a complementary relationship.

In Hinduism and Buddhism the situation is more complex. Traditionally, the monks and contemplatives have been
loved and admired. They have articulated and embodied a
mystical dimension which influences many aspects of Eastern thought. To varying degrees they have served in a liminal capacity in which the "monastery" is perceived to be
the focal point for spiritual and cultural animation. Today
the scene is changing rapidly. The contemplative is often
perceived as a legendary guru, endowed with a wisdom
which is quaint and somehow out of tune with the contemporary secularized world. Indeed, many people in both
East and West consider the monastic settlement to be an
edifice of bygone days and the monks as "the last of the
Mohicans."

A New Charter for Interiority

The monastic and contemplative life seems to be out
of tune with the spiritual yearnings of the contemporary
world. It needs a new liminal space to address the crucial
issues of interiority for the twenty-first century. Archetypally, the monastic experience — for male and female alike
— witnesses to a reality that is deeply ingrained in the fabric of human life. The marriage of the yin and the yang is
nowhere more truly realized than in the contemplative life.
The monastic person gives human and earthly expression
to the hopes and aspirations of all the great mystics; the
monastery is mysticism institutionalized.

Without this grounding, the mystical vision would fail to
take root in our culture and would fail to be the catalyst for
renewal and transformation. I am not equating monasticism
and mysticism, but I don't believe that one can survive without the other. When the contemplative life loses touch with
the profoundly holistic ambience of mysticism, it fails to connect meaningfully with people, with the earth, and with the
surrounding culture.

What do I mean by mysticism? Stevens captures much of
its depth and richness in this description:

> Mysticism is the art of becoming fully conscious. It is
> the way of removing the filters. It is the path to getting
> fully in tune with reality. Mysticism is a new way of

being that transforms everything it touches. It puts me
in touch with my deepest self, my hidden powers. So
profoundly does it transform me that the mystic state is
described as touching the divine.[1]

Contrary to popular opinion, mysticism has a distinctively human, earthly, and ecological, as well as spiritual,
significance.[2] Indeed, it seems to be a unique feature of mysticism that it can hold together the polarities and opposites
of existence. The mystic maintains simultaneously an inner
relationship with the mysterious, unchanging, all-powerful
God, alongside a sense of being at home in the fragmented
reality of daily life. The mystical pursuit is one of integration, holding together the diverse energies of universal life.

A resurgence of mysticism is occurring. "All in all,"
writes Johnston, "mysticism is in the air we breathe; and
it promises to be even more in the air of the new age into
which we are moving."[3] Mystical seekers emerge from many
strange places, even from agnostic and atheistic backgrounds. Of particular interest is the convergence of science
and mysticism in recent years.

Science and religion are considered to be classic enemies.
This is a facile and grossly exaggerated perception. It has
some foundation in the strong opposition of the Catholic
church to most scientific discoveries of the eighteenth and
nineteenth centuries. Outside Catholicism, the opposition has
not been so pronounced.

The distinction is also superficial in the sense that many
of the leading scientists of the twentieth century — for instance, Einstein, Bohr, Schrodinger, Heisenberg — openly
acknowledge that they too are in search for truth, which remains incomplete without including the spiritual dimension.[4]
The following is just one of many statements verifying the
scientific, spiritual orientation:

> Science can only be created by those who are thor-
> oughly imbued with the aspirations towards truth and
> understanding. This source of feeling, however, springs
> from the sphere of religion. To this there also belongs
> the faith in the possibility that the regulations valid for
> the world of existence are rational; that is comprehen-
> sible to reason. I cannot conceive of a genuine scientist

without that profound faith. The situation may be expressed by an image: science without religion is lame,
religion without science is blind.[5]

Moreover, the leading theories and most of the major
discoveries of twentieth-century physics project science more
and more away from inert matter toward the underlying
"energy" that sustains all creation.

Science and spirituality are on the same highway and, in
fact, traveling in the same vehicle. They are even talking the
same language, but are often blind to their common pursuit
because of old prejudices. We need some "facilitators" whose
own spiritual depth enables them to see where differences
are transcended and connections are established. The people
supremely equipped for this challenging task are contemplatives, those who ground the mystical vision for humanity.
Their agenda in our new scientific age is what I wish to explore for the remainder of this chapter.

The Scientific Pursuit

Our reflections rest on the following conviction: What the
new physics is striving to articulate has remarkable similarities with the basic mystical values of the contemplative life.
Religious can enable the physicists to rediscover the spiritual
dimension at the heart of creation.

Contemporary science is an exciting and intriguing endeavor. Atoms, as the basic units of the material of the
universe, were first named by the Greek philosopher An-
axagoras (500–428 B.C.). For over two thousand years, atoms
were considered to be indivisible and indestructible (hence
the term: elementary particles). Not until the English chem-
ist John Dalton (1766–1844) noted that atoms have different
weights and combine to form compounds did physicists
doubt the atomic theory. It took another one hundred years
to establish the actual existence of atoms through the pioneering work on electrons by John J. Thompson in 1896.
Finally, in 1909, the New Zealand physicist, Ernest Ruther-
ford, established the basic architecture of the atom, which
consisted of a central nucleus comprising a ball of tightly
bound protons and neutrons and surrounded by a cloud

of orbiting electrons. Most of the mass is contained in the nucleus.

The splitting of the atom at the beginning of the twentieth century led to a proliferation of subatomic particles, numbering about ninety naturally occurring elements which have been identified on earth and about a dozen that have been produced artificially. Among the better known are electrons, protons, neutrons, bayrons, mesons, hadrons, leptons, and quarks. The most recently discovered are the quarks whose intriguing "arrangement" was only established in 1984.

As atomic theory developed, scientists discovered four fundamental forces in nature: gravity, electromagnetism, weak nuclear, and strong nuclear. They are all thought to operate through the agency of particles called "gauge bosons," which metaphorically may be compared to a rugby ball creating an interaction between players as a game progresses. How the four forces interrelate became the focus of scientific research throughout the 1970s, pioneered by Steven Weinberg and Sheldon Glashow of Harvard University and Abdus Salam of Imperial College, London.

Instead of the original four, we now have three major forces: the electroweak, the strong nuclear, and gravity. Physicists believe that the discovery of a new unifying link between the electroweak and the strong force is imminent; this pursuit they have named the grand unification theory (GUT). Moreover the scientific community is convinced that scientists, in the not too distant future, will discover a theory to explain the essential unity of all life in the universe. Already they have named it the TOE (theory of everything) theory.

This background provokes us to ask two questions: "What are the scientists pursuing?" and second, "What is the archetypal significance of their discoveries?" The scientists themselves claim that they are pursuing the ultimate building blocks of matter. They wish to establish what this world is made of and how it came to be. I suggest that the scientific pursuit is a great deal more complex, and is a mystical exploration into the meaning of life itself.

Science, Mystery, and Contemplation

A mystical dimension is observable in the scientific spec-
ulations of the ancient Greeks; so many "unknowns" only
made sense by adopting the paradigm of a mysterious universe. We often assume that contemporary science sets out
to eradicate spiritual reality, accepting only what can be
"proven." This is a gross simplification which does injustice
to the scientific method and to the great scientific pioneers of
the twentieth century.

Albert Einstein (1879–1955) remains the central figure in
exploring the new scientific paradigm. A Jew and German
by birth, he was essentially a free thinker whose God was
the one who "reveals himself in the harmony of all being."
His deeper faith can be gleaned from these oft-quoted words
from a recording made in 1932: "The finest thing we can
experience is mystery. It is the fundamental emotion that
is at the roots of true science. Those who cannot know it,
those who cannot admire, those who are no longer capable
of experiencing a sense of wonder, might as well be dead."

Einstein's fame centers on his discovery of relativity,
the special theory in 1905 and the general one in 1916. Both
theories challenge the traditional common-sense notions that
space and time are objective realities existing independently.
The special theory states that the motion of the observer
partly determines how reality is perceived. Our world is
not an absolute entity endowed with definitive categories of
space and time. Instead, we live in a space-time continuum
measured relative to the observer's perception.

The general theory is an application of the same principles on a global scale. Planets move in their orbit not because of some postulated force of gravity but because of the
fact that space in our universe is curved rather than linear.
In other words, planets move relative to the space-curvature
of the universe.

To the non-scientist, the theory of relativity may seem
obscure, but to the mathematician and physicist, it has the
fascination and beauty of poetry. The theory states that the
world is one and everything in it is interrelated; therefore,
everything is of relative importance. Creating hierarchies of

importance from the absolute to the relative is a human construct which fails to do justice to the mystery, beauty, and interrelatedness of universal life. In a sense, the relativity theory invites us to turn upside-down many of our common-sense notions. Zukav expresses it rather poetically: "If the universe has a heartbeat, its rate depends upon the hearer."[6]

We are dealing with creation-centered mysticism. We are also exploring concepts and ideas that have profoundly changed our attitudes to the world, reminding us that our tendency to dominate and control nature is alien to the scientific pursuit itself. Taken to its logical conclusions, Einstein's vision is about rediscovering our place in a universe where there must be no absolute dictators, but where all life forms can live together in mutual interdependence.

This new mystical orientation also underpins another great discovery of the twentieth century, namely quantum theory. It was originally proposed by Max Planck (1858–1947) in 1900 when he discovered that the energy of heat radiation is not emitted continuously (in "logical" mechanical sequences) but appears in the form of "energy packets" which Einstein called "quanta" and recognised as fundamental aspects of nature. Although Einstein contributed to the formulation of the quantum theory (along with Werner Heisenberg, Erwin Schrodinger, Max Born, Neils Bohr, and others), he could never accept its unpredictability, defending his position to the end of his life with his oft-quoted quip: "God does not play dice with the universe."

Scientists have great difficulty in translating quantum theory into daily language. Its fundamental tenet is that objects in the world around us only make sense in terms of the context to which they belong; for example, if I look at a house in the distance, my perception and awareness of that house has as much to do with the environmental/geographical context of the house as with the house itself. We perceive reality in wholes, not as isolated, independent units.

> To the naive realist the universe is a collection of objects. To the quantum physicist it is an inseparable web of vibrating energy patterns in which no one component has reality independent of the entirety; and included in the entirety is the observer.[7]

Quantum theory, therefore, articulates the same aspirations as those of the great mystical traditions of humanity.
It issues an invitation to transcend the transitoriness and
man-made distinctions of daily life in order to connect with
the more holistic and unifying energies. It goes even further
and suggests that linear thought is a human fabrication that
undermines rather than enhances our human capabilities.
Humans are innately endowed with a lateral (holistic) capacity to perceive and understand, what Karl Pribram called a
holographic brain capable of comprehending life holistically
rather than in piecemeal fashion. The dividing line between
science and spirituality, between physics and contemplation,
becomes extremely thin; perhaps, it too, is one of our human
linear constructs.

The Holistic Paradigm

Relativity and quantum theories set the scene for what
Capra calls the transition from the old, mechanical paradigm
of Newtonian science and Cartesian philosophy to the new
holistic model. For Newton, the whole is equal to the sum of
the parts; all of life and each aspect of life can be perceived
as a machine consisting of basic parts which can be changed
or modified by intervention, thus influencing the whole. In
the holistic paradigm, the whole is greater than the sum of
the parts; moreover, the whole is contained in each part as
in a hologram.[8] And intervention takes on quite a different
meaning: it is no longer that of the technocrat seeking to
manipulate and control but rather that of a catalyst who
creates the conditions for the whole to unfold in accordance
with its own innate evolutionary tendency.[9] The mastery of
control and domination has yielded pride of place to gentle
and contemplative stewardship.

Where does this leave the contemporary scientist? I don't
know of any physicist today who rejects either relativity or
quantum theory. Moreover, Neils Bohr's principle of complementarity (that at subatomic levels, "objects" consist of both
particle and wave properties) and Werner Heisenberg's principle of uncertainty (matter does not exist with certainty in
terms of a particle's speed and position but will tend to exist
in one or other capacity) are widely accepted in the scientific

community. Scientists spend most of their time working with "unknowns," and words such as uncertainty, relativity, complementarity, interconnectedness, elegance, and beauty are extensively used in scientific exploration. Despite the popular emphasis on quantification, verification, and objectivity, scientists operate essentially in the realm of spirit.

The spiritual underpinnings become blatantly obvious in the nailing of the quarks. The most recent episode in the pursuit for the "ultimate building blocks" began in the early 1960s when Murray Gell-Mann at Caltech (California) and George Zweig at CERN (near Geneva) independently accounted for a vast array of newly discovered particles which they called aces (Zweig) and quarks (Gell-Mann), the name that has prevailed. Physicists became very excited and many felt that at long last the basic constituents of matter were about to be revealed. The sixth and final quark was discovered in 1984. The physicists named it "top" or "truth," hoping that it was the breakthrough that would enable them to piece together the jigsaw of universal life.

They were in for a shock! Physicists discovered that quarks functioned only in relationships of two and threes (not in individual isolation), and their activity was predominantly that of wave-like patterns of energy with (apparently) no objective, independent existence. All attempts to bombard individual quarks out of their relational, wave-like existence have failed. Many scientists reluctantly conclude that nature abhors naked quarks, but a substantial number are determined to continue the atom-bashing and are demanding the erection of more elaborate particle-accelerators to isolate and identify the elusive "building blocks."

Two categories of scientists are beginning to emerge: those locked into the mechanistic ideology, who, despite all the breakthroughs of the twentieth century, are unable to transcend the functional, utilitarian, materialistic perception of life. They want more and bigger particle-accelerators (physical objects) to procure the physical evidence for what they consider to be a purely physical universe.

The second category still comprises a minority but one that is coming to prominence. Without necessarily adopting religious language or ideas, physicists of this orientation readily acknowledge the spiritual undercurrents. They feel that the discovery of the quarks could well mark the end of the pursuit of "building blocks": life is not about the assemblages of physical units but about wave-like interrelationships of energy. The more adventurous feel that if the pursuit is to continue it has to move onto a new plane; hence, the dialogue between scientists and mystics unique in our time.[10]

Big Bang and Supersymmetry

What I call the mystical orientation emerges strongly in two aspects of contemporary scientific scrutiny: the big bang theory and supersymmetry theory. Regarding the former, the emphasis has shifted from what happened in the first few minutes of life on earth to what happened in the first one second![11] In our ordinary experience, a second is so short that we cannot imagine much happening in that tiny space of time. Yet, among physicists today there is a large measure of agreement that something of immense human and global significance took place in the first second of time. That conviction, and the immense time and effort put into its exploration, convinces me that contemporary physicists operate out of a supra-human time scale, something akin to the Christian perception that with God there is no before or after, but only an instantaneous "awareness." We are into the realm of mystical experience!

Alongside the new sense of time is a conviction that cannot be scientifically verified but which scientists believe has to be correct. That conviction concerns "supersymmetry." This is one of the elegant theories for which concrete evidence may never be possible simply because the concept is so vast. Its starting point is the simple observation that many aspects of nature, such as a snowflake or a raindrop, comprise a highly complex but elegant structure. Therefore, the basic building blocks should be construed as loop-like strings with the harmonic vibrating qualities of strings on a musical instrument (hence, the concept "superstrings"). An image of a highly artistic universe begins to emerge.

Supersymmetry seeks to safeguard both the complexity and unity of life. It postulates a ten- (or eleven-) dimensional

universe and highlights the forces for unity and synchronic-
ity at work in the universe. Beyond these elaborate concepts are the theories of a superforce and a superlaw; Paul
Davies introduces both these concepts with a distinctively
divine flavor.[12] And our culmination is appropriately called
a Theory of Everything, which is a fundamental aspiration of
mysticism in all ages and in every culture of humanity.

Bridging the Spiritual Vacuum

The scenario I have depicted attempts to trace the philosophy (dare I say, spirituality) of science in the twentieth
century. Why then has so much scientific exploration culminated in consumerism, hard technology, arms production,
and the atom bomb? And why hasn't the underlying spiritual thrust led scientists to devote their wisdom and expertise to resolving some of the great catastrophes of our time;
for example, earthquakes, monsoons, food-production, and
disease eradication?

We are confronted with a perceptual vacuum. Many
physicists seem to be blind to the mystical dimensions of
their explorations. Could it be that most are still operating
out of the old mechanistic paradigm, while acknowledging
(intellectually) the developments of the twentieth century?
Science is taught today in elementary schools all over the
world, but what are we teaching our children? Are we teaching mechanistic, academic theories substantiated in labora-
tory experiments but largely disconnected from daily life, or
are we teaching the skills to wonder, admire, and explore the
elegance and beauty of the universe?

It seems such a tragic waste of resources to deprive our
culture of this vast and fascinating body of wisdom and
information. The artificial gap between science and religion
(which seems to be more the fault of the church than of
scientists) must be bridged. It is my contention that those
who specialize in the contemplative dimension of the vowed
life should pioneer this breakthrough.

Why the contemplatives? First, nobody is better equipped
to appreciate and comprehend the mystical elements of the
scientific pursuit than those schooled in contemplation. By
contemplation, I mean the gift of being able to feel and

perceive in depth. It is a disposition which has been suc-
cinctly described by Boros.

> Contemplation seeks more than to "establish facts" and
> to "get to know" the world. . . . It desires the world
> for its own sake, in its original power and sacredness.
> It gives itself up to experience, which thus attains a
> heightened reality. Moments of contemplative vision are
> moments lived intensely, times of totally experienced
> humanity, of immediate recognition, of unchecked
> vitality. . . .
> Contemplation is there when a man is walking and
> then suddenly stops and turns, his senses wide open,
> his spirit exposed. He desires only to become so totally
> one with his experience that at that moment the experi-
> ence itself becomes a message. . . .
> Through contemplative vision a man experiences for
> himself something of the perfection inherent in the most
> insignificant things and events. Thus there develops,
> out of contemplative vision, that which is entrusted to
> all men who have become inward — the Kingdom of
> God: that kingdom of danger and audacity, of eternal
> beginning and becoming, of the Spirit that is open and
> inward.[13]

I suggest that it is the task of the modern contemplative
to articulate and translate for the contemporary scientist the
deeper experiences of scientific exploration. Moreover, the
contemplative can also be a supreme bridge builder between
the technically nebulous world of the scientist and that of
the "ordinary" person, who often feels divorced from this
repository of holistic wisdom. The contemplative doesn't
have to be a scientist, but the scientist and contemplative
have a great deal in common.[14] It is unchartered territory
awaiting its hour of dialogue.

Once the dialogue begins to take place, it will quickly
become obvious that communication is only a first step.
Mystics of all ages and all cultures point to the limitations
of human language, and nobody is more aware of this than
the contemporary scientist. Already some scholars employ
mythical concepts, such as that of the "dance of creation and
destruction,"[15] or the discovery of the quarks as a "koan
experience,"[16] to captivate the sense of mystery. Drawing
parallels between Western science and Eastern mysticism

is but a first step to an experiential encounter where exploration and contemplation become synonymous.

The Art of Meditation

Meditation is the initial practical step toward realizing this goal. It is a word with a wide range of meanings. Many people consider it to be the exclusive realm of priests, nuns, and monks. At another extreme, it is viewed as an Eastern idea which sensible Westerners should avoid. Etymologically, it means to stand at the center; hence the description frequently used: centering prayer. Meditation is a skill that enables me to gather the diverse energies of feeling and attention so that I become grounded in the center of my being. It is a process that facilitates inward movement (interiority rather than introspection), a calming down of sensations and feelings, a mental alertness, and an overall disposition of openness and receptivity to life.

Meditation is a type of tuning-up process, centering me in my own "heart," but also grounding my experience in a way that connects meaningfully with the conscious energy of life. Starcke captures this dual function with clarity and precision:

> Technically, this is what meditation accomplishes. We are starting a journey with our conscious mind. That conscious mind is like the one-eighth of an iceberg which appears above the ocean. The seven-eighths not apparent to the naked eye is the subconscious. Beyond the subconscious is the collective unconscious, the noosphere, universal consciousness, or the total Godhead. This collective unconscious is like the ocean in which all the icebergs float. This ocean is not only the means of communication between all the icebergs, but it is the collection of total truth to which we, as individual icebergs, have access. Through meditation we contact that total truth, we transcend our finite limitations and we communicate with each other.
>
> Meditation is simply the name we put on whatever means we use in order to turn within and go from our conscious, through our unconscious, into the experience of pure truth or God.[17]

In current secular language, meditation is sometimes described as "the technology for a new age of consciousness."

With every scientific breakthrough there is a corresponding set of technological skills to apply the new information. For the electronic age, we invented television, videos, etc. For the information age, we invented computers. For what many predict to be an emerging age of psychic evolution, where consciousness rather than matter binds the universe together, we need a new global, supra-material technology, namely meditation.

The contemplatives of all religious traditions are the custodians of the ageless wisdom of meditation. Unfortunately, they have tended to guard and seclude this precious gift with a plethora of ritual and spiritualized accretions, to such a degree that it lost appeal to society. But like all archetypal values, it could not remain dormant. Today, it is surfacing in a variety of forms and proving to be one of the tools uniting the spiritual traditions of East and West.

Despite these developments, meditation is still very much a fringe issue clouded by an other-worldly spiritual mystique. Contemplatives need to rescue it and translate it into forms suitable for our times, as John Main did in the 1970s with the Centering Prayer tradition.[18] Our scientists need the profound wisdom of meditation, simply to be better scientists. All people have the same need if they are to comprehend and appreciate the scientific mysticism which has such profound ramifications for life on our planet.

We began this chapter by recalling the unique impact of the monks on medieval Europe. In all cultures, right across the world, the monastic people, the specialists in the contemplative life, are custodians of archetypal values precious for earthly and human civilization. Among these values is the gift of meditation. In our time it is an urgently needed wisdom to enable us to make the crucial evolutionary transition from the mechanistic to the holistic age. Without the complementary skills of both the contemplative and the physicist, that transition will be difficult to negotiate.

In medieval Europe, the contemplatives were a force for transformation in the shift from the declining Roman empire to the emergence of the illustrious Middle Ages. Today, the transition is one of global magnitude and the transformation is spiritual (psychic) rather than physical.

If the contemplatives can rise to this challenge and break out of their cloistered enclaves, where too often the Spirit has been strangled in archaic ritualism, then it will be a new day for religious life.

Conclusion to Part Four

It is painfully obvious that the present world order is out of tune with the fundamental aspirations of humanity. Our earth is broken up into nations which differentiate, religions which divide, races which dominate one another, and a scandalous polarization between the extortionist North and the impoverished South.

Deep in our hearts none of us desires this state of affairs and many long for a better world: united, reconciled, healed, and made whole once more. This, too, is the vision of the kingdom which Jesus came to proclaim: a world marked by right relationships of justice, love, and peace. Indeed, it is a fundamental aspiration of all humanity.

As we approach the twenty-first century, we experience a growing awareness of the need to live in greater unity and work in greater harmony. We realize that, under God, the earth is ours, our one and only home. On this planet, we either learn to live together or we exterminate one another. We have had more than enough bitterness, bloodshed, and division, pollution and incarceration, exploitation and manipulation. We want to become new people; we want to make a fresh start.

What do religious — monks, ascetics, sisters, brothers — wish to bring to this new world? A cosmetic religion of saffron robe, ascetic prowess, archaic institutions, and insipid spirituality? Or a vision of new possibilities marked by courageous action and fresh initiatives? Religious are called to adopt a strategy that: (a) becomes passionately committed to just and loving relationships; (b) overtly and vociferously confronts the control and exploitation of people and of the earth's resources; (c) courageously explores alternative lifestyles for the marginalized and oppressed; and (d) challenges and empowers people to discern God's evolutionary plan for our universe.

In this way, religious rediscover and enable others to understand their call to be:

Liminal people: set apart to articulate more radically the dreams and aspirations shared by all people of good will;

Archetypal people: whose values challenge and inspire the surrounding culture to love more deeply, treat more gently, and listen more attentively to the unfolding vision of the next millennium;

Prophetic people: whose call is to liberate the power within people and within our universe by denouncing all that is alien to human meaning and endorsing all that releases the transforming power of God's kingdom.

Above all, religious need to take renewed responsibility for their charismatic identity. Religious are a global movement, not just a religious phenomenon; they have a message and mission from and for the world and not merely an agenda from or for any one church; they have a sacred history which does not justify a nostalgia for the past but never ceases to point to the future. Finally, religious are about the creation of a new world (the transformation of the kingdom) which often demands a readiness to part with the institutions sanctioned by time and tradition.

It is this transition from the closed (old) to the open (new) system that will make the heaviest demands on the adaptability and creativity of religious. Times of transition (at least in the Christian tradition) bring out the best and worst in them. Historically, the majority never make it, but there is enough evidence to suggest that revitalization is a possibility for all. The ultimate destiny of religious is in the hands of God, but God has supreme respect for human freedom. God will only condemn religious to extinction when they have chosen to condemn themselves.

I have described what I perceive to be the religious life of the future: global, eclectic, transcending nation, race, and religion. I trust it is a vision worthy of the aspirations of all who work for a better world. If it is, then it is also worthy of the great tradition of religious life which has served our culture so well in the past.

Like all institutions in today's world, religious are in a state of change and transition; the missionary and apostolic models of the recent past are dying. What I have attempted to depict is a new vision, a global myth of the twenty-first century. Somewhere in that complex and challenging dream are the seeds of new life, sprouting in the barren desert, as we glimpse the promised land of a new tomorrow.

Endnotes

ONE: A Panoramic Overview

1. David Miller and Dorothy Wertz, *Hindu Monastic Life*.

2. Vandana, *Gurus, Ashrams and Christians*.

3. Quoted in Mayeul de Dreuille, *From East to West: Man in Search of the Absolute*, p. 40.

4. Irmgard Schloegl, *The Zen Way*, p. 33.

5. Vandana, chapters 1 and 2.

6. Cf. Amyot in John Moffitt, *A New Charter for Monasticism*, pp. 59–60, 66–67.

7. Melford E. Spiro, *Buddhism and Society*, p. 345.

8. Amyot in Moffitt, p. 64.

9. "Nuns in Revolt," *India Today*, March 15, 1987, p. 81.

10. Michael Nazir-Ali, *Islam: A Christian Perspective*, p. 61.

11. A. H. Jones, "Tariqah," *The Encyclopedia of Religion*, vol. 14, pp. 342–352.

12. Richard C. Martin, *Contributions to Asian Studies: Islam in Local Contexts*, p. 29.

13. B. D. Metcalf in Martin, pp. 62ff.

14. Roy Wallis, *The Elementary Forms of the New Religious Life*.

15. A. H. Dammers, *Lifestyle: A Parable of Sharing*. Donald Bloesch, *Wellsprings of Renewal*. Andrew Lockley, *Christian Communes*. David Clark, *Basic Communities*.

16. "Pro Mundi Vita Bulletin," no. 62, 1976. Ian and Margaret Fraser, *Wind and Fire*.

17. Clark, *The Liberation of the Church*.

18. John Wraw, "An Active Community of Coptic Orthodox Nuns," *Sobornost*, vol. 8, pp. 47–50.

19. R. P. Beaver, "The Rise of Monasticism in the Church of Africa," *Church History*, vol. 6, pp. 350–372.

20. Meier, in Bernard Lewis, *The World of Islam*, p. 121.

TWO: Liminal Identity

1. Mircea Eliade, *Shamanism: Archaic Techniques of Ecstasy*.

2. Sr. Donald Corcoran, *Skudlarek* (1982), pp. 250–253.

3. Eliade, pp. 508–509.

4. Eliade, pp. 215ff., 300ff., 326ff.

5. Eliade, p. 181.

6. Eliade, p. 508.

7. Eliade, p. 316.

8. Eliade, p. 117.

9. Eliade, p. 9.

10. Eliade, p. 6.

11. Eliade, p. 13.

12. Eliade, p. 76.

13. Eliade, pp. 145–153.

14. Eliade, pp. 11, 15.

15. Eliade, p. 64.

16. Richard Endress, "The Monastery as a Liminal Community," *American Benedictine Review*, vol. 26, pp. 142, 148.

17. Endress, pp. 146–147.

18. Endress, p. 147.

19. Victor Turner, *Dramas, Fields and Metaphors*, pp. 202–203.

20. Turner, "Liminality, Kabbalah and the Media," *Religion*, vol. 15, pp. 205–217.

21. Turner, *Image and Pilgrimage in Christian Culture*, pp. 4, 7.

22. Derwas J. Chitty, *The Desert a City*, p. 15.

23. Endress, p. 148.

24. Turner, *Dramas, Fields and Metaphors*, p. 268.

25. Turner, p. 172.

26. *Gaudium et Spes*, no. 4.

THREE: Archetypal Values

1. Mircea Eliade, *Cosmos and History: The Myth of Eternal Return*.

2. Anthony Stevens, *Archetype: A Natural History of the Self*.

3. Quoted in Aniela Jaffe, *The Myth of Meaning in the Work of C. G. Jung*, pp. 158, 159.

4. Ray L. Hart, *Unfinished Man and the Imagination*, p. 298.

5. Stevens, p. 142.

FOUR: Prophetic Possibilities

1. Anthony Stevens, *Archetype: A Natural History of the Self*, pp. 215ff.

2. John Davies, "The Prophetic Community," *Community*, no. 37, pp. 1–2.

3. Walter Brueggemann, *The Prophetic Imagination*.

4. Sandra Schneiders, *New Wineskins: Re-imagining Religious Life Today*. Evelyn Woodward, *Poets, Prophets and Pragmatists: A New Challenge to Religious Life*.

5. Johannes Metz, *Followers of Christ*, pp. 12–13.

6. Werner Heisenberg, *Physics and Philosophy*.

7. Fritjof Capra, *The Tao of Physics*.

8. "Religious and Human Promotion," foreword, *L'Osservatore Romano*, January 26, 1981.

FIVE: The Historical Paradigm

1. Oscar Cullmann, *The Johannine Circle*. Raymond Brown, *The Community of the Beloved Disciple*.

2. David Knowles, *From Pachomius to Ignatius*. S. Hilpisch, *Benedictinism Through Changing Centuries*. Geoffrey Moorehouse, *Beyond All Reason*.

3. Raymond Hostie, *Vie et Mort des Ordres Religieux*.

4. L. Cada, *Shaping the Coming Age of Religious Life*.

5. Hostie, p. 312.

6. Cada, p. 53.

7. Derwas J. Chitty, *The Desert a City*, p. 66.

8. Arthur Voobus, *History of Asceticism in the Syrian Orient*, vol. 1, pp. 259–266. Chitty, p. 126.

9. Daniel Rees, *Consider Your Call: A Theology of Monastic Life Today*, pp. 43–56.

10. Herbert Workman, *The Evolution of the Monastic Ideal*, pp. 233–234.

11. Armand Veilleux, "The Evolution of the Religious Life in its Historical and Spiritual Context," *Cistercian Studies*.

12. R. Fitz & L. Cada, "The Recovery of Religious Life," *Review for Religious*, vol. 34, p. 698.

13. Voobus, *History of Asceticism in the Syrian Orient*, vol. 2, pp. 327, 338ff.

14. Workman, pp. 6–12. James Mohler, *The Hersey of Monasticism*, pp. 54ff.

15. Rees, p. 370.

SIX: A New Look at the Origins of Religious Life

1. W. K. L. Clarke, *The Ascetical Works of St. Basil*, p. 14. Herbert Workman, *The Evolution of the Monastic Ideal*, pp. 6–10.

2. W. H. C. Frend, *Martyrdom and Persecution in the Early Church*, pp. 547ff.

3. W. H. Mackean, *Christian Monasticism in Egypt*, pp. 36ff. M. Ohlig-slager, "De-Hellenization of Monastic Life," *American Benedictine Review*, vol. 18, pp. 517–530. Armand Veilleux, "The Abbatial Office in Cenobitic Life," *Monastic Studies*, vol. 6, pp. 3–45.

4. Arthur Voobus, *History of Asceticism in the Syrian Orient*, vols. 1 and 2.

5. Jean Gribomont, "Le Monachisme un Sein de l'Eglise en Syrie et en Cappodoce," *Studia Monastica*, vol. 7, pp. 7–24. G. Nedungatt, "The Covenanters of the Early Syriac-speaking Church," *Orientalia Christiana Periodica*, vol. 39, pp. 191–215, 419–444. Robert Murray, "The Exhortation to Candidates for Ascetical Vows at Baptism in the Ancient Syrian Church," *New Testament Studies*, vol. 21, pp. 59–79.

6. Jean Leclercq, "Monastic Profession and the Sacraments," *Monastic Studies*, vol. 5, pp. 59–85.

7. Nedungatt, p. 444.

8. Veilleux, p. 8. Gribomont, p. 17.

9. Veilleux, p. 7.

10. F. C. Burkitt, *Early Eastern Christianity*, pp. 130, 150.

11. Nedungatt, p. 428.

12. Nedungatt, pp. 431–432.

13. Dom David Amand, *L'Ascese Monastique de Saint Basile*.

14. On Basilian monasticism, see Gribomont; Paul Fedwick, *The Church and the Charisma of Leadership in Basil of Caesarea*.

15. Daniel Rees, *Consider Your Call: A Theology of Monastic Life Today*, pp. 43–56.

16. Owen Chadwick, *John Cassian*, pp. 50ff.

17. Veilleux, p. 6.

SEVEN: The Vitality Curve: Growth and Decline

1. Thomas F. O'Meara, *Holiness and Radicalism in Religious Life*.

2. Gerald A. Arbuckle, *Strategies for Growth in Religious Life; Out of Chaos: Refounding Religious Congregations*.

3. Elisabeth Kübler-Ross, *On Death and Dying*.

EIGHT: Refounding and Revitalization

1. Gerald A. Arbuckle, *Out of Chaos: Refounding Religious Congregations*, pp. 11–28.

2. L. Cada, *Shaping the Coming Age of Religious Life*, p. 60.

3. Arbuckle, pp. 88–111.

NINE: Community and Intimacy (Celibacy)

1. Mayeul de Dreuille, *From East to West: Man in Search of the Absolute*, p. 12.

2. Mary Bateson, "Origin and Early History of Double Monasteries," *Transactions of the Royal Historical Society*, vol. 13, pp. 139–198.

3. David Clark, *The Liberation of the Church*, pp. 136–139.

4. Sandra Schneiders, *New Wineskins: Re-imagining Religious Life Today*, pp. 252–255.

5. Evelyn Woodward, *Poets, Prophets and Pragmatists: A New Challenge to Religious Life*, p. 18.

6. Clark, p. 15.

7. I use the term "socializing myth" rather than the theological concept of "revelation" because the great Eastern religions do not have a deposit of revealed truth as understood in the Christian or Judaic sense.

8. Clark, pp. 27ff.

9. "Religious and Human Promotion," *L'Osservatore Romano*, January 26, 1981, no. 24.

10. M. Ohligslager, "De-Hellenization of Monastic Life," *American Benedictine Review*, pp. 517–530.

11. Schneiders, "Non-Marriage for the Sake of the Kingdom," *Widening the Dialogue: Reflection on Evangelica Testificatio*, pp. 133–134.

12. Schneiders, pp. 156–163.

13. Max Thurian, *Marriage and Celibacy*, pp. 22–23, 44. Donald Georgen, *The Sexual Celibate*, pp. 104–124. William F. Kraft, *Sexual Dimensions of Celibate Life*, pp. 51–93.

14. Wilfred Harrington, "Christian Celibacy," *Supplement to Doctrine and Life*, p. 31.

15. Roger Balducelli, "The Decision for Celibacy," *Theological Studies*, vol. 36, pp. 226–229.

16. Balducelli, p. 233.

17. Raimundo Panikkar, *Blessed Simplicity: The Monk as Universal Archetype*, pp. 33–34.

18. Aloysius Roche, *The First Monks and Nuns*, p. 91.

19. Bernard Häring, *Acting on the Word*, p. 138.

20. Marilyn Ferguson, *The Aquarian Conspiracy*, pp. 426ff.

TEN: Listening in Order to Discern (Obedience)

1. Fritjof Capra, *The Turning Point*, pp. 10–11. Capra claims that the cultural transition taking place is marked by three outstanding features: the breakdown of patriarchy, the rise of feminism, and the oil crisis.

2. Adrian Van Kaam, *The Vowed Life*, p. 17.

3. Van Kaam, p. 14.

4. Capra, pp. 37ff.

5. J. Lipnack & J. Stamps, *The Networking Book*, p.2.

6. John Lozano, *Discipleship: Toward an Understanding of Religious Life*, p. 222.

7. Lozano, pp. 224, 227.

8. John Futrell, *Making an Apostolic Community of Love*, p. 161, n. 24.

9. For further reading, *Studies in the Spirituality of the Jesuits*, see Futrell, "Ignatian Discernment," vol. 2, pp. 47–88. J. J. Toner, "A Method for Communal Discernment of God's Will," vol. 3, pp. 121–154. Ladislaus Orsy, "Toward a Theological Evaluation of Communal Discernment," vol. 5, pp. 139–196.

10. Cf. J. T. Lienhard, "On Discernment of Spirits in the Early Church," *Theological Studies*.

11. John Shea, *Stories of God*, p. 181.

ELEVEN: Resources for Sharing and Caring (Poverty)

1. Alejandro Cussianovich, *Religious Life and the Poor: Liberation Theology Perspective.* V. F. Vineeth, *Call to Integration: A New Theology of Religious Life.* John Lozano, *Discipleship: Toward an Understanding of Religious Life.* Leonardo Boff, *God's Witnesses in the Heart of the World.* Sandra Schneiders, *New Wineskins:Re-imagining Religious Life Today.*

2. Quoted in Boff, p. 106.

3. Boff, p. 103.

4. Cussianovich, pp. 137, 138.

5. Peter G. Van Breeman, *Called by Name*, pp. 272–273.

6. Albert Nolan, *Jesus Before Christianity*, p. 113.

7. Boff, p. 108.

8. Schneiders, p. 101.

TWELVE: Justice That Liberates

1. "Religious and Human Promotion (R.H.P.)," *L'Osservatore Romano*, January 26, 1981, nos. 1–12.

2. R.H.P., no. 1/3.

3. R.H.P., no. 1/4/A.

4. R.H.P., no. 1/2.

5. R.H.P., no. 6E.

6. R.H.P., no. 10/A & C.

7. R.H.P., no. 11–12.

8. Sandra Schneiders, *New Wineskins: Re-imagining Religious Life Today.*

9. R.H.P., no. 3/E.

10. Fritjof Capra, *The Turning Point.* Peter Russell, *The Awakening Earth.*

11. Theodore Roszak, *Person/Planet*, p. xxx.

12. James Lovelock, *Gaia: A New Look at Life on Earth.*

13. Erich Jantsch, *The Self-Organizing Universe.*

14. Paul Davies, *The Cosmic Blueprint.*

15. Jean Baker Miller, *Toward a New Psychology of Women.* Carol S. Robb, *Making the Connections: Essays in Feminist Social Ethics.* Mary Jo Weaver, *New Catholic Women: A Contemporary Challenge to Traditional Religious Authority.*

16. R.H.P., no. 15.

17. Leonardo Boff, *God's Witnesses in the Heart of the World*, pp. 247–248.

THIRTEEN: From Asceticism to Aestheticism

1. William Edward Hartpole Lecky, *History of European Morals*, vol. 2, p. 107.

2. Derwas J. Chitty, *The Letters of St. Anthony the Great.*

3. Louis Bouyer, *The Spirituality of the New Testament and the Fathers*, p. 319.

4. Aidan P. Cusack, "The Temptation of St. Benedict: An Essay at Interpretation Through Literary Sources," *American Benedictine Review*, vol. 27, pp. 143–163.

5. On the interpretation of hagiography, cf. Ludolf Muller, "The Theological Significance of a Critical Attitude in Hagiography," *The Ecumenical Review*, vol. 15, pp. 279–282.

6. *Interpreter's Dictionary Supplement*, 1976, p. 947.

7. Bouyer, p. 313.

8. Chitty, *The Desert a City.*

9. Theodore Roszak, *Person/Planet*, p. 285.

10. George Aschenbrenner, "Active and Monastic: Two Apostolic Lifestyles," *Review for Religious*, vol. 45, pp. 653–668.

11. R. Arbesmann, "Fasting and Prophecy in Pagan and Christian Antiquity," *Traditio*, vol. 7, pp. 1–71.

12. *Sacramentum Mundi* (1968), vol. 2, p. 335.

13. Aloysius Roche, *The First Monks and Nuns*, p. 70.

14. *Shorter Rules*, no. 89.

15. G. Nedungatt, "The Covenanters of the Early Syriac-speaking Church," *Orientalia Christiana Periodica*, vol. 39, pp. 431–432.

16. On spiritual marriage, see Rosemary Rader, *Breaking Boundaries: Male/Female Friendship in Early Christian Communities*, pp. 62–71.

17. Herbert Workman, *The Evolution of the Monastic Ideal*, p. 97.

18. Chitty, *The Letters of St. Anthony the Great*, p. viii.

19. Edward Stevens, *An Introduction to Oriental Mysticism*, pp. 81–88, 131–135.

FOURTEEN: New Ecumenical Horizons

1. Eileen Barker, *New Religious Movements*. James Beckford, *New Religious Movements and Rapid Social Change*.

2. Diarmuid O'Murchu, "How to Revitalize an Order in Decline," *Religious Life Review*, 1983, vol. 22, pp. 132–144.

3. Matthew Fox, *Original Blessing: A Primer in Creation Spirituality*.

4. A valuable resource for this task is the Vatican II document, *Gaudium et Spes*. Also, the 1981 document "Religious and Human Promotion" contains many ideas explored in this book.

5. *Mutuae Relationis*, 1978, no. 12.

6. Paul F. Knitter, *No Other Name?: A Critical Survey of Christian Attitudes Toward the World Religions*.

7. The teaching is consistent with the vision of the Second Vatican Council, as enunciated in *Gaudium et Spes* and its Declaration on the Relationship of the Church to Non-Christian Religions, *Nostra Aetate*. It is also faithful to *Evangelii Nuntiandi* (cf. no. 15).

8. Knitter, p. 223.

9. Knitter, pp. 205ff.

10. Walbert Buhlmann, *The Coming of the Third Church; The Church of the Future: A Model for the Year 2001*.

11. Sandra Schneiders, *New Wineskins: Re-imagining Religious Life Today*, pp. 266ff.

FIFTEEN: On Monks and Atoms!

1. Edward Stevens, *An Introduction to Oriental Mysticism*, pp. 15–16.

2. Walter Stace, *The Teachings of the Mystics*.

3. William Johnston, *The Inner Eye of Love: Mysticism and Love*, p. 9.

4. Ken Wilber, *Quantum Questions: Mystical Writings of the Great Physicists*, 1984.

5. Albert Einstein, *Out of My Latter Years*, p. 26.

6. Gary Zukav, *The Dancing Wu Li Masters: An Overview of the New Physics*, p. 167.

7. Paul Davies, *Superforce: The Search for a Grand Unified Theory of Nature*, p. 49.

8. Ken Wilber, *The Holographic Paradigm and Other Paradoxes*.

9. Erich Jantsch, *The Self-Organizing Universe*.

10. Fritjof Capra, *The Tao of Physics*. Zukav. Rene Weber, *Dialogues with Saints and Sages*.

11. John Gribben, *In Search of the Big Bang*.

12. Davies, *Superforce; The Cosmic Blueprint*.

13. Ladislaus Boros, *In Time of Temptation*, pp. 80, 82, 83.

14. Rene Weber, *Dialogues With Saints and Sages*.

15. Capra, pp. 249ff.; Zukav, pp. 230–237.

16. Capra, pp. 273ff.

17. Walter Starcke, *The Gospel of Relativity*, p. 33.

18. Neil McKenty, *In the Stillness Dancing: The Journey of John Main*.

Reference Bibliography

Amand, Dom David. *L'Ascese Monastique de Saint Basile*, Editions de Maredsous, 1948.

Arbesmann, R. "Fasting and Prophecy in Pagan and Christian Antiquity." *Traditio*, 1949, vol. 7, pp.1–71.

Arbuckle, Gerald A. *Strategies for Growth in Religious Life*. Slough: St. Paul Publications, 1986.
Out of Chaos: Refounding Religious Congregations. London: Chapman & New York: Paulist Press, 1988.

Aschenbrenner, George. "Active and Monastic: Two Apostolic Lifestyles," *Review For Religious*, 1986, vol. 45, pp.653–668.

Balducelli, Roger. "The Decision for Celibacy." *Theological Studies*, 1975, vol. 36, pp.219–242.

Barker, Eileen. *New Religious Movements*. New York: Edwin Melen Press, 1982.

Bateson, Mary. "Origin and Early History of Double Monasteries." *Transactions of the Royal Historical Society*, 1989, vol. 13, pp.139–198.

Beaver, R.P. "The Rise of Monasticism in the Church of Africa." *Church History*, 1937, vol. 6, pp.350–372.

Beckford, James. *New Religious Movements and Rapid Social Change*. New Dehli: Sage Publications, 1986.

Biot, Francois. *The Rise of Protestant Monasticism*. Dublin: Helicon, 1963.

Bloesch, Donald. *Wellsprings of Renewal*. Grand Rapids, Michigan: Eerdmans, 1974.

Boff, Leonardo. *God's Witnesses in the Heart of the World*. Chicago: Claret Centre for Resources in Spirituality, 1981.

Boros, Ladislaus. *In Time of Temptation*. London: Burns & Oates, 1968.

Bouyer, Louis. *The Spirituality of the New Testament and the Fathers*. London: Burns & Oates, 1960.

Brown, Raymond. *The Community of the Beloved Disciple*. New York: Paulist, 1979.

Brueggemann, Walter. *The Prophetic Imagination*. Philadelphia: Fortress Press, 1978.

Buhlmann, Walbert. *The Coming of the Third Church*. Slough: St. Paul Publications, 1974.
The Church of the Future: A Model for the Year 2001. Slough: St. Paul Publications, 1986.

Bunnag, Jane. *Buddhist Monk: Buddhist Layman*. New York: Cambridge University Press, 1973.

Burkitt, F.C. *Early Eastern Christianity*. London: J. Murray, 1904.

Cada, L. et al. *Shaping the Coming Age of Religious Life*. New York: Seabury Press, 1979.

Capra, Fritjof. *The Tao of Physics*. London: Flamingo Books, 1975.
The Turning Point, London: Flamingo Books, 1982.

Chadwick, Owen. *John Cassian*. New York: Cambridge University Press, 1968.

Chitty, Derwas J. *The Desert a City*. Oxford: Blackwell, 1966.
The Letters of St. Anthony the Great. Oxford: SLG Press, 1975.

Clark, David. *Basic Communities*. London: SPCK, 1977.
   The Liberation of the Church. Birmingham, England: NACCAN, 1984.
Clarke, W.K.L. *The Ascetical Works of St. Basil*. London: SPCK, 1925.
Cullmann, Oscar. *The Johannine Circle*. Minneapolis, MN: SCM Press, 1974.
Cusack, Aidan P. "The Temptation of St. Benedict: An Essay at Interpre-
   tation Through Literary Sources." *American Benedictine Review*, 1976,
   vol. 27, pp.143–163.
Cussianovich, Alejandro. *Religious Life and the Poor: Liberation Theology
   Perspective*. Dublin: Gill & Macmillan, 1979.
Dammers, A.H. *Lifestyle: A Parable of Sharing*. Northampton: Turnstone
   Press, 1972.
Davies, Paul. *Superforce: The Search for a Grand Unified Theory of Nature*.
   London: Unwin Paperback, 1984.
   The Cosmic Blueprint, London: Heinemann, 1988.
Davies, John. "The Prophetic Community." *Community*, 1983, no. 37,
   pp.1–2.
de Dreuille, Mayeul. *From East to West: Man in Search of the Absolute*. Ban-
   galore: Theological Publications, 1975.
Eckenstein, Lina. *Woman Under Monasticism, 500–1500*. New York: Cam-
   bridge University Press, 1896.
Einstein, Albert. *Out of my Latter Years*. New York: Philosophical Library,
   1950.
Eliade, Mircea. *Cosmos and History: The Myth of Eternal Return*. New York:
   Torch Books, 1959.
   Shamanism: Archaic Techniques of Ecstasy. New York: Pantheon Books,
   1964.
Endress, Richard. "The Monastery as a Liminal Community." *American
   Benedictine Review*, 1975, vol. 26, pp.142–158.
Fedwick, Paul. *The Church and the Charisma of Leadership in Basil of Caesarea*.
   Toronto: Pontifical Institute of Mediaeval Studies, 1979.
Ferguson, Marilyn. *The Aquarian Conspiracy*. London: Paladin Books, 1982.
Fitz, R. & L. Cada. "The Recovery of Religious Life." *Review for Religious*,
   1975, vol. 34, pp.690–718.
Fox, Matthew. *Original Blessing: A Primer in Creation Spirituality*. Santa Fe:
   Bear & Co., 1983.
Fraser, Ian & Margaret. *Wind and Fire*. London: British Council of
   Churches, 1986.
Frend, W.H.C. *Martyrdom and Persecution in the Early Church*. Oxford:
   Blackwell, 1965.
Futrell, John. *Making an Apostolic Community of Love*. St. Louis: The Insti-
   tute of Jesuit Sources, 1970a.
   "Ignatian Discernment." *Studies in the Spirituality of the Jesuits*, 1970b,
   vol. 2, pp.47–88.
Goergen, Donald. *The Sexual Celibate*. New York: Seabury Press, 1974.
Goldberg, Michael. *Theology and Narrative*. Nashville: Abingdon, 1981.
Gribomont, Jean. "Le Monachisme un Sein de l'Eglise en Syrie et en Cap-
   podoce." *Studia Monastica*, 1965, vol. 7, pp.7–24.
Gribben, John. *In Search of the Big Bang*. London: Bantam/Corgi Books,
   1986.
Griffiths, Bede. "The Monastic Order of the Ashram." *American Benedictine
   Review*, 1979, vol. 30, pp.134–145.

Halkenhauser, J. "Religious Life in the Reformed Churches of Europe." *Religious Life Review*, 1987, vol. 37, pp.30–36.

Hammett, R. & L. Schofield. *Inside Christian Community*. New York: Le Jacq Publishing Co., 1981.

Hannay, James. *The Spirit and Origin of Christian Monasticism*. London: Methuen, 1903.

Häring, Bernard. *Acting on the Word*. Leominister: Fowler Wright, 1975.

Harrington, Wilfred. "Christian Celibacy." *Supplement to Doctrine And Life*, 1976, vol. 14, pp.29–43.

Hart, Ray L. *Unfinished Man and the Imagination*. New York: Herder & Herder, 1968.

Healy, S. & B. Reynolds. *Social Analysis in the Light of the Gospel*. Dublin: Folens & Co., 1983.

Heisenberg, Werner. *Physics and Philosophy*. London: Allen & Unwin, 1963.

Hilpisch, S. *Benedictinism Through Changing Centuries*. Collegville: St. John's Abbey Press, 1958.

Holland, J. & P. Henriot. *Social Analysis: Linking Faith and Justice*. New York: Orbis Books, 1980.

Hostie, Raymond. *Vie et Mort des Ordres Religieux*, Desclee de Brower, 1972. (English edition available from the Center for Applied Research in the Apostolate, Washington D.C.)

Jaffe, Aniela. *The Myth of Meaning in the Work of C.G. Jung*. Zurich: Daimon, 1984.

Jantsch, Erich. *The Self-Organizing Universe*. Oxford: Pergamon Press, 1980.

Johnston, William. *The Inner Eye of Love: Mysticism and Religion*. London: Collins, 1978.

Jones, A.H. "Tariqah." *The Encyclopedia of Religion* (M. Eliade, ed.), 1987, vol. 14, Macmillan & Co., pp.342–352.

Jones, Alan. *Soul Making: The Desert Way of Spirituality*. London: SCM Press, 1985.

Jones, Kenneth R. *Ideological Groups: Similarities of Structure and Organisation*. London: Gower, 1984.

Knitter, Paul F. *No Other Name?: A Critical Survey of Christian Attitudes Toward the World Religions*. London: SCM Press, 1985.

Knowles, David. *From Pachomius to Ignatius*. Oxford: Clarendon Press, 1966.

Kraft, William F. *Sexual Dimensions of Celibate Life*. Dublin: Gill & Macmillan, 1979.

Kübler-Ross, Elisabeth. *On Death and Dying*. London: Tavistock, 1970.

Leclercq, Jean. "Monastic Profession and the Sacraments." *Monastic Studies*, 1968, vol. 5, pp.59–85.

Lewis, Bernard. *The World of Islam*. London: Thames & Hudson, 1976.

Lienhard, J.T. "On 'Discernment of Spirits' in the Early Church." *Theological Studies*, 1980, vol. 41, pp.505–529.

Lipnack, J. & J. Stamps. *The Networking Book*. London: Routledge and Kegan Paul, 1986.

Lockley, Andrew. *Christian Communes*. London: SCM Press, 1976.

Lovelock, James. *Gaia: A New Look at Life on Earth*. New York: Oxford University Press, 1979.

Lozano, John. *Discipleship: Toward an Understanding of Religious Life*. Chicago: Claret Center for Resources in Spirituality, 1980.

Mackean, W.H. *Christian Monasticism in Egypt*. London: SPCK, 1920.

Martin, Richard C. *Contributions to Asian Studies: Islam in Local Contexts.* Leiden: E.J. Brill, 1982.

McKenty, Neil. *In the Stillness Dancing: The Journey of John Main.* London: Darton, Longman & Todd, 1986.

Metz, Johannes. *Followers of Christ.* London: Burns & Oates, 1978.

Meyendorff, John. *Byzantine Theology: Historical Trends and Doctrinal Themes.* New York: Fordham University Press, 1979.

Miller, David & Dorothy Wertz. *Hindu Monastic Life.* London & Montreal: McGill-Queen's University Press, 1976.

Miller, Jean Baker. *Toward a New Psychology of Women.* Boston: Beacon Press, 1976.

Moffitt, John. *A New Charter for Monasticism.* Notre Dame, IN: University of Notre Dame Press, 1970.

Mohler, James. *The Heresey of Monasticism.* New York: Alba House, 1971.

Moorehouse, Geoffrey. *Beyond All Reason.* New York: Weidenfeld & Nicholson, 1969.

Muller, Ludolf. "The Theological Significance of a Critical Attitude in Hagiography." *The Ecumenical Review,* 1962/63, vol. 15, pp.279–282.

Murray, Robert. "The Exhortation to Candidates for Ascetical Vows at Baptism in the Ancient Syrian Church." *New Testament Studies,* 1974, vol. 21, pp.59–79.

Navone, John. *Towards a Theology of Story.* Slough: St. Paul's Publications, 1977.

Nazir-Ali, Michael. *Islam: A Christian Perspective.* Exeter: The Paternoster Press, 1983.

Nedungatt, G. "The Covenanters of the Early Syriac-speaking Church." *Orientalia Christiana Periodica,* 1973, vol. 39, pp.191–215, 419–444.

Nolan, Albert. *Jesus Before Christianity.* London: Darton, Longman & Todd, 1977.

Ohligslager, M. "De-Hellenization of Monastic Life." *American Benedictine Review,* 1967, vol. 18, pp.517–530.

O'Meara, Thomas F. *Holiness and Radicalism in Religious Life.* New York: Herder & Herder, 1973.

O'Murchu, Diarmuid. "How to Revitalize an Order in Decline." *Religious Life Review,* 1983, vol. 22, pp.132–144.
   Coping With Change in the Modern World. Cork: Mercier Press, 1987.

Orsy, Ladislaus. "Towards a Theological Evaluation of Communal Discernment." *Studies in the Spirituality of the Jesuits,* 1973, vol. 5, pp.139–196.

Nereman, Y. & Y. Kirsh. *The Particle Hunters.* New York: Cambridge University Press, 1986.

Panikkar, Raimundo. *Blessed Simplicity: The Monk as Universal Archetype.* New York: Seabury Press, 1982.

Pribram, Karl. *Languages of the Brain.* New York: Prentice Hall, 1971.

Radar, Rosemary. *Breaking Boundaries: Male/Female Friendship in Early Christian Communities.* Mahwah, NJ: Paulist Press, 1983.

Rees, Daniel. *Consider Your Call: A Theology of Monastic Life Today.* London: SPCK, 1978.

"Religious and Human Promotion," (R.H.P.) initially published in *L'Osservatore Romano,* January 26, 1981.

Robb, Carol S. *Making the Connections: Essays in Feminist Social Ethics.* Boston: Beacon Press, 1985.

Roche, Aloysius. *The First Monks and Nuns*. London: The Catholic Book Club, 1945.

Rossetti, S. "The Celibacy Experience." *Review for Religious*, 1982, vol. 41, pp.660–677.

Roszak, Theodore. *Person/Planet*. London: Gollancz, 1979.

Russell, Peter. *The Awakening Earth*. London: Routledge & Kegan Paul, 1982.

Schloegl, Irmgard. *The Zen Way*. London: Sheldon Press, 1977.

Schneiders, Sandra M. "Non-Marriage for the Sake of the Kingdom." *Widening the Dialogue: Reflection on Evangelica Testificatio*. Ottawa: Canadian Religious Conference, pp.125–197, 1974.
New Wineskins: Re-imagining Religious Life Today. Mahwah, NJ: Paulist Press, 1986.

Shea, John. *Stories of God*. Chicago: The Thomas More Press, 1978.
Stories of Faith. Chicago: The Thomas More Press, 1980.

Skudlarek, William. *The Continuing Quest for God*. Collegeville: The Liturgical Press, 1982.

Slade, Herbert. *Contemplative Intimacy*. London: Darton, Longman & Todd, 1977.

Spiro, Melford E. *Buddhism and Society*. London: Allen & Unwin Ltd., 1971.

Stace, Walter. *The Teachings of the Mystics*. New York: New American Library, 1960.

Starcke, Walter. *The Gospel of Relativity*. London: Thurstone Books, 1974.

Stevens, Anthony. *Archetype: A Natural History of the Self*. London: Routledge & Kegan Paul, 1982.

Stevens, Edward. *An Introduction to Oriental Mysticism*. Mahwah, NJ: Paulist Press, 1973.

Tambiah, S.J. *World Conqueror and World Renouncer: A Study of Buddhism and Polity in Thailand*. New York: Cambridge University Press, 1976.

Thurian, Max. *Marriage and Celibacy*. London: SCM Press, 1969.

Toner, J.J. "A Method for Communal Discernment of God's Will." *Studies in the Spirituality of the Jesuits*, 1971, vol. 3, pp.121–154.

Trimingham, J. Spenser. *The Sufi Orders in Islam*. Oxford: Clarendon Press, 1971.

Turner, Victor (& Edith). *The Ritual Process: Structure and Anti-Structure*. Chicago: Aldine, 1969.
Dramas, Fields and Metaphors. Ithaca, NY: Cornell University Press, 1974.
Image and Pilgrimage in Christian Culture. Oxford: Blackwell, 1978.
"Liminality, Kabbalah and the Media." *Religion*, 1985, vol. 15, pp.205–217.

Van Breeman, Peter G. *Called by Name*. Denville, NJ: Dimension Books, 1976.

Vandana. *Gurus, Ashrams and Christians*. London: Darton, Longman and Todd, 1978.

Vanier, Jean. *Community and Growth*. London: Darton, Longman and Todd, 1980.

Van Kaam, Adrian. *The Vowed Life*. Denville, NJ: Dimension Books, 1968.

Veilleux, Armand. "The Abbatial Office in Cenobitic Life." *Monastic Studies*, 1968, vol. 6, pp.3–45.
"The Evolution of the Religious Life in its Historical and Spiritual Context." *Cistercian Studies*, 1971.

Vineeth, V.F. *Call to Integration: A New Theology of Religious Life.* New York: Crossroad, 1979.

Voobus, Arthur. *History of Asceticism in the Syrian Orient,* Vol.1: *The Origins of Asceticism: Early Monasticism in Persia.* Louvain, 1958.

Vol.2: *Early Monasticism in Mesopotamia and Syria.* Louvain, 1960.

Wallis, Roy. *The Elementary Forms of the New Religious Life.* London: Routledge and Kegan Paul, 1984.

Weaver, Mary Jo. *New Catholic Women: A Contemporary Challenge to Traditional Religious Authority.* New York: Harper & Row, 1985.

Weber, Rene. *Dialogues With Saints and Sages.* London: Routledge and Kegan Paul, 1986.

Wilber, Ken. *The Holographic Paradigm and Other Paradoxes.* Boston and London: New Science Library, 1982.

Quantum Questions: Mystical Writings of the World's Great Physicists. Boston & London: New Science Library, 1984.

Woodward, Evelyn. *Poets, Prophets and Pragmatists: A New Challenge to Religious Life.* Notre Dame, IN: Ave Maria Press, 1987.

Workman, Herbert. *The Evolution of the Monastic Ideal.* London: Epworth Press, 1913.

Wraw, John. "An Active Community of Coptic Orthodox Nuns." *Sobornost,* 1986, vol. 8, pp.47–50.

Zukav, Gary. *The Dancing Wu Li Masters: An Overview of the New Physics.* London: Flamingo Books, 1979.